Second Edition

STUDY
ABROAD
101

By

Wendy Williamson

Agapypubl......

Study Abroad 101

Copyright © 2004, 2008 by Wendy Williamson

Second Edition

International Standard Book Number: 978-0-9721328-4-8

Library of Congress Catalog Card Number: 2008906256

First published in 2004

Agapy Publishing
Charleston, IL
Website: www.agapy.com

Printed in the United States of America

Table of Contents

III. Prepare for your Trip

IV. Be Healthy and Safe

V. Manage your Money and Life

VI. Live in another Country

VII. Get along with the Locals

VIII. Maximize your Trip: Top Secrets

IX. Life after Study Abroad

Introduction (words of wisdom)

So, you want to study abroad. Studying abroad can be one of the most rewarding experiences of a lifetime. For this reason, there are hundreds upon thousands of opportunities vying for your business in the industry. With so many possibilities to choose from, it is important to focus on what you want and need for your education. Think <u>not</u> where you'd like to go on vacation, but on what you need to enhance your qualifications and marketability, for the career you hope to achieve.

While study abroad can be wonderful in its own rite, it is not easy, or at least it shouldn't be! Living in another country is difficult, and to some degree, it is uncomfortable. At times, it takes a great deal of patience and perseverance to get through the days. Remember that study abroad is not supposed to be a break from or a vacation during college; it is supposed to be a challenging part of your college experience that allows you to grow in your persona and your professional expertise.

It is not study abroad, but the appropriate challenge in study abroad that is valuable to you as a college student. Just think about how you'd turn out if all of your college classes were super-easy; where there is no challenge, there is little growth. Before you decide to go abroad, <u>choose an experience</u> (study or vacation). If you are looking for a vacation, then don't go through school…do it separately for a lot less money! Lastly, do not put vacations on your resume; employers catch on fast.

No matter how you choose to go abroad (study or vacation), the information in this book should be useful. It is my hope that this book will answer most of your questions about study abroad and equip you with the information that you will need to make sound decisions before, during, and even after your experience. If you decide to take the challenge, then learn as much as you can. Pack your awareness, knowledge, and skills and get ready to come back with more

Part I.

Get a Grip on
the Basics

1. Why should I study abroad?

The World is a book, and those who do not travel read only a page. ~*St. Augustine*

It's a lot fun, it's a great experience, it will change your life, it will enhance your education, so on and so forth. I'm sure this isn't anything you haven't already heard or else you wouldn't be reading this book. Don't forget why you're in college, to get an education so you can eventually have a career and do whatever it is that you want to do with your life. Toward the achievement of this goal, it is important to look at what you have to offer from the perspective of employers.

Between 1995 and 2005, US college enrollment increased by 23%, from 14.3 million to 17.5 million (US Department of Education, National Center for Education Statistics), and is expected to continue increasing through 2014. According to the 2006 American Community Survey, conducted by the Census Bureau, 39.7% of the US population between the ages of 18 and 24 were enrolled in a US college degree-granting program. This means there is a lot of competition!

Think about it...more people are applying for the same jobs, and many of these people have strong qualifications along with college degrees and good grade point averages, thanks to grade inflation driven by consumerism. It's no wonder why college students are so busy enhancing their education with other activities that set them apart from their peers. Without internships, work experience, international knowledge, and leadership positions, their credentials will lose value.

One activity that can greatly enhance your credentials is study abroad. This is because our cultural, economic, and political systems are becoming more dependent on and are integrating more fully with those across the planet. Consequently, foreign language skills, international experience, cultural knowledge and expertise, and cross-cultural abilities are advantageous from the perspective of many employers. The good news is study abroad opportunities are not saturated like colleges and universities; only between one and two percent of all US college students study abroad per year.

While it is not widely published, some institutions such as Texas A&M University and the University of Minnesota have researched the outcomes of study abroad experiences as they pertain to post-graduate employment. Their findings suggest that graduates with international experience are provided with more offers of employment and higher starting salaries than those without. Call it a hunch, but I think that study abroad is becoming the cutting-edge degree enhancer of the century. The more global your degree, the better prospects you'll see!

In addition to what study abroad can do for your degree and future job prospects, it can increase your self-understanding, boost your self-confidence, speed up your maturity, enhance your interest in studying, help you decide on a major/minor, heighten your foreign language skills, develop an open mind, and influence your life for the better (2004, *The Benefits of Study Abroad* by Mary M. Dwyer, Ph.D. and Courtney K. Peters, www.TransitionsAbroad.com).

What will you be highlighting when you graduate?

_____ College Degree

_____ Grade Point Average

_____ Work Experience

_____ Professional References

_____ Extracurricular Activities

_____ **Study Abroad Experience**

---

2. What if I'm not in college yet?

The early bird catcheth the worm. ~John Ray

If you're in high school, and you are planning to study abroad during college, then you are in a wonderful position to have this book in hand! While you may not realize it now, where you choose to go to college could severely enable or disable your study abroad opportunities and experiences. Just because a recruiter mentioned study abroad in a presentation you saw, does not mean you will be able to do what you want or need to do. You must (and I mean absolutely must) understand the inner-workings of study abroad at your top choices. I do not want to overload you with details, but briefly, this is what you need to know and consider in your decision:

Level of Support
- Is there a study abroad designee or office? If not, what kind of support will you receive?
- Is there a website with information that is easy to follow, which explains the study abroad process?
- How many advisors work in the study abroad office compared with how many students study abroad?
- Are the policies, processes, and procedures fair and easy to grasp? Is paperwork online?
- Are students satisfied with the level of support they receive from the designee/office in charge?

Program Options
- Does the university have its own programs and/or partners, and are you interested in any of them?
- Are there different paths to the same destination (direct enroll, third party, consortium, faculty-led)?
- If their programs and/or paths aren't appealing to you, then would the institution allow you to go on another

program you find on your own? If so, what is the likelihood of another program being approved?

- If you decide to go on another program, do you get valuable credit that counts in your study plan? Are additional problems/costs incurred? What are the drawbacks of not going on one of their programs?

Academic Credit

- Are you enrolled while away? If not, then you will lose all institutional benefits and may even have to reapply to your university upon returning!
- Do you receive *transfer credit* or *resident credit*? This can also influence your financial aid package; usually resident credit would offer more financial aid.
- Does credit come in as pass/fail or does it average into your grade point average? How will it appear on your official transcript (for jobs, graduate school, etc.)?
- Is study abroad linked to academic requirements? In other words, can you get major, minor, and general education credit or will you just get electives?
- Do faculty/departments run programs? This may or may not be relevant to you. Faculty-led programs can be an excellent way to get to know your professors.

Financial Aid

- What financial aid (federal, state, private, etc.) can you use for study abroad, and with which study abroad programs can you use it?
- When can you get financial aid? For example, some institutions will not give aid to students if they are enrolled in less than six credits.
- Are you enrolled while away? Home institution enrollment is necessary for you to receive institutional benefits, financial aid, and grants/scholarships.
- Does the institution offer any scholarships or other incentives to study abroad? Some talk the talk, but

don't walk the walk by offering scholarships to enable low and middle-class students to study abroad.

<u>Actual Costs</u>
- What are you paying for when you study abroad? It is a good idea to compare costs for similar programs at different colleges and universities. Some institutions waive tuition while you are away (so you can pay the partner's tuition), but others charge you no matter what (and you end up paying tuition twice). Some institutions charge a program cost and/or admin fees either at cost or way above cost. It varies dramatically.
- Whom do you pay and how do you pay for your study abroad program? Sometimes you pay your university and sometimes you pay the host/provider.
- What are the refund policies for whomever you pay?
- What is included and not included in the fees?

Case Studies - So let's practice! You want to study abroad, but you're just not sure when or where, and you're not ready to figure it all out until you go to college. You've researched study abroad at your top four institutions. How might this information factor into your decision about where to go?

1. SEEMSEASY COLLEGE

- **Level of Support**: They have a study abroad office with lots of good support, and 80% of students study abroad, many of which rave about the experience.
- **Program Options**: There are a limited number of options. You're not permitted to participate in any sort of Non-SEEMSEASY program for unspoken reasons.
- **Academic Credit**: Your credit will transfer without complications. If you pick the right program, then you will fulfill the requirements you need to stay on track.

- **Financial Aid**: All of your regular financial aid will apply as if you were taking classes on campus.
- **Actual Cost**: $25,000 tuition per semester to attend any study abroad program, all-inclusive. They purchase your airfare and give you the ticket.

2. NOBUDGET UNIVERSITY

- **Level of Support**: They have a study abroad office with some support, and 5% of students study abroad.
- **Program Options**: There are many more options than at SEEMSEASY COLLEGE. You CAN participate in a Non-NOBUDGET program if your petition is approved (which is likely).
- **Academic Credit** Approved credit will transfer. If you pick the right program, then you will get what you need to stay on task and graduate on time.
- **Financial Aid**: You can use your financial aid on any approved program, regardless of length or type. You have to be enrolled as a full-time student, but not all your courses have to be taken through study abroad.
- **Actual Cost**: Waives tuition and regular fees. Instead, they charge a $300 study abroad *administrative fee* and *program fees* (at cost). Programs are not all-inclusive; students purchase their own airfare and may have to pay for other things on their own. Budgets are on the website and include estimated figures for everything (airfare, housing, program fees, admin fees, passport, visa, etc.). You notice that total estimated costs range from $1,500 to $12,000.

3. ONYOUROWN UNIVERSITY.

- **Level of Support**: There is one faculty member, who advises students, but it is only part-time and there is no office or website designated for study abroad.

- **Program Options**: Doesn't have its own programs or partners, so you have to find one on your own.
- **Academic Credit** You can get transfer credit if you have a transcript sent to the university when you re-enroll, after your program.
- **Financial Aid**: The University requires that you withdraw while away and does not award financial aid or give you any other benefits as a US student.
- **Actual Cost**: It depends on the program you choose.

4. PROPRIETARY COLLEGE

- **Level of Support**: They have a study abroad office and appear to have adequate support staff for the number of students that study abroad.
- **Program Options**: With only 15 options, you can acquire permission to go on a non-PROPRIETARY program, but you do not get any aid and your credit comes in as transfer credit (which is not listed as a study abroad program on your transcript).
- **Academic Credit**: Gives you their academic credit for only their programs and partners.
- **Financial Aid**: Gives you financial aid for only their programs and partners.
- **Actual Cost**: Varies per program. Ranges from 8K to 18K for a semester abroad, or whatever else you find on your own through the Non-PROPRIETARY track.

Informed decisions make better futures! I'm sorry to say that I hear a hefty number of complaints from students about the practices at their home institutions. I cannot stress enough the importance of choosing a *study-abroad-friendly* college or university that fits your own particular needs. Maybe you don't mind paying a lot of money in exchange for additional help and support. The differences between institutions vary, and your decision about where to attend can result in much time, energy, and money either lost or gained.

3. What kind of credit can I get?

Experience, travel - these are as education in themselves. ~ **Euripides**

Most institutions have a process in place to approve study abroad coursework for major, minor, general education, and elective credits. Make sure that your courses are integrated with your study plan by having each one pre-approved before you go abroad. While it may not always be possible to do this before departure, you can usually do it via email from abroad, before your classes begin.

To save yourself some hassle, always have more courses pre-approved than you plan to take, in case of schedule changes or cancellations. If you end up taking courses that you did not get pre-approved, then get them approved as soon as possible. Know the drop/add procedures at your host institution, so you don't waste any energy if you need to make a change. Being planful in the beginning saves time and frustration in the end.

More than being planful, it is imperative that you know the rules before you begin your experience. For example, many colleges and universities will not award credit for coursework taken at institutes or training centers; some will not transfer courses in certain subjects; some limit the number of credits you can receive for study abroad experiences; and some limit the amount of time you can study abroad.

Credit is never automatic. Thus, it is important to ask if you are not given the information upfront. In addition to the rules at home, you may also encounter regulations at your chosen host institution. Some hosts will not let foreigners take certain courses and some of the courses have prerequisites or require a full year of study, etc. Every year I encounter students who find themselves abroad and in a quandary over their courses.

When it comes to processing credit from study abroad, every college and university is different. At various schools, grades earned while studying abroad are factored into the GPA. It is just as common for schools to record grades for study abroad courses that do not factor into the GPA. Still, at other schools, students receive pass/fail or transfer credit for their studies abroad. Some do a combination of the above.

The cause for so many differences is campus culture. Those institutions that calculate study abroad courses into the GPA are focused on the *academic* experience. They believe that students do less partying and miss fewer classes when they view their grades as important. Those institutions that do not factor grades into the GPA are more focused on the *personal* aspects of the experience, and believe that the added stress of GPA can prohibit students from taking healthy risks. For this reason, you will receive either *resident* or *transfer* credit for your studies abroad. The differences are explained below:

A. Resident Credit. A student is enrolled in either the home institution's courses or a placeholder designated for study abroad. In case of a placeholder, credit evaluation is contingent on a host or provider transcript of the courses, credits, and grades taken through the program. After the host transcript is received and evaluated, the placeholder is deleted. Then, the institution's equivalents, credits, and grades are recorded on the home transcript.

B. Transfer Credit. A student takes a leave of absence from the home institution to study abroad and re-enrolls upon returning. There may or may not be a placeholder that allows the student to receive financial aid and other institutional benefits while he/she is away. Transfer credit is dependent on a host transcript with the student's actual courses, credits, and grades. This kind of credit may not be considered as resident credit, and may be limited.

Below are some different kinds of credit that you can explore for your study abroad experience, beyond the commonplace.

Internship Credit. This category of credit offers students an opportunity to gain important international work experience. Typically, study abroad internships are initiated by a student, and arranged in collaboration with an academic department or within the parameters of a study abroad program. In addition to working, students must complete academic requirements. This type of credit is becoming popular! See section #17.

Independent Study. An independent study course is a great opportunity to earn academic credit by engaging in research or completing a project related to a study abroad experience, outside of the formal classroom environment. A student who is interested in knowing more about a topic not covered in the regular curriculum may propose an independent study to any regular fulltime member of the department faculty. This type of credit is excellent for the self-motivated student.

Experiential Credit. This academic credit can be awarded to a student who has learned through international experiences certain competencies, which are indisputably equivalent to or superior to that which could have been acquired on the home campus. This type of credit may involve a supporting paper or portfolio. While not common in the field of study abroad, it shouldn't be overlooked for people who have lived, studied, or worked extensively in an international environment.

Examination Credit. This academic credit may be awarded if, after an international experience, a student passes an exam designed to measure the learning objectives of study abroad courses that were taken abroad. This type of credit is most common with foreign-language learning, but is also available for other subjects. Check your home institution's catalog for more information, specific to your college or university.

Tips for unaccredited Schools, Institutes, and Centers

Your university may not transfer study abroad courses from an unaccredited school, institute, or center. Notwithstanding, there may still be a way for you to acquire valuable credit. A few accredited colleges and universities will evaluate your study abroad courses for a fee. Not only will they evaluate your courses, but they will also record them on an accredited transcript. You can use then this official transcript to transfer the same credits to your university. The fee for this service may go up to $1000. Ask your host school, center, or institute for information. They may already have an arrangement.

4. How will it fit into my college degree?

Nothing that is worth knowing can be taught. ~*Oscar Wilde*

This is a difficult question to answer because it depends on many factors: type of college degree, field of study, career path, chosen program, recognition of your chosen program, etc. The bigger, scarier question you can ask yourself is how your degree is going to help you meet your job aspirations if you do not enhance it with something else, like study abroad.

With the steady increase in the number of bachelor's degrees awarded every year, the competition is great among college graduates for jobs. Data suggests that most college graduates are employed, but not all in positions that require a college education. According to the 2006 *Current Population Survey* and *American Community Survey* (both US Census Bureau), about 22% of men and 25% of women who held bachelor's degrees and worked full time, year-round, earned less than or equal to the median earnings for high school graduates. These earnings were $31,715 for men and $20,650 for women.

So, ask yourself what's going to set you apart, when it comes time to apply for the ideal job? The finest jobs are nabbed by those who can distinguish themselves from their competition, and convince employers that they are best choice. Sometimes it is clear in our minds that we are best choice, but we have a hard time convincing others. Face the facts; there are lots of people who can do a great job. Who gets the second glance? Who gets in the front door? Who gets the interview? These are questions you should be asking yourself right now. Last but not least, who interviews well and gets the job?

Interpersonal, leadership, and intercultural skills are vital to many careers. Flexibility, innovation, and autonomy are also important. The good news is that these skills and character traits are often linked with study abroad, and can be linked to you, if you make wise decisions before, during, and after your study abroad experience. If you choose a program because it looks easy and fun, or because you are looking for a summer vacation, then employers will detect this at some level of the screening process. If you are selected for an interview, then chances are you will be asked about your experience and to articulate what it did for you and your education.

It doesn't matter what your major is or what kind of job you wish to obtain, study abroad can be beneficial to all students and to you. You may think that what you've learned (how to study, how to manage time, how to treat people, how to solve a problem, etc.) is universal; when in fact, it is cultural. Such presumptions can limit your understanding and capability in an ever more interdependent world. Even that which does transcend culture may be strategized or expressed differently. Take mathematics for example. By discovering how another culture solves mathematical equations, students unavoidably develop awareness, knowledge, and skills, which transfer to many multicultural classrooms. Knowing how students think and process information in another culture can greatly benefit schoolteachers that work with a diverse group of children.

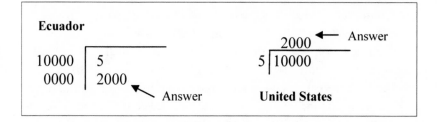

Ecuador

```
10000  | 5
 0000  | 2000  ← Answer
```

```
        2000  ← Answer
5 | 10000
```

United States

Similar to mathematics, you will discover that the world has a variety of strategies for obtaining the same or similar results. In business, different management styles are valued, but the process is still management. In art, different expressions are taught, but the product is still beauty. In education, different teaching styles are utilized, but the objective is still learning. Being exposed to different cultural expressions will enhance your education; however, you may not understand how it fits into your degree until after you graduate, find a job, and get your feet wet in the workforce. There is just something about hands-on experience that helps us to understand our education and how to make better decisions as a result.

5. Will study abroad delay graduation?

Nothing happens unless first a dream. ~Carl Sandburg

With careful planning, studying abroad does not have to delay your graduation. In fact, it can speed up your graduation in some instances. I have seen Spanish majors complete all their language requirements in one or two semesters, and German majors get 20 credits for one semester of study abroad. It all depends on the program, the credit evaluation process, and the norms at your college or university. Ask and seek out this information before you begin your journey. Find out what is customary at your institution and what courses you can take, to stay on the right track. If you can get courses pre-approved for your major, minor, and/or general requirements, then you shouldn't have a problem graduating on time.

If financing your college education is a concern for you, and you've had to work while taking classes, studying abroad can sometimes help. At a number of public institutions, out-of-state and international students study abroad for less than they would otherwise pay to take classes on campus or at a private US college or university. This may be the case when in-state tuition is included in the study abroad program fees—that is, when tuition is not a separate expense. In the same regard, home tuition and fees may also be waived, for students who participate in unsponsored programs. While it depends on many factors and your home/host institution, studying abroad may even accelerate your big day and diploma!

Consider summer programs if you have a very strict schedule of classes during the academic year, but you still want the opportunity to study in another country. Summer programs offer short-term opportunities for you to fulfill coursework and have an international experience at the same time. At my university, Education majors have to take most courses on campus (for certification purposes), but can participate in one or two faculty-led programs and/or COST (the Consortium of Overseas Teaching) if they wish to study abroad. In all three of these cases, students get valuable academic credit towards their degree and lose no time whatsoever towards graduation. Actually, they can get more credit for less time and cost!

6. Do I need to know a foreign language?

A man who does not know foreign language is ignorant of his own. ~ Johann Wolfgang von Goethe

You don't need to know a foreign language in order to study abroad. There are more options available to you if you speak another language, or want to study another language, but a foreign language is not a requirement and doesn't have to be a part of your international package. Australia, New Zealand, various parts of Africa, Canada, and the United Kingdom are all English-speaking areas that can provide unique cultural experiences to students who have no interest in developing foreign language skills.

If you decide to study abroad in English, don't be mistaken, studying in another country that speaks English can be like learning a foreign language. Sometimes, it's even harder. If you are going to the UK, then check out *The (Very) Best of British: the American's Guide to Speaking British* by Mike Etherington (www.effingpot.com). The *British to American Translator* is also useful, www.translatebritish.com. If you're thinking about Australia, then check out the website, *How to Speak Australian* (www.howtospeakaustralian.com).

If you want to study abroad in a country, but you do not speak the language, then consider an *Island Program*. This type of program offers courses and activities conducted in English. It may also offer some introductory foreign language schooling. The nice thing about learning a foreign language, in a country where it is spoken, is that you have the opportunity to practice outside of class. While Island programs can be valuable to the beginner, they do not facilitate the same growth as *Immersion Programs*. It would be rare for Island participants to develop a high degree of cultural awareness, knowledge, and skills, or to develop fluency in the foreign language.

In addition to island programs, there are plenty of American institutions overseas. *Schiller International University* is just one American university with campuses in several different countries. Quite a few American institutions were founded by missionaries. The American College of Beirut was founded by Daniel Bliss. The American University of Cairo was set up with similar ideals. Today, going to one of these institutions (and many more) is like getting a US education overseas. You can take classes simultaneously at host-country public/private colleges and universities for a more diversified experience.

7. Isn't study abroad just for rich kids?

Wealth is the ability to fully experience life. ~*Henry David Thoreau*

No, study abroad is not just for rich kids; it's for everyone! I direct international education at a public institution, where students can study abroad for less than what it costs to stay on campus and take a full load. This is because we waive our tuition for programs that are <u>not</u> faculty-led or exchange. We do this because most of our partners require that students pay them tuition. This is advantageous for our students because host tuition is oftentimes less than ours. Room and board may also be less costly in cities where cost of living is low.

Cities with a lower cost of living	Cities with a higher cost of living
<u>Latin America</u>: Buenos Aires (Argentina), Quito (Ecuador), San Jose (Costa Rica), Santiago (Chile) <u>Europe</u>: Athens (Greece), Prague (Czech Rep), Lisbon (Portugal), Sofia (Bulgaria), Warsaw (Poland)	Amsterdam, Beijing, Copenhagen, Dublin, Geneva, Hong Kong, London, Milan, Madrid, Moscow, Osaka, Oslo, Paris, Rome, Seoul, Singapore, Shanghai, Sydney, St. Petersburg, Tokyo, Vienna, Zurich

Even though you can study abroad for less than what it costs to stay at home, don't base your decision solely on the cost. If you're an English major, then London may be your best bet, even though the cost of living is high. Also, pay attention to what's included in the price of a program, and what is not included, as well as how much additional money you would need to spend. Third-party provider programs often include major tourist attractions and other excursions, and since they get group rates, it may be less costly than going on your own.

Are you debating between 2-3 different programs, or trying to decide whether you should direct enroll or go through a third-party provider? If so, then copy and complete the following budget worksheet for each program that you are considering.

Budget Worksheet

Program Name:	
Program Fee (may include some items below) Includes: _____ _____ _____	
Home Tuition (if applicable)	
Host Tuition (if applicable)	
Home Fees (if applicable)	
Host Fees (if applicable)	
Accommodations (room, apartment, family)	
Utilities (if not included above)	
Meals (anything not included above)	
Roundtrip International Airfare	
On-site Transportation (to/from airport)	
Local Transportation (to/from class, store, etc.)	
Books/Supplies	
Passport/Photos	
Student visa (if applicable, check w/consulate)	
Immunizations	
Insurance (health, travel, etc.)	
Required Field Trips	
Optional Travel (other places you want to see)	
Miscellaneous (incidentals and spending money)	
Other:	
Other:	
Total Estimated Cost	
Scholarships (Guaranteed)	-
Scholarships (Possible)	-
Total Adjusted Cost	

8. Can I get financial assistance?

I know at last what distinguishes man from animals; financial worries. ~ **Romain Rolland**

Federal financial aid can be used for study abroad if (a) credit is earned and (b) the home institution approves the academic credit earned toward the student's degree. The law states that students cannot be denied federal aid simply because they are studying abroad. The only type of federal aid that is difficult to use is *work-study awards*, because of employer limitations and reporting restrictions. However, it is sometimes possible to convert a work-study award into a Perkins loan. Ask your financial aid officer for more information and details.

FAFSA is required for nearly every type of aid: Grants (Pell, TEACH, FSEOG, SMART, etc.), Perkins Loans, Plus and Stafford Loans, Public State Funding, and many study abroad scholarships. The FAFSA is usually the first step to any type of public aid or assistance and is based on your financial need according to your Estimated Family Contribution (EFC). Get started by visiting http://studentaid.ed.gov after January 1 for the following academic year and completing the FAFSA by June 30, or your State's deadline, whichever is earlier.

Depending on your state's legislation, state-funded assistance may follow you abroad or may be restricted to in-state use. The same is true of private scholarships. It is best to check with your home institution and the provider of your financial assistance. If you are planning to use your financial aid to study abroad, you must maintain full-time enrollment in a degree-granting program, and have your study abroad courses pre-approved for credit before you leave. In addition, the total cost of your program must be documented and verifiable by the Office of Financial Aid.

A variety of factors influence one's eligibility for financial aid and seem to change from one institution to another. At my university, it used to be that state-funded aid could only be used to pay for our tuition. For study abroad, this meant that it could only be used to pay for tuition on exchange programs. After we changed the way in which we recognized/recorded study abroad credit on the academic transcript (resident credit factoring into the GPA), students could use their state-funded aid more broadly to cover host tuition and fees that go outside of the university.

In addition to the financial aid you may already have, and the transferable scholarships you've secured through your college or university, you can apply for other grants and scholarships earmarked for study abroad. Don't underestimate their value; I've met several students who have received more financial assistance than necessary for their study abroad experience. Unfortunately, there isn't too much available for the above-average student who wants to go to London or Sydney. Most nationally known scholarships favor nontraditional and non-English-speaking locations.

Regardless of where you would like to go or what you want to study, it is wise to allow yourself plenty of time to research and apply for scholarships (if you have need). There are many search engines and databases available to help you find good matches, many of which are earmarked for study abroad.

Note: If you're planning to be gone for more than a semester, it is wise to give a homebound and trustworthy parent, friend, or relative *Power of Attorney* to watch over your financial aid and other assets, while you are abroad. Power of Attorney is a legal instrument used for the primary purpose of delegating lawful and signature authority to another. There are several different types of authorized delegations. Paperwork/Forms can be obtained on the Internet or through your attorney, and are usually filed in the County Clerk's Office.

Tips/Databases/Channels for finding
Study Abroad Grants and Scholarships

- Fast Web: http://www.fastweb.com
- FinAid.org: http://www.finaid.org
- IIE Passport Study Abroad Funding Database: www.studyabroadfunding.org
- International Education Finance Corporation: www.iefc.com (for loans)
- International Education Financial Aid: www.iefa.org (for scholarships)
- International Scholarships Premier Database: www.internationalscholarships.com
- University of Minnesota Scholarships Database: www.umabroad.umn.edu/financial/scholarships
- Diversity Abroad offers scholarships for low income minority students and hosts a searchable database: www.diversityabroad.com/scholarships
- Your institution's scholarship list, your financial aid office, and various national opportunities.
- Your Academic Department (may have scholarships for its students to study abroad). In higher education, you have to ask. Sometimes this type of aid is not so apparent on the surface or may not even be available unless you ask for it and the Department Chair finds something through colleagues or friends.
- The employers of your parents or grandparents (often have scholarships available for college students).
- Any associations, organizations, churches, clubs, or social groups, in which you and your parents belong.
- Your fraternity or sorority may support study abroad.
- Keep an eye on the *Senator Paul Simon Study Abroad Foundation Act* of 2007 (H.R. 1469, S.991), which is a visionary bill in Congress that could result in some serious cash for study abroad programs and students in the future (maybe by the time you read this book).

Prominent Study Abroad Scholarships

Boren Undergraduate Scholarships/Graduate Fellowships
Funded by the National Security Education Program for
students planning to study languages in areas of the world
that the United States seeks to know better.

Eligibility	Undergraduate or graduate student. US citizenship, and working toward a college degree at a US post-secondary institution.
Location	Africa, Asia, Central and Eastern Europe, Eurasia, Latin America and the Caribbean, and the Middle East
Length	Preference given to full academic year
Amounts	Undergraduates receive up to $20,000 and graduates receive up to $30,000
Deadline	Late January for the following academic year
Website	www.worldstudy.gov/boren

Bridging Scholarship – Funded by the Association of
Teachers of Japanese Bridging Project, this scholarship is for
undergraduate students who plan to study in Japan

Eligibility	US Citizenship or Permanent Residency in the United States. Working on an undergraduate degree in a US post-secondary institution.
Location	Japan
Length	Semester or longer
Amounts	$2500 to $4000
Deadline	April for the following Fall or Academic Year. October for the Spring semester.
Website	www.colorado.edu/ealld/atj/Bridging/scholarsh ips.html

DAAD Scholarships – These scholarships are funded by the German Academic Exchange Service and are available for undergraduate to post-doctoral students with well-defined research or study projects that make a sojourn in Germany essential.

Eligibility	Varies for the different scholarships. Must be planning to study and/or conduct research in Germany. High academic standards expected.
Location	Germany
Length	Semester or longer
Amounts	Awards range from $2000 to actual expenses
Deadline	Depends on the scholarship
Website	www.daad.org

Freeman-Asia Scholarship – This scholarship is funded by the Institute of International Education and is for US citizens with freshmen, sophomore, and junior standing, who are planning to study in East or Southeast Asia.

Eligibility	Undergraduate (American) with demonstrated financial need. See website for a full list of eligibility requirements.
Location	East or Southeast Asia
Length	Summer (eight weeks or longer), Semester, or Academic Year
Amounts	Summer: up to $3000 Semester: up to $5000 Academic Year: up to $7000
Deadline	March for the following Summer. April for Fall/Academic Year. October for Spring/Early Academic Year.
Website	www.iie.org/programs/freeman-asia

Fulbright Scholarships – These scholarships are funded by the Fulbright Commission, to increase mutual understanding by the people of the United States and the people of other countries. They may be used for studying, teaching, and/or conducting research abroad.

Eligibility	US citizen. Must be a graduating senior or hold a B.S., B.A., master's degree, or be a doctoral candidate or young professional/artist.
Location	East Asia/Pacific Region, Europe and Eurasia, Near East/North Africa and South and Central Asia, Sub-Saharan Africa, Western Hemisphere
Length	Depends on the type of award
Amounts	Award amounts vary but can be substantial
Deadline	October for the following academic year
Website	www.iie.org/fulbright or www.cies.org

George J. Mitchell Scholarship – This scholarship is funded by the US-Ireland Alliance; scholars must be enrolled in a graduate degree program or certificate program offered by an institution of higher learning, in Ireland or Northern Ireland. The application deadline is in October.

Eligibility	US citizen between 18 and 30 years of age with academic excellence, intellectual distinction, an outstanding record of leadership, and a strong commitment to community and service. Must hold Bachelor's degree from accredited institution before beginning scholarship.
Location	Ireland or Northern Ireland
Length	Academic Year
Amounts	Tuition, housing, a $12,000 stipend, and international travel
Deadline	October for the following academic year
Website	www.us-irelandalliance.org

Gilman International Scholarship – This federally funded scholarship is for students with financial need who are also planning to study abroad anywhere in the world. Deadlines are in October and April.

Eligibility	US citizen and undergraduate in good academic standing. Must be receiving, or will be receiving a Pell Grant at the time of application or during the study abroad term.
Location	Anywhere except Cuba or countries on the State Department's list for travel warnings
Length	At least four weeks in one country, so long as it is in the Fall, Spring, or Academic Year terms (can't be only summer).
Amounts	Up to $5000
Deadline	April for programs between the following July and October. October for programs between the following December and April.
Website	http://www.iie.org/programs/gilman

Japanese Government (Monbukagakusho) Scholarship – This scholarship is funded by the Japanese government for research students, teacher training students, undergraduate students, Japanese studies students, college of technology students, special training college students, as well as *Young Leader's Program* students.

Eligibility	Varies per track
Location	Japan
Length	Varies per track
Amounts	Varies per track
Deadline	There is no application form, but instead, the host university (in collaboration with the home university) submits nominations on your behalf.
Website	www.studyjapan.go.jp/en/toj/toj0302e.html

JASSO Short-term Student Exchange Scholarship (formerly AIEJ) – This scholarship is funded by the Japan Student Services Organization and is designed to promote friendships between Japan and several other countries.

Eligibility	Must qualify for and be participating in a Japanese academic-year exchange program through your university.
Location	Japan
Length	Three months to one year
Amounts	It provides for a stipend of ¥80,000 per month, and a relocation allowance of about ¥150,000 upon arrival
Deadline	There is no application form, but instead, the host university (in collaboration with the home university) submits nominations at the time you apply to the program.
Website	www.jasso.go.jp

Language Flagship Program – Funded by the National Security Education Program.

Eligibility	US citizen who has an *advanced-low* proficiency in the appropriate foreign language and a *superior* proficiency in English. Must have an undergraduate degree and cannot be employed by the federal government.
Location	Designated locations to study Arabic, Chinese, Korean, Persian/Farsi, Russian, and Eurasian Languages.
Length	Two years both domestic and overseas
Amounts	Tuition, a modest stipend, and support for health insurance and travel costs
Deadline	January of every year
Website	http://thelanguageflagship.org or www.iie.org/programs/nsep/flagship/default.htm

Marshall Scholarship – The British government established this full-ride scholarship to thank the United States for its assistance during World War II.

Eligibility	Sophomore. Very competitive, see website. Must graduate with a 3.7 GPA or higher.
Location	United Kingdom, any university
Length	Two years of graduate study
Amounts	Varies according to the circumstances, place of residence, selected university, etc. Tends to be about £20,000 per year on average.
Deadline	Submit the application in mid-September, at least two or more years before obtaining a bachelor's degree.
Website	www.marshallscholarship.org

Rhodes Scholarship – Funded by the Rhodes Trust, this full-ride scholarship provides generous stipends for study at Oxford in the United Kingdom.

Eligibility	Recipients must be between 18 and 24 years old and complete a bachelor's degree.
Location	United Kingdom, University of Oxford
Length	Two years of study, with the possibility of renewal for a third year
Amounts	A maintenance allowance adequate to meet necessary expenses for term-time and vacations, as well as necessary costs of travel to and from Oxford. After submitting your application, additional grants may be approved for research purposes or study-related travel.
Deadline	October 1, in the fall of your senior year
Website	www.rhodesscholar.org

Rotary Ambassadorial Scholarship – Funded by the Rotary Foundation for graduate study in a field related to Rotary's objectives of world peace, international understanding, eliminating disease, conquering hunger, or fostering literacy.

Eligibility	Applicants must contact their nearest Rotary club to determine whether funding is available, ask about deadlines, and obtain the application forms and materials.
Location	Various locations available
Length	Academic Year
Amounts	Up to up to $26,000 for students and qualified professionals who apply early.
Deadline	Varies per district, but plan to submit about one and a half years in advance
Website	www.rotary.org

Rotary Cultural Ambassadorial Scholarship – Funded by the Rotary Foundation to undergo intensive study of a foreign language and cultural immersion.

Eligibility	Applicants must contact their nearest Rotary Club to determine whether funding is available, ask about deadlines, and obtain application materials. Must have at least one year of training in the language to be studied.
Location	15 languages offered in 29 countries
Length	Three or six months
Amounts	$10,000 to $15,000
Deadline	Varies per district, but plan to submit about one and a half years in advance
Website	www.rotary.org

Tips for your study abroad scholarship applications!

- Start EARLY! Start NOW! It is not uncommon for application deadlines to be a year or more prior.
- Know what each committee is looking for and think about how your achievements fit with their criteria.
- Make your application stand out from the rest, in a positive way, and this does not mean orange paper.
- The goals of your application should be to convince your readers that you are one of the best candidates.
- Write a different essay/statement for each scholarship and explain how you best match its unique criteria.
- Write well and answer all the questions presented in the application and/or the personal statement.
- Include your most significant experiences and how they've influenced your life and career goals.
- Focus on a few of your key experiences and do not include too much information that can overwhelm.
- Unify your academic achievements, personal beliefs, and key experiences into a definite theme.
- Focus on your education and how study abroad will enhance your career goals in addition to your life.
- Have others review your writing and offer advice.
- Take your essay to the Writing Center on campus and to your Study Abroad Office for review and advice.
- Re-read and re-write. Edit, edit, and edit your essay.
- Eliminate any unnecessary length and redundancy.
- After you have edited thoroughly, then proofread and check for grammatical and spelling errors.
- Submit before deadlines; submit well in advance.
- Save some information for your interview. Your essay should not be a catchall, but rather a teaser.
- Demonstrate desirable traits like flexibility, maturity, adaptability, communication, independence, etc.
- Display your leadership potential, your commitment to a better world, and clear goals for the experience.

9. What if it just costs too much?

Whatever you have, spend less. ~ Samuel Johnson

If you attend an out-of-state public institution, check into the study abroad tuition and fees. At some institutions, there is a great advantage for out-of-state and international students to study abroad because in-state tuition rates are included in the program fees, or regular tuition/fees are waived so the student can pay the provider or host directly. This can amount to huge savings towards your college education, if you can pay less to study abroad than you would to take courses on campus.

If out-of-state tuition is still applicable, or if you pay hefty tuition rates at a private college or university, then consider enrolling at a public in-state institution just to study abroad and then transfer credit to your out-of-state or private home institution afterwards. Sometimes this won't work for various reasons (i.e. you have to be enrolled full-time for a semester or year before you can study abroad). Moreover, if you are using financial aid, look carefully if or how it will transfer.

There's no law that says you can't be enrolled at two or more colleges at the same time. Students often enroll at a local two-year college and a four-year college or university in order to save money on tuition. So why not enroll in a private/out-of-state institution of your choice and a public in-state institution so as to save money on study abroad? Think about it; it makes sense. If your home institution gives you a hard time about it, then explain that you don't have the money to study abroad any other way and you'd really like the opportunity.

Also, there is no law against taking time off. Students usually have the right to take some time off from classes before they are booted from the institution. They may withdraw to earn money, so why not to study abroad? Our students can study abroad for less than it costs to stay (on in-state tuition).

41

10. When and for how long can I go?

He travels best that knows when to return. ~ *Thomas More*

The answer to this question depends on the policies at your institution. Every college and university has its own policies about when and for how long students can receive credit for studying abroad. If there are policies about *when*, then your freshmen and/or senior year may be restricted. If there are policies about *how long*, then you may be restricted to only a semester or year, or two years at the most.

The real question is how many academic requirements can you fulfill by studying abroad through your home institution? Generally, the more requirements you still have to fulfill, the easier it is to find study abroad opportunities and replacement courses to match. For instance, if you have fulfilled all your general education requirements on campus, then your study abroad program choices are limited to those that can help you fulfill your major, minor, and elective requirements.

Late sophomore or junior year is a good time to study abroad because you've adjusted to college, you should have a major declared, and you don't have to worry about graduating and looking for a job as soon as you return. However, there is no hard or fast rule about the best time to go abroad. My advice is to think and plan a year or two in advance. Planning can help you hold off on certain requirements that you are able to fulfill when you study abroad.

In addition to considering the academic factors that have an effect on your study abroad experience, it is also important to think about your personal experience. Consider the climate in conjunction with activities, and the time you'll have after the program. For example, Australia's summer vacation is from December to February; so if you study there from July to November, you will have part of summer to enjoy afterwards.

11. Is study abroad safe?

While it depends on where you study, the majority of students feel safer abroad than they do in the US. Violent crimes are less common in study abroad. More prevalent are purse/bag snatchers and pickpockets who rob unsuspecting tourists, not used to such criminals. I was eating in a Barcelona café when apparently a man walked in, lifted a woman's purse, and then left without anyone noticing his actions. When she realized that her purse was gone, the owners played back the video surveillance. It showed how he did it, but his identity was concealed by a large cowboy hat that covered his face.

Regardless of where you live and travel, health and safety is never a guarantee. We will all die someday from something; we can only hope that it is from natural causes at a very old age. While destiny is not in our hands, we can do things that reduce our risk for illnesses, accidents, and death. We can use good judgment and street smarts, and make wise decisions about everything. Don't be careless, thinking that *it* cannot or will not happen to you. Preventable illnesses, accidents, and death happen to the most unsuspecting people, every day.

While certainly you could be hurt by a number of things in any country, including the United States, international travel does pose some unique risks. To reduce these risks, you have to (1) be aware of them; (2) do all you can to take necessary precautions against them; and (3) plan, plan, plan! A few things that come to mind are jet lag, motion/altitude sickness, travelers' diarrhea, parasites, viruses, diseases, bacterial infections, sunburn, insect bites, auto accidents, and drowning. You should research the risks that are relevant to your host city and country, as well as other areas you will explore.

Sometimes it happens that we get informed, but we don't use the information wisely. For some reason, students tend to take more risks while they are traveling than they would normally take at home. I'd like to caution you in this area. Picking up your passport doesn't mean putting down your brain. Educate and protect yourself! Information is empowering and making good decisions with that information helps you to be healthy and safe. Get informed, use sound judgment, and weigh your behaviors and actions against possible consequences. When we are *young and indestructible*, it is easy to forget about the least favorable results (immediate and long-term).

Let's look at an example…we all know that cigarette smoke is directly linked to lung cancer, yet look at how many people smoke. Smoking is one of the world's leading causes of death (see www.globalhealth.gov), yet college students who have said "no" to smoking all their lives, take it up overseas and become addicted. Maybe it is really peer pressure or our strong sense of invincibility that is the world's leading cause of death! People smoke for different reasons, but it's not a bad idea to ask yourself why you choose to smoke and if the benefits are more valuable than the possible consequences. Would you trade a lifetime of smoking for 10 years of life, or would you rather lose 10 years than give up cigarettes?

It is human nature to be caught up in the moment and say that you'll be more careful later, but really, the time to be careful is now. The time to pay attention to you and your body is now. If you don't, later may never come, or worse, it may be miserable. Take it from someone who has experience. For one reason or another, I had a hard time understanding my mortality when I was in my teens and twenties, and therefore didn't always use my common sense and take precautions. I ended up with giardia, amoebas, and shoulders problems from carrying too much weight around. That mistake has cost me several surgeries and now a lifetime of pain management. I also didn't wear sunscreen or hats, so I hope that I don't get skin cancer later in life, too. Being smart now, will pay off later if you are willing to make several small changes.

What you have to do is give up your sense of invincibility and *decide rationally* how much risk you're willing to take in life, and how you can reduce risk even more, every second of your existence. To do this correctly, you have to be mature enough to understand the potential consequences of your decisions and behaviors. You should then engage in those behaviors because you believe that the short- and long-term benefits of participating are more valuable than the least probable result, after you have done everything you can to reduce the risks. Risks are necessary and healthy for full enjoyment of life. We take a risk every time we get into a car, train, or plane. We take risks when we eat certain foods. You took a risk when you decided to go to college and study abroad!

To be honest, it wasn't that I thought carrying a heavy back-pack was more important than my shoulders or not wearing a hat was worth the risk of getting skin cancer. I guess I just never knew the risks, or I didn't think they pertained to me. More often than not, we tend to think we're invincible and it often takes a major wake-up call for us see otherwise. A few years ago, I knew a young man who decided one night to get drunk with his friends and get up on top of the car to surf. Unfortunately, he never saw another day. When the car took a turn, he flew off, hit his head, and died within a few hours. What a wakeup call this was to the other boys that were in the car. My cousin was his best friend and happened to be driving that night. You can probably imagine his grief.

While bad things do happen, and sometimes safety is beyond our control, we can take certain measures to reduce our risk in otherwise risky situations. If you can reduce your risk from death to injury (by getting trained and wearing appropriate protective gear), or you can reduce your probability of getting sick from 95% to 15% (by taking certain precautions), then you can still enjoy life to its fullest, from an audacious point of view. Nobody is asking you to be a hermit and nobody expects you to eliminate risk. Just learn the dangers and do small things to reduce your risk for injury and death. Below are a few examples of how you can manage.

Activity	Risk	Reduce Risk	Eliminate Risk
Living in and/or visiting a place with malaria	Contracting the disease	Take the right prophylaxis.	Don't live or visit any areas that have malaria.
Riding a motorcycle	Accident or even death	Wear a helmet, and follow other road/safety rules.	Don't drive or ride motorcycles at all.
Taking a taxi	Assault, accident, or even death	Take a legal taxi and don't travel alone. Always wear a seatbelt.	Walk instead of taking a taxi, and choose your path judiciously.
Drinking the juice at a café	Bacteria and/or parasites	Eat at a café that boils/treats water for the juices.	Don't drink juice at the café; drink soda instead.
Going to a bar	Assault	Don't let your food/drink out of sight. Don't drink more than you can be alert.	Don't drink when you go to the bars, or simply don't go to the bars at all.
Bungee jumping	Injury or even death	Go with a reputable company, get trained, and wear the right equipment	Don't go bungee jumping; go for a walk instead.
Working in the hot sun	Sunburn, long-term skin cancer	Wear hats and sunscreen with a high SPF.	Do go out in the sun; stay indoors instead.

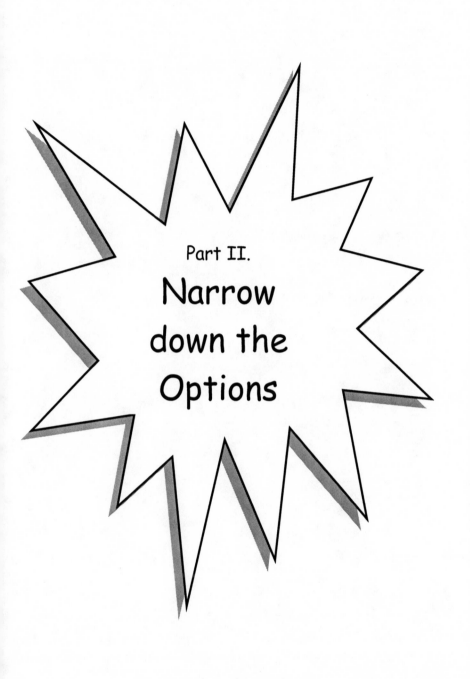

Part II.

Narrow down the Options

12. When should I get started?

It's never too early to plan your study abroad experience. If you didn't start your planning in high school, then ideally you should start during your freshman year of college. By starting this early, you will have more program options available to you than you would have if you started later. After you select a program, you can better manage your study path, *before* you go abroad. Hold off taking requirements that you can fulfill abroad, and in the meantime, take courses that are not offered through your study abroad program.

Traditionally, the junior year has always been viewed as the best time for students to study abroad. However, this tradition is changing. College students are now studying abroad during all phases of their education, even during graduate school and summer vacations. When you choose to study abroad depends on your academic and personal circumstances. It is a good idea to schedule an appointment with your Academic Advisor to talk about how you can best accommodate your plans.

If you're thinking about doing an academic-year abroad, then a traditional four-year college plan might look like this:

Freshman	Gather information from a variety of sources; choose a location and program. Research and apply for scholarships.
Sophomore	Apply to a program, continue to apply for scholarships, and plan your experience.
Junior	Spend the year living and studying abroad. Get to know the culture and the locals.
Senior	Incorporate the experience into your life, your resume, and your career goals. Leverage your study abroad experience for potential jobs.

13. What are my program options?

Nobody ever did, or ever will, escape the consequences of his choices. ~ *Alfred A. Montapert*

To understand your options, first identify the department or office on campus that helps students study abroad, and then go there. If your home institution doesn't have a study abroad designee or process in place, then inquire about being absent for a semester or two and then transferring credit in through other channels. If you're not yet in college, and study abroad is important to you, then find out how it all works at your top choices, before you decide where to go (this is important).

In any case, it is imperative to work closely with the office or the designee on campus. Doing this will make your life a lot easier when it comes to financial aid, course approvals, credit evaluation, and health and safety issues, among other things. If you ignore or bypass policies and procedures, and do things your own way, then keep in mind that you will probably have difficulties obtaining assistance, applying your financial aid, receiving credit for coursework, etc.

While some colleges have an array of study abroad options, others have only a select few, and still others don't have any, in which case students have to creatively find ways to obtain credit for studying abroad. It comes down to what you can do for credit. Institutions have different policies in this regard. Some accept credit for only their sponsored programs, or a list of approved partners, while others accept credit from any foreign institution recognized by its Ministry of Education.

Your university may (a) own and operate its own programs, (b) rely on outside partners, and/or (c) allow students to select external programs of their choice (with approval). Either way, there are five common paths to studying abroad for credit.

Path	Description	Advantages/Disadvantages
Exchange (Partner)	You study at University X, and a student from University X studies at your institution. You and the other student pay regular tuition rates to your home institutions.	The least expensive when the tuition cost at the host institution is greater than what you pay at home. The number of participants is always limited (making it more competitive).
Direct Enroll (Partner or Non-Partner)	You apply directly to the host institution (through its international student office), enroll in courses available to international students, and make your own travel arrangements.	Second least expensive, but can also be time consuming. Requires independence and foreign language skills (for some countries). Best suited for those comfortable with international travel.
Consortium (Partner)	Your institution has an agreement with a group of programs that belong to different institutions. The processes may be simple or they may be complex. Arrangements made on your behalf may be minimal or extensive.	Usually more expensive than a *Direct Enroll*, but less than a *Provider*. An extra level of service is generally extended, but it requires you to make a lot of your own arrangements for courses, housing, transportation, etc.
Third-Party Provider (Partner or Non-Partner)	A company submits the admissions materials on your behalf and makes most arrangements for you (classes, housing, orientation, etc.). Onsite directors and excursions are common. Everything is taken care of for you or very explicit instructions are provided (i.e. visa).	Most costly, but usually a high degree of service for students who want to save time and energy. Best suited for those who have not traveled abroad alone and/or want a high level of support. Also good for those who don't want to spend extra money/time planning their excursions, insurance, etc.
Home-Owned and Operated (sponsored by your college or university)	Either your university owns overseas facilities and contracts all the staff OR your university sends a faculty member abroad for the sole purpose of teaching a course to its students. The group may travel about or stay put.	May or may not be costly, depending on the location/ length, and the institution sponsoring the program. There are higher standards of care and expectations in a *university-owned/operated* program. Faculty and staff are usually well trained.

Example of a Third-Party Provider

There are many choices for third-party providers. Academic Programs International (API) is one example of a respectable third-party program provider. They contract with overseas academic institutions and housing; they organize excursions and cultural events, manage offices and fulltime staff in each program location, and provide many or all of the *extras* that students might need throughout the time they spend studying abroad (insurance, mobile phones, 24/7 on-site support, etc.). The most distinguishing aspect of API is that it was founded by four knowledgeable women (who are now all mothers), with significant experiences abroad, as well as in the field of international education. API emphasizes not only academics, but on providing tools to help students succeed academically, culturally, and personally. They have an online resource BKA *Toolbox* to help students maximize their experiences abroad. For information about API, visit: www.academicintl.com.

Example of a Home-Owned and Operated Program

Many colleges and universities own and operate programs. They may or may not permit students from other colleges and universities to participate. Harlaxton College is a 100-room Victorian manor located in the English midlands. Students live and study at the manor along with their faculty members and other Harlaxton staff. Harlaxton is owned and operated by the University of Evansville, and it was cited amongst the top 25 programs in *The Student's Guide to the Best Study Abroad Programs* (Tannen, G. & Winkler, C., 1996, Pocket Books: NY). Harlaxton offers a full curriculum, with courses taught by resident British Faculty and Visiting Faculty from a wide variety of Partner Schools and disciplines. Harlaxton is most renowned for its intensive British Studies course, and its unique and noteworthy student-learning experience. For more information, visit http://www.harlaxton.ac.uk.

14. Where do I search for programs?

Man cannot discover new oceans unless he has the courage to lose sight of the shore. ~ **Andre Gide**

The study abroad program you eventually choose should fit into your schedule, complement your character, and help you achieve your personal, academic, and career-oriented goals. Below are the most popular resources for searching programs.

- **Australian-Universities.com** - Complete guide to Australian universities and colleges with rankings, schools, history, groupings, and links to home pages.

- **British Council United States** – If you want to study in the United Kingdom (England, Wales, Scotland, or Northern Ireland), check www.britishcouncil.org/usa.

- **Campus France** – A French governmental agency that helps students plan and carry out a period of study in France. www.campusfrance.org

- **Goabroad.com** – Search their directories with over 12,000 opportunities abroad, updated daily including study abroad, internships, volunteer opportunities, teach abroad, language schools and much more.

- **IIEPassport.org** – An online, searchable database of study abroad programs. You can search by language, country, and subject. It is one of the best directories online for identifying programs.

- **IIE Passport: Academic Year Abroad** and **IIE Passport: Short-Term Study Abroad**– These directories are similar to iiepassport.org, but include more comprehensive information, listing over 6000 study abroad programs offered by accredited US and foreign institutions. Most study abroad offices have these directories on hand, but if not, you can purchase them through IIE (www.iiebooks.org).

- **International Handbook of Universities** – First published in 1959, this handbook is a good resource when looking for accredited colleges and universities around the world. It provides data on 8,300 higher education institutions. It is published every two years by Palgrave Macmillan, and is available for review in most study abroad offices.

- **Peterson's Search for Study Abroad Programs** – A complete online directory of more than 1800 overseas programs at over 350 institutions in the US and around the world. They also publish a book called *Study Abroad [*current year*]*. It includes academic programs, volunteer work, internships, financial aid, health and safety, and travel opportunities. Visit their website: www.petersons.com/stdyabrd/us.asp.

- **StudyAbroad.com** – A comprehensive directory of study abroad programs (including short-term summer opportunities), internships, service learning, and volunteer abroad programs, high school study abroad, intensive language programs and more, all searchable by subject, country, or city.

- **StudyAbroadDirectory.com** – A busy website sponsored by Studyabroad.com, with an online database of international programs and travel tools/ resources. Study abroad programs are searchable by country, subject, and term.

- **Study Abroad 2000+** – A 640-page trilingual guide to study abroad opportunities and scholarships, published by UNESCO. Best of all, this English-Spanish-French guide is free and can be accessed at www.unesco.org/education/studyingabroad. Click on "Networking" and then on "Study Abroad."

- **StudyAbroadLinks.com** - A searchable web directory featuring thousands of study abroad opportunities and resources worldwide.

- **Study South Africa** – If you're interested in going to South Africa, you must visit www.studysa.co.za, the International Education Association of South Africa.

- **Transitions Abroad** – A web portal with plenty of resources for students planning to study abroad. It also has an online directory of study abroad programs. See the website: www.transitionsabroad.com.

- **UNESCO Portal for Higher Education Institutions** This portal provides access to higher education institutions sanctioned by either government or other competent authorities. You can find information about higher education, accreditation, quality assurance, and related subjects in various countries. The portal serves as an entry point to each country's information; it is not a centralized database or international list. www.unesco.org/education/portal/hed-institutions

- **University of Minnesota** - This guide has over 1,500 programs, including work and volunteer opportunities. www.istc.umn.edu

- **Worldwide Colleges and Universities** – A resource with web links to colleges and universities around the world. www.globaled.us/wwcu

15. What if I have special circumstances?

Man needs difficulties; they are necessary for health.. ~**Carl Gustar Jung**

a. Strong Religion

Religion is one of those things that many Americans practice but don't always understand or talk about. Nonetheless, your religion may influence where you'd like to study abroad. You may want to learn more about *your own* religion or you may want to learn about *another*. I call myself a Christian, but I lived with an African Muslim family while training with the Peace Corps. At first, I was shaken because of the differences in our religious views. However, I grew to love my homestay family, and became best of friends with their daughter.

Living with and befriending a family with a very different religious orientation was no cakewalk, but it was a growing experience. We exchanged much dialog around religion and I questioned both their religious views and mine. More importantly, I found answers. In the end, their commitment to Allah deepened my faith in Jesus Christ. Even though they are still Muslim and I am still Christian, I am better because of them. Instead of following after the masses, I went off the beaten path and found my own version of truth.

More than being exposed to various religions, you can also *study* them around the world. Europe and the Middle East are often considered a goldmine of religious relics and can be a wonderful place to learn and undertake study/research. There are several study abroad programs that specialize in religious studies. Studying your religion in its birthplace or its early stages of evolution can be an eye-opening experience. Also, studying other religions can help you understand people from a new perspective. Who knows, maybe you'll end up being a college professor or using your knowledge in other ways.

Finally, if you are religious, then you should investigate the acceptance of your religion in the country you wish to visit. Some countries don't tolerate the beliefs and/or practices of certain religions, and it would be best for you to either not go to one of those countries and/or not exhibit your beliefs while you're there. This is a tough decision that only you can make, based on what you hope to get out of your experience. The most popular destinations are normally tolerant of different religions and beliefs, although one may dominate the culture.

Religion & Ethics – An Encyclopedia of world religions. www.bbc.co.uk/religion/religions

Sacred Text Archive – Claims to be the largest freely available archive of online books about religion, mythology, and folklore on the Internet. www.sacred-texts.com

Wikipedia Religious Intolerance – A nice article on religious intolerance with the ability to look up discrimination/persecution by victimized group. http://en.wikipedia.org/wiki/Religious_intolerance

World Religions Index – The objective of this site is to give Christians an understanding of other faiths and religious philosophies. wri.leaderu.com

---

b. Graduate Student

There are many opportunities for graduate students to study abroad. Ask your advisor about the prospects in your field. In some programs, graduate students can complete internships and practicum. In other cases, graduate students travel abroad for teaching and research purposes. If you're researching any human subjects, don't forget that each participant must give his/her *informed consent* before taking part in your study. An informed consent is written agreement to voluntarily take part in research, after having been advised of the purpose. This is an important ethical regulation governed by the US Office for Human Research Protections.

Graduate students usually have two major concerns when it comes to study abroad: (a) fulfilling academic requirements with little flexibility, and (b) financing the experience, since graduate assistantships cannot frequently be transported off-campus. However, through careful and creative arrangements, nothing is impossible. Valuable credit can usually be obtained if your academic department has its own programs or if the experience can satisfy internship, practicum, research, and/or independent study requirements. Graduate advisors may also substitute course requirements with similar courses abroad, or allow required electives to be complete through study abroad.

There's no comprehensive list of graduate-level study abroad programs. Consult a variety of resources in the same way that you did when you were searching for a graduate school in the US. While investigating your options, look into how colleges and universities are adding international dimensions to their curricula, relevant to your field. If you are looking for a short experience, there are lots of faculty-led programs looking for students within particular disciples. For example, in Student Affairs, there are study abroad courses like *Disability in a Diverse Society* (Michigan State), *Issues in College Student Development* (St. Cloud State), *International Perspective on Education and Social Reform* (New York Univ.), *Comparing Educational Systems* (Clemson Univ.), and more. Our School of Biology just started an *Ethnobotany in China* program that has really taken off with our M.S. Biology students.

Choosing a study abroad experience to enhance your graduate studies is probably going to take some time and planning. The following resources may prove useful in this process:

- **International Graduate Schools** – An international graduate programs directory searchable by academic discipline. http://international.gradschools.com

- **International Graduate** - Graduate and postgraduate courses for students worldwide who want to study abroad. www.internationalgraduate.net

- **Universities Worldwide** – A searchable database with direct links to universities around the world, organized by country. http://univ.cc

- **UIUC College and University Rankings** – Use this collection of databases to discover rankings around the world. www.library.uiuc.edu/edx/rankint.htm

- **US Department of Education** – The International Education Programs Service (IEPS) administers various programs that complement graduate study. www.ed.gov/about/offices/list/ope/iegps/index.html

In addition to looking at program opportunities, you should look into funding, especially if you're conducting research. The following sites may be useful in this process:

- **American Association of University Women** - Offers fellowships, grants, and awards for Women Scholars: www.aauw.org/education/fga

- **FundSource** – Funding in behavioral and social sciences. www.decadeofbehavior.org/fundsource

- **Grants.gov** – Find and apply for federal government grants. More than $400 billion. www.grants.gov

- **InfoEd International (SPIN)** – A database of international funding opportunities. www.infoed.org/new_spin/spinmain.asp

c. Partner and/or Kids

Students with partners and children are taking advantage of study abroad opportunities. If it is your dream to go abroad, then don't let anything get in your way. More nontraditional students are going back to college, and more study abroad programs are taking spouses and children into consideration. Your study abroad office can help you make arrangements for your family (housing, daycare, and/or school).

One of the biggest excuses I hear from people is they can't study abroad because they are tied down to responsibilities at home. This is really not fair to you or your family. Children and spouses can benefit from your studying abroad just as much as you can, and it's good for them, too. Putting a little variety into your lives can only enrich your family in the long run. While it takes preparation to make special arrangements, there are many rewards for both you and your family.

I know a single Mexican-American mom who took her eight-year old daughter when she studied abroad in Mexico. Both had a wonderful and unforgettable experience returning to their motherland and learning about their ancestral heritage. They particularly enjoyed living with a host family that took care of their everyday chores like cooking and laundry. While mom was taking classes at the university, her daughter was going to school at an American-style elementary school.

If you are interested, then inquire and discover. There are two websites that you may find helpful in this process. The *Office of Overseas Schools* (www.state.gov/m/a/os) provides a nice directory of elementary and secondary schools for dependents of American citizens, and *Transitions Abroad: Family Travel* (www.transitionsabroad.com/listings/travel/family) provides links to a plethora of resources for families, including books, articles, exchanges, rentals, homestays, hostels, etc.

d. Minority (here or there)

If you are a student of color, planning to study someplace that is devoid of color, you may have some questions about what to expect. Will you encounter racial bias and prejudice? Will people make unfair judgments based upon the color of your skin? How will things be different from what you experience at home? What things will be the same?

On the contrary, you may be excited because you are going to a part of the world where you will represent a member of the majority for the first time in your life. How will it feel to see your own race represented, from the taxi driver all the way up to the president of the country? How will locals perceive you? How will your culture be different from theirs?

Regardless of what you think you know, it is important to investigate your race in the country you would like to visit. Whether gawked at or glanced over, you will at least know what to expect and how to respond to racial prejudice. A few noteworthy color-country combinations are Blacks in Spain, China, and Japan; Koreans in Ecuador; Native Americans in Russia; and Whites in Japan.

I once advised a member of the college football team, who studied abroad in Japan, but had a hard time adjusting. People gawked at him, laughed at him, and called him a giant every time he went out into public. Some even stopped to take his picture because he looked so strange and different to them. Needless to say, he wasn't amused. He decided to come home early, halfway through his program. Just remember, people are learning about you just as much as you are about them.

If you are white, then you may be considered a minority in certain areas of the world. As a result, you may experience what it feels like to represent the minority, similar to what people of color experience in many parts of the United States. While it doesn't compare to a lifetime of being a minority in a nation, it's important to get a glimpse of this reality, as it will help you become more sensitive to people of color.

If you are a student of color, consult the following resources and look into special scholarship opportunities only available to minority students. Most importantly, know what you might encounter and how to deal with such encounters.

- **Diversity Abroad** – This website promotes study abroad opportunities, grants, and scholarships for multicultural students. www.diversityabroad.com

- **Diversity Issues in Study Abroad** – An excellent compilation of quotes by Brown University students addressing issues of diversity in study abroad. http://www.brown.edu/Administration/OIP/pdf_docs/ diversity_st_abroad01.pdf

- **Resources to Support Underrepresented Students** Scholarships that support underrepresented students. http://www.globaled.us/plato/resources.html

e. Disability or Challenge

There are two federal laws in place to protect the educational rights of individuals with disabilities. The first is *Section 504 of the Rehabilitation Act of 1973*. This law strictly prohibits discrimination on the sole basis of disability in any program or activity receiving federal financial assistance. According to the *Civil Rights Restoration Act of 1987*, if a higher education institution accepts even one US dollar of federal funding anywhere, in any area or department, then this law applies to and infects the entire institution. See the following website for more information: www.usdoj.gov/crt/ada.

The second is Title II of the *Americans with Disabilities Act* (ADA). This law applies to all government and commercial entities, including study abroad. It prohibits discrimination against individuals with qualified disabilities in all services, programs, and activities, regardless of whether they are public or private. For detailed information about this law, see the following ADA-related websites at http://www.ada.gov and http://consumerlawpage.com/brochure/disab.shtml. Also, read about your rights and responsibilities specific to international education at www.miusa.org/publications.

In light of these laws and our inability to control situations and circumstances in foreign countries, most universities and colleges strive to provide *reasonable* accommodation, unless it would fundamentally alter the study abroad program. It is however the responsibility of the student to disclose his/her disability to the appropriate campus official, early on in the process, and be straightforward about the type of assistance that is needed. Since overseas sites have different types of accessibility, try to identify several programs that meet your academic interests/needs.

Mobility International USA (MIUSA), serves as the National Clearinghouse on Disability and Exchange (NCDE). This fine organization strives to increase study abroad opportunities for people with disabilities and provide student assistance that helps ensure successful international experiences. Visit their website at www.miusa.org. It is full of helpful information, as well as publications, videos, and programs. Consider one of their books, *Survival Strategies for Going Abroad: Strategies for People with Disabilities*.

Another good source of information for students and advisors is http://www.umabroad.umn.edu/access, maintained by the University of Minnesota. Access Abroad was created through national FIPSE funding. It was a collaborative venture among many universities, and is considered a national resource in the field of international education. Check out their sampling of programs around the world that accommodate students with disabilities, and the section highlighting student experiences. Their *Student Checklist* is also very helpful.

While there may not be countless options for students with physical disabilities, more universities around the world are becoming accessible. Whatever your wants/needs may be, it is important to be proactive and transparent. Being open and honest with your study abroad advisor and your disability services coordinator, about the kind of accommodations you need, is critical to finding the right program for you. Don't be bashful; your advisors are more than willing and able to help. They want you to have a successful and positive experience.

Inclusion International – A global federation of family-based organizations advocating for the human rights of people with intellectual disabilities worldwide.
www.inclusion-international.org

Disability Information for Students and Professionals – A website for students who are studying in the field of disability, as well as professionals working within it.
www.abilityinfo.com

Making it Happen – A documentary highlighting the accommodations and opportunities abroad for students with both apparent and non-apparent disabilities.
www.abroad.pitt.edu/makingithappen.html

---

f. Nontraditional

If you're a nontraditional student, and you are planning to study abroad, fear not. There may be younger students around you, but age-diversity can be a good thing. Chances are you'll enjoy this unique opportunity to interact primarily with a new generation of students. You may be able to offer them a fresh and different perspective throughout their studies abroad. On the other hand, you may find yourself doing things that you never thought feasible or possible at your age!

Whether or not to live in the residence halls is up to you, but I've found that older students either prefer to live apartment-style or with a host family. It really depends on your way of life, your goals, and your flexibility. It also depends on the culture in the part of the world where you will be living. In France, for example, host families usually don't work out as well as they do in Spain or Latin America. Sometimes host families don't work at all for adults who are accustomed to living by themselves and on their own.

As a nontraditional student, you may also consider alternative long-term opportunities. If you can make the commitment, the US Peace Corps is an excellent way to live and work in another culture without the typical worries of study abroad. Unlike study abroad, the Peace Corps pays for international and local transportation, language/technical training, health care services, and provides an adequate salary to sustain you while abroad. In addition, Peace Corps sets aside a monthly stipend for you, available after your service (mini-retirement). I've known many retirees who joined the Peace Corps and had the time of their lives.

If you're 50+, take a look at Elderhostel (www.elderhostel.org) or Elder Treks (www.eldertreks.com) for more opportunities.

9. Dietary Restrictions

If you are a vegetarian or have certain food allergies or other restrictions, you will need to plan accordingly. If you live with a host family, then they should be able to accommodate your special needs. If you live on your own, it's a lot easier to decide what to eat and not to eat, but there are also drawbacks and other considerations. No matter where you live, your diet is always manageable if you're willing to take the extra steps necessary to ensure restrictions are met.

In some places, it will inevitably be harder than in others to hold to a special diet. For example, if you are a vegetarian in Spain, you may find it difficult to eat healthy at restaurants, depending on the level of your vegetarian restrictions. Don't think you'll always be able to prepare your own food because Spaniards love to go out to eat, and often! I once traveled to Spain with a vegetarian, and all she ate was cheese and bread. I don't think she was able to find too many vegetable dishes.

If you are able and willing, then be flexible. Vegetarians may choose to eat vegetables that are cooked in the same pot with meat; because that's the way they are prepared. By virtue of the fact that you've decided to study in another country, you should try different foods. Many countries take great pride in their cooking. To miss ethnic cuisine is to miss at least some culture. I was a vegetarian when I went into the Peace Corps, but chose to eat meat that wasn't injected with hormones.

If you are allergic to certain foods, or have another medical reason for maintaining a certain diet, then there's no room to be flexible. I met a man who was mildly allergic to wheat. Whenever he'd eat anything with wheat, he'd break out with a rash. He was able to bend the rules here and there, but not much. I also met someone who had a severe allergy and she had to be extremely careful with what she ate. One teaspoon of peanut butter could have hospitalized or killed her at worst.

Green Earth Travel, LLC – Caters to travelers who desire to maintain their vegetarian and vegan lifestyle, throughout the world. www.vegtravel.com

SelectWisely – Customized travel translation cards for food allergies and special diets. www.selectwisely.com

h. Lesbian, Gay, Bisexual, Transgendered

If you fall into the category of LGBT, then you definitely need to learn about the social and cultural norms surrounding friendship, dating, homophobia, and dress in the host culture that you are contemplating for study abroad. You should also find out if the legal system offers protection (or harm) when sexual orientation is involved.

What is considered normal for you at home may elicit a very different reaction in another country (negative or positive). You may be discriminated against, or at worse, you could be harmed. It's good to be aware of widespread attitudes, beliefs, and behaviors, and modify your situation accordingly. Think about your safety first; you have nothing to prove.

See the regional information section of the International Gay and Lesbian Human Rights Commission (www.iglhrc.org) to learn about what is happening in different countries around the world. Also, see the Department of State *Country Reports on Human Rights Practices* (http://www.state.gov/g/drl/hr). These are excellent places to start your research.

Gay.com – Worldwide travel destinations and topics for gays and lesbians. www.gay.com/travel

Gayguide.net – An online network connecting gay people and communities around the world.

ILGA Europe – A must-see for travelers to Europe. I was especially impressed by their easy to use *LGBT Guide to Europe* (country by country). www.ilga-europe.org

International Lesbian and Gay Association – This group is working for the human rights of LGBT people. In the search box, type "State-sponsored Homophobia" for a report on laws prohibiting same sex activity between consenting adults. Type "World Legal Survey" to access a map on legislations affecting LGBT people around the world. www.ilga.org

NAFSA Rainbow SIG – An excellent resource for students who are gay, lesbian, bisexual or transgendered, and looking for practical advice regarding their study abroad experience. www.indiana.edu/~overseas/lesbigay

16. How should I select a program?

The shoe that fits one person pinches another; there is no recipe for living that suits all cases. ~**Carl Gustav Jung**

Knowing yourself (and accepting who you are) is the key to finding your best-fit study abroad programs. For example, if you like living in a small town and are somewhat reserved, it's probably not a great idea to start your experience out in an enormous city. It's not that you couldn't manage, but you'd probably have a richer experience in a smaller city, where you could live with a family, make friends easily, and walk or ride a bike to class. Study abroad is challenging enough, don't push yourself too far.

During my first stint in the Peace Corps, I was placed in a small African village to live and work. My village was very remote and there were only about 1000 people who lived there. My job was to teach health education. Even though I didn't like my job much, I felt comfortable with the people and community, made some good friends along the way, and knew who to speak with and where to go for all of my needs. As a result, I had a positive experience that I wouldn't trade for anything in the world.

During my second tour in the Corps, I was placed in an urban youth development job in Quito, the capital city of Ecuador. While the job was definitely more exciting, it was extremely hard for me to adjust to life in the big city. Thus, I asked the Peace Corps for reassignment to a small village. They told me that the only way that they could reassign me was if I gave up youth development work and went back to health education. I decided it was worth the sacrifice, and so I moved to a small village in the Andes Mountains.

To save yourself some headaches and from having to jump through hoops and more hoops, it is best to figure out what you *want* and *need* before you commit yourself to a study abroad program and location. Studying abroad is one of those things that you will fondly remember for the rest of your life, so take some time to think about what you want to get out of this door-opening opportunity. Think about fit, not glamour and excitement. Think about what might be best for you, not what someone else said was awesome.

Far too often, students make decisions about where to study based on hearsay. One student said it was awesome, so others think it must be a good fit for them, too. You don't decide on a major or career because your friend told you it was cool, so don't do it with study abroad. Preferably, your study abroad program and location should augment your education and future career, fit your personality, and challenge you to grow. You should be able to coherently explain to an employer why you selected a program and how it advanced your goals.

As you can imagine, there is a lot to consider when vetting study abroad programs: dates, duration, subjects, eligibility, credit, price, cost of living, instruction, housing, and location.

You should also look at program types and structures. It can be overwhelming if you don't have some idea of what you want before getting started. Nonetheless, your first step is to figure out what you want/need in a study abroad experience. The more careful you are about complementing your personal characteristics and career goals with a study abroad program, the better chance you'll have for a successful experience.

The following worksheet will help you bring together all the factors that should be considered when vetting programs, and should guide you to make better choices.

First-Step Worksheet

Why do you want to study abroad? (ex. personal growth, academic enrichment, career goals)

_____

_____

_____

_____

_____

Where are you interested in going? (Don't rule out non-traditional locations as they are becoming more popular.)

_____

_____

_____

_____

_____

What do you hope to accomplish? (ex. improve foreign language skills, learn another culture, etc.)

_____

_____

_____

_____

Would you prefer a special type of environment and/or atmosphere? (ex. big city, small town, etc.)

_____
_____
_____
_____

What do you like to do in your spare time? (fun activities)

_____
_____
_____
_____

What kind of courses do you plan to take? (subject matter)

_____
_____
_____
_____

How do you want/need study abroad coursework to factor into your degree program? (The more you choose, the more options you will have when it comes to selecting a program.)

◘ General Education ◘ Major ◘ Minor

◘ Internship ◘ Language ◘ Independent Study

_____
_____
_____
_____

How long do you want to be gone? (Note, most students wish they signed up for longer than they did… a semester goes by really fast.)

◘ 1-6 weeks ◘ Semester ◘ Academic Year

When can you be gone? (Check all that apply and circle one or two preferences.)

◘ Fall ◘ Winter Break ◘ Spring

◘ Spring Break ◘ Summer

In what languages are you willing/able to take classes?

◘ English or ◘ Another language: _____

Are you interested in learning another language?

◘ No ◘ Yes: _____

Your current level: _____

What kind of housing best suits your goals?

◘ Hostel or Hotel   ◘ Flat or Apartment

◘ Host Family   ◘ Residence Hall

_____
_____

Do you have any special needs? (vegetarian, disability, etc.)

_____
_____
_____
_____
_____

What size and type of institution/classroom best suits you?

Institution Size: ◘ Small ◘ Medium ◘ Large
Classroom Size: ◘ Small ◘ Medium ◘ Large
Type: ◘ Americanized ◘ Foreign (something new)

How important is total cost in your final selection?

◘ Not important   ◘ Somewhat important

◘ Very important   ◘ I cannot go without help

How much money do you have to spend? (include any financial aid that will apply to study abroad) _____

How much independence do you desire? (The more support and/or structure you want or need, the more costly the program in comparison with others in the same location.)

Very comfortable asking questions or figuring things out on my own.	Not comfortable asking questions or figuring things out on my own.
Lower Cost	Higher Cost
Less structure needed ← →	More structure needed

Other notes:

_____
_____
_____
_____
_____
_____
_____
_____
_____
_____

Take this worksheet to your study abroad office so a trained advisor can help you identify some best-fit programs just for you, from the options available at your institution. When you begin to narrow down your options, then talk to students who have gone before you and review student evaluations. There are many resources that can help you in this process:

- **Abroadbuzz.com** – A relatively new site designed specifically for students to leave feedback about study abroad programs.

- **Abroadviews.com** – A new website dedicated to volunteer, internship, and study abroad program reviews from students who have gone before.

- **Allabroad.us** – An online forum where you can find a mentor, and get your questions answered by those who have studied abroad.

- **Iagora.com** – Currently, the most comprehensive option for student reviews on various aspects of a study abroad program. http://www.iagora.com/istudy

While all of this may seem overwhelming, it's really not once you figure out what you want/need. It's also quite rewarding when you've come to a decision based on sound logic rather than dust in the wind. One thing that people tend to overlook in their youth is that each decision they make in life leads to another, which unfolds into a journey that leads to who, what, where, when, why, and how they continue to exist. When you get to be my age, you see that where you've ended up was all based on your decisions along the way. Then you have either an epiphany or a midlife crisis. ☺

So let's assume that you're interested in Australia, Spain, and Argentina. You would love to visit all of these countries but can only pick one for study abroad. The reason why you want to study abroad is to improve your Spanish skills. You also want to see more of the world and make international friends. Based on your goals, Spain and Argentina seem like the most viable options for a study abroad experience, since you will not be able to improve your Spanish skills much in Australia. After gathering some basic information about Argentina and Spain, you just can't seem to decide between the two.

From here, let's say that you determined from the worksheet that you want to study abroad for a full year, improve your Spanish skills, live with a host family, be instructed in both English and Spanish, and take classes in your major. You also would like to live in a small city with easy access to outdoor sports activities, and the experience can't cost any more than you receive in financial aid because you don't want to take out more loans. Moreover, you've decided that an integrated program would better fit your personality and goals. With a set of criteria like this, it is much easier to shop for programs.

You analyze the program types and structures in each of these countries and narrow down your preferences in both Spain and Argentina. Because you're an adventurous person and one of your goals is to learn the language and culture, you choose an integrated program. From an advising standpoint, an *integrated program* is the best choice for your goals. An integrated program provides a level of structure that enables students to get involved in the local language, community, and culture. Conversely, an *island program* tends to cluster international students together within a tight framework that encourages community with other international students (or American students) rather than with locals.

With these specifications, you find only two programs that seem to suit all your needs/wants. One is in Spain, and the other one is in Argentina. You apply to both and are admitted without delay. Because cost is a major determining factor for you, and the cost of living in Argentina is somewhat lower than in Spain, you lean towards Argentina. You also like the outdoor activities that Argentina has to offer. Finally, you always wanted to see the other side of the equator. Voila, a decision! You take out your paperwork for Argentina and start filling it all out. Doesn't it feel good to come to sound decision based on your personal preferences and academic goals? I hope you have a magnificent experience, and I look forward to hearing about it after you return home!

17. What if I want to do an internship?

The world is your school. ~ **Martin H. Fischer**

In addition to studying abroad, students may choose to intern or volunteer abroad for academic credit. More universities are approving international internships en lieu of domestic ones, and some are even offering credit for volunteer experiences, or service learning. There is a broad range of options from working full-time to on a part-time basis while taking regular courses abroad. If you are required to complete an internship or service-learning component as part of your degree, then consider something international for a variety of reasons.

International internship and volunteer opportunities exist in just about every field. There are plenty of positions with a challenging level of responsibility. Plus, you get the benefit of obtaining hands-on experience in another part of the world. The downside of interning/volunteering abroad is that it is hard to find positions that are paid, mainly because of visa restrictions, and you have to cover the costs associated with your airfare, accommodations, food, and daily transportation. Depending on how you locate and organize your internship, you may end up paying much more. If you're having trouble finding something on your own, ask your professors if they have any ideas. Sometimes a professor will have contacts in an organization or company abroad that is looking for help.

If you are unable to find something on your own, or through your college or university, and/or you don't have the time and energy to make all the arrangements, then think about going through an agency and paying for an internship or volunteer program. An agency (third-party provider) offers professional coordination services, saving you time and frustration in the process. Such coordination may include interview assistance, job placement, accommodations, visa/permit help, customer support, and language lessons. It is nice to have this level of assistance when arranging an internship experience abroad, but doing it all by yourself is not impossible either. It depends on what you want and need.

In order for you to obtain credit for an internship or volunteer project, it needs to be career-related and you need to have it pre-approved toward your internship and/or service-learning requirements. Academic credit can be obtained and validated with an official transcript from your program provider, or by pre-arranging an evaluation with a professor who is willing to work with you or with your internship coordinator. Make all arrangements BEFORE you select or even start looking for an experience, as you may find there are restrictions and hurdles to unravel and manage. Working out credit is the first thing you should do, after identifying your options.

Regardless of whether you are interested in finding a paid provider or in finding something on your own, you can begin at Transitions Abroad (www.transitionsabroad.com); type the word "Internships" in the Google search box. In the list that comes up, select the link that reads "Internships Abroad: Top International Internship Programs." This page has the most comprehensive information available on learning, teaching, working, and volunteering as an international intern. Another good website is internationalcenter.umich.edu/swt, run by the University of Michigan. Finally, Michigan State publishes a thorough Directory of International Internships; you can buy it at www.isp.msu.edu/students/internships/intlguide.

If you are determined to save money, and you want to find something on your own, then look for volunteer opportunities with NGOs and see if you can work out academic credit on your campus. Many NGOs are looking for volunteers. Check out Idealist.org and VolunteerAbroad.com for listings. Also, consult with your department/faculty because they may have contacts with NGOs already, from their own experiences in the field. If you haven't figured it out yet, it's always easier to get somewhere when you know somebody. This seems to be true across all cultures, and even more so outside of the US.

If you're interested in South America, then visit the South American Explorers Club at www.saexplorers.org. They have a lot of information and resources for travelers, and a section for volunteer listings. You have to be member to access this section of the website, so if you're sure that you're going to South America, then it is probably worth the investment. One thing I like about Latin America in general is that the cost of living tends to be low, and it doesn't cost an arm and a leg to fly there either. For the UK, consider BUNAC; for technical specialties consider IAESTE; for Germany consider CDS.

An alternative to going abroad is to work with a company or organization that has an international focus or branch. This is a good option if you're looking for an international career such as foreign policy. Look at the websites of big NGOs, the US Department of State, and the Foreign Policy Association (www.fpa.org). The federal, state, and city governments may also have internships in their international trade offices. Visit studentjobs.gov for information on government agencies with opportunities. See section #99 for career-related resources. The opportunities are vast; all you have to do is search.

Internship/Volunteer Resources

- **AIESEC** – The world's largest student organization, arranges international job exchanges. www.aiesec.org
- **Association for International Practical Training** Provides educational and professional exchange programs in many countries. http://www.aipt.org
- **Alliances Abroad** – Offers customized internship, work, teach, and volunteer programs around the world. http://www.allianceabroad.com

- **American-Scandinavian Foundation** – Placements in Scandinavia, http://www.amscan.org/training.html
- **Amity Volunteer Teachers Abroad** – A nonprofit organization that organizes teaching exchanges around the world. http://www.amity.org
- **BUNAC** – Work programs in the UK, Australia, New Zealand, Canada, South Africa. http://www.bunac.org
- **CCUSA** – Summer camp and adventure jobs around the world. http://www.ccusa.com
- **CDS International** – Internships in Argentina, Germany, Russia, and Spain. http://www.cdsintl.org
- **CIEE Work Abroad** – Work abroad opportunities in 30+ countries (Australia, Canada, France, Germany, Ireland, New Zealand, and more). http://www.ciee.org
- **Dave's ESL Café** – Job center for ESL teaching opportunities. http://www.eslcafe.com
- **English Job Maze** – ESL/EFL job center and search. http://www.englishjobmaze.com
- **Foundation for Sustainable Development** – Short-term work in Bolivia, Ecuador, Nicaragua, Tanzania, Peru, and Uganda. http://www.fsdinternational.org
- **French American Chamber of Commerce** – Offers internships in France. www.ccife.org/usa/new_york
- **Global Experiences** – A program provider, specializing in international internships and work experience abroad. www.globalexperiences.com
- **Habitat for Humanity International** – Building homes around the world. http://www.habitat.org
- **How to live your Dream of Volunteering Overseas** A book, http://www.volunteeroverseas.org/html
- **IASTE** – Technical internships and exchanges all around the world. http://www.iaeste.org
- **Interexchange** – Provides a wide range of work & travel, volunteer, internship, and *au pair* programs around the world. http://www.workingabroad.org

- **Intern Abroad** – A nice directory of internship opportunities. http://www.internabroad.com
- **International Cooperative Education (ICE)** – Arranges for students to work as paid interns in an array of employment fields. www.icemenlo.com
- **International Honors Program** (IHP) – Unique comparative studies of social, environmental, and political issues. www.ihp.edu
- **International Internships and Volunteer Network** Promotes International Internship and Volunteer programs. http://www.rtpnet.org/~intintl
- **JET** – Language teaching opportunities in Japan. www.us.emb-japan.go.jp/JETProgram/homepage.html
- **Jobs Abroad** – A nice directory of employment opportunities. http://www.jobsabroad.com
- **Proworld** – A provider of work abroad projects determined by community need as well as your skills and interests. http://www.myproworld.org
- **Teach Abroad** – A nice directory of teaching opportunities. http://www.teachabroad.com
- **TEFL.com** – The world's largest database of English language teaching jobs. http://www.tefl.com
- **Transitions Abroad** – A web portal for work abroad and overseas travel. http://www.transitionsabroad.com
- **Volunteers for Peace** – A directory of international volunteer projects in 100+ countries. www.vfp.org
- **Volunteer Abroad** – A nice directory of volunteer opportunities. http://www.volunteerabroad.com
- **Volunteer International** – International volunteer work and internships. www.volunteerinternational.org
- **World Teach** – Opportunities to teach abroad. Based at Harvard University. http://www.worldteach.org
- **WWOOF** – Worldwide opportunities on organic farms. Volunteer on organic farms in exchange for your room and board. http://www.wwoof.org

18. Am I finally ready to apply?

We are always getting ready to live, but never living. ~ **Ralph Waldo Emerson**

Let me make myself clear…if the process you went through to choose a study abroad program wasn't as complex or more than it was for you to choose a college or university for which to study and obtain an undergraduate or graduate degree, then you're probably not ready to apply. If you're sure that you've weighed the pros and cons and found a program that is a good fit for all your academic and personal goals, then by all means start filling out the application materials.

First, it's important that your application is truthful. If your GPA isn't up to par, don't exaggerate or mislead. GPAs are never rounded to the nearest ten; a 2.75 is NOT a 3.0. Your chances of getting into a program are greater if you're honest, than if you're dishonest on your application, even if your GPA is lower than the minimum requirement! Dishonesty is usually discovered, because most study abroad offices verify the information that you put on your application.

If required, write a strong statement about your academic and personal goals for study abroad, and check for spelling and grammatical errors. The purpose of a statement should be to demonstrate your thought-provoking goals and good writing skills. Poor writing is a red flag for many decision makers. If you can't think clearly or write well, then you won't succeed on essay questions that sometimes count for half your grade in many study abroad programs.

So what makes a strong application? While it depends on the program, decision makers are generally looking for:

- At least the minimum eligibility requirements
- A match between your goals and the program

- Scholastic achievement and motivation to succeed
- Strong references that support you studying abroad
- The likelihood of you being a positive ambassador for your school, community, and country
- The likelihood of your having a healthy and safe experience, and not endangering yourself or others

Finally, include any pertinent health information and special needs (if not in the application, in the paperwork you receive after you are admitted to the program). This is critical so that your advisor can help to accommodate your particular needs. It might be necessary to find a counselor while you're abroad or it may be that you require a notetaker for a disability that you have declared. You may need to attend AA meetings in your host country or find a host family that can support your vegan diet. Whatever the need, early disclosure is critical.

After you've filled out and submitted your application before the deadline, sit back and wait for the results. Depending on the program, there may be several decision makers involved. In case of an exchange program or partner program through your study abroad office, the host or provider usually makes the final decision. Depending on the program and country, this may take longer than one would expect. If you don't hear back within a reasonable time period (longer than a month), then call your study abroad advisor to find out what's going on. He/she may be able to provide you with status updates.

19. What if the deadline has passed?

A deadline is negative inspiration. Still, it's better than no inspiration at all.
~ Rita Mae Brown

Study abroad programs are advertised with deadlines, which do not mean much if enrollments are lower than expected. Because program fees and profit margins are established by a predictable number of *payees* (enrollees), anything less can drive a program into the red. If this happens, then program personnel have three choices: (a) to take a loss, (b) to cancel, or (c) to extend the application deadline. Most will opt to extend their deadline en lieu of the other two choices, unless a negative profit margin is part of the start-up business plan.

If the application deadline has passed, you may still be able to get into a program. When space is available, and warm bodies are needed to make a program cost-effective, your chances are good, provided that you meet the minimum requirements. The deadlines for Summer/Fall programs are usually between February and May. The deadlines for Spring programs tend to fall between September and November. Although deadlines may be extended, study abroad offices get busy around this time of year, and therefore may not get around to posting them right away. Don't assume you've missed the boat; ask.

If you're applying after the deadline, chances are you'll have to do a number of other things late, too. So, look before you leap. You may need to apply late for a passport, obtain a visa, sign up for courses, make sure you have enough financial aid, visit your doctor for a physical checkup, get recommended and required immunizations, have your courses pre-approved, arrange for your housing, and purchase your airfare. This is why it is always better to apply early, because the time it takes for passports and visas doesn't fully depend on you.

Believe it or not, it is possible to obtain a same-day passport. You must provide proof that you are leaving within three working days to qualify for this same-day service and you typically have to go to a major passport office (like Chicago or D.C.). It takes about four to six hours to process. I knew a professor who was denied entry on the plane because her passport was due to expire within 6 months. She had to pay an extra $60 for expedited service, but she was able to get a new passport and get on a plane the next day.

20. How can I get a dual/joint degree?

It's not your blue blood, your pedigree or your college degree.
It's what you do with your life that counts. ~ Millard Fuller

The US and Europe have taken very different approaches to student mobility. The approach of student mobility in the US has been labeled as *vertical*. Students typically complete an undergraduate degree at one US institution and then pursue a graduate degree at another. In the course of obtaining their degrees, students study outside of the US, but only for short periods of time, or via formal international partnerships.

The approach to student mobility in Europe has been labeled as *horizontal*, mainly because of the Erasmus Program. This program allows European students to spend between three to twelve months at another college or university in Europe, by recognizing and transferring all of the academic credits to the home institution. The program was launched in 1987, and its major objective is to reach 3 million by 2010.

These approaches have opened up different education abroad opportunities, such as *dual* and *joint degrees* on both sides of the Atlantic. A *joint degree* means that more than one college or university's name is on the diploma, which is being offered jointly and awarded by two or more different institutions. A *dual degree* is the articulation of a college degree from two or more institutions, each awarding its own.

Dual/joint degree programs are available for undergraduate and graduate studies; however, the majority of programs are for graduate studies. While there are many more programs in Europe than there are in the US, we are trying to catch up. For example, San Diego State University (SDSU) manages a dual-degree program called *Project Amigos*, which allows management majors to spend two years at SDSU and two years at the Guadalajara campus of Tec de Monterrey, one of Latin America's top business schools. American students who have minimal Spanish spend their first year taking classes in English, along with intensive Spanish language training, and their second year taking business classes taught in Spanish.

Another example is EUCHEMUSA (funded by ATLANTIS), a dual-degree program in Chemistry between two European and two US universities, with elective classes in language and culture. The ATLANTIS Program is an EU-US Cooperation that provides funding for the development of dual and joint degree programs between Europe and the United States. For a list of approved projects, and many new degree options, visit http://ec.europa.eu/education/programmes/eu-usa and look at the "Selected Projects" that have been approved since 1996.

Another option, which is unrelated to dual/joint degrees, is to complete your college degree abroad. A good place to start your research is www.collegeabroad.com, an online directory of worldwide colleges and universities that offer full degree programs, taught in English. Consider a dual-degree option from the Università Bocconi and Central European University that combines the study of European business practices and American management style, with the new challenges of the emerging economies. The opportunities are endless!

Part III.

Prepare for
your Trip

21. I was accepted, now what?

Congratulations feels great but is never enough.
Here's the big checklist. ~ **Wendy Williamson**

_____**TALK TO YOUR PARENTS**. It's important that you talk to your parents (or other family members) before making any final decisions about a program. Allowing parents to be involved in the process will help them to help you in certain aspects of planning and preparation. Don't underestimate the value of their support.

_____**ACCEPTANCE PAPERWORK**. Fill out, sign, and return any acceptance paperwork, including contracts. Some of these contracts will limit a program's liability and some will hold you accountable for certain behaviors and/or events. Read this paperwork carefully and make sure you understand everything, including payment and refund policies.

_____**COURSES**. If you haven't already done so, select and verify your courses and have them pre-approved to replace academic requirements in your degree program. Select twice as many as you plan to take, in case of cancellations. Every college and university has a different process in place for approving study abroad coursework.

_____**HOUSING**. Select and secure your housing overseas. It is important that you do not wait until the last minute to find housing, because space is often limited (especially for on-campus housing, when available).

_____**FINANCIAL AID**. Make sure your financial aid is in order. If your university doesn't already have one on file, your host may have to complete a *Consortium Agreement*, certifying that they will not administer Title IV financial aid for you (it will come from your home institution instead).

_____**PASSPORT & VISA**. You must apply for a passport and then a visa (if applicable). See section #22, *What about passport and visa?*

_____**HEALTH**. Schedule a medical checkup with a doctor and see section #23, *What about my health?*

_____**SAFETY**. Learn the best approaches to staying safe in the countries you'll be visiting and see section #24, *What about my safety?*

_____**AIRFARE**. Purchase your international airfare. See section #25, *What should I know about flights?*

_____**INTERNATIONAL ID**. An ISIC or other card is optional. See section #26, *Do I need an International ID?*

_____**INSURANCE**. Purchase good international health insurance (if not pre-arranged by your university/provider). See section #27, *What about insurance coverage?*

_____**REGISTRATION**. Register with the Dept. of State in the countries that you'll be visiting (name, passport number, dates, and location) via https://travelregistration.state.gov if you're a US citizen or a permanent resident. Otherwise, register with your country's equivalent. Examples:

- UK: www.fco.gov.uk/en/travelling-and-living-overseas/Locate/
- Canada: www.voyage.gc.ca/main/sos/rocapage-en.asp
- New Zealand: www.safetravel.govt.nz/beforeugo/index.shtml#registration
- Japan: www.anzen.mofa.go.jp

_____**ORIENTATIONS**. Attend any recommended or required pre-departure orientations, organized by your home university (usually a good source of helpful information).

_____**ARRANGEMENTS**. You will need to arrange your personal affairs while away.

_____Designate someone to be your *Power of Attorney* to take care of and settle problems while you're away. www.ilrg.com/forms/powatrny.html

_____Make arrangements for your bills. Nowadays you can set most of your bills to pay online, including your credit cards. Again, a Power of Attorney or trusted parent/friend can help you if your Internet access is limited.

_____Make arrangements to vote from abroad, if applicable. You will need to vote by *absentee ballot*. Visit the Federal Voting Assistance Program for information about the process: http://www.fvap.gov or http://www.votefromabroad.org.
- Democratsabroad.org
- Repulicansabroad.com
- Overseasvotefoundation.org

_____Make arrangements to take the GRE, LSAT, GMAT, or MCAT (if you plan to attend graduate school upon return).

_____Make arrangements to register for classes while you are abroad for the semester when you return.

_____Make arrangements to secure housing for the semester that you return to your home campus. Also, don't forget to cancel any home-campus housing contracts for the time that you'll be absent.

_____Drop any courses you might have registered for if/when you thought you'd be on campus for the time that you'll be studying abroad.

_____If you're going to buy a rail pass for Europe, do it before you leave the US, to get the best prices.

_____Ask your parents to arrange an international calling plan/method from home so they can call you affordably when you are abroad. We usually buy calling cards on the Internet; try www.zaptel.com or www.callcasa.com to compare rates.

_____Make sure your addresses with schools, banks, services, etc. are updated to your permanent address, where someone is checking and taking care of your mail while you are away.

_____**DOCUMENTS**. Gather and prepare the appropriate documents for emergency planning and purposes.

_____Renew your plastic. You don't want to find yourself with an expired passport, driver's license, health insurance card, ATM cards, or credit cards. Change your ATM pin to only four digits because overseas ATMs can *eat* cards with longer ones.

_____Make at least two copies of your passport (the page with your photo and information) and airline itinerary. Leave one with your family and plan to take several with you (in different parts of your luggage).

_____Write down your credit/debit card information on a sheet of paper, with numbers to call in case of loss or theft. Code your personal information, in case someone else finds the list. Make two copies, one to leave with your family (or trusted friend), and one to take with you. If you don't want to write it all down, then make front and back copies (at least two) of all your cards, and leave one set with someone at home.

_____Notify your banks when you will be traveling and where, so they don't put a false fraud-alert on your cards and stop service. Nowadays, suspicious activity often triggers automatic deactivation.

_____Write down these and other relevant telephone numbers for emergency purposes.
- Overseas Citizens Services: 1-888-407-4747, from overseas: 202-501-4444 (death, arrest, detention, robbery, missing persons, and other crisis involving American citizens after hours).
- Office of Children's Issues: 1-888-407-4747, from overseas: 202-501-4444 (international parental child abduction, international adoption, recorded information on custody and adoptions, denial of passports to minors in certain situations such as abductions)
- Go to http://usembassy.state.gov, locate your host country, and write down the embassy contact information (office-hour and emergency phones).
- Write down your host country's local 911 and emergency phone numbers. For a handy list, visit http://www.sccfd.org/travel.html
- Write down your home and host institution's emergency phone numbers.

_____Carry your passport OR a copy of your passport AND emergency telephone numbers at all times. Keep copies of everything, separate from what you carry with you.

_____ You can register valuables that have a serial number, or a distinguishing mark with US Customs, before you leave (to avoid questionable duty when you return). Just fill out a *Certificate of Registration* (Customs Form #4455) and bring it, along with the item, to a Customs Office/Station to have it certified.

_____**AWARENESS**. Learn as much as possible about the host country and culture.

_____Learn about the country and culture, including its history and how physical surroundings (natural resources, geography, climate, population, etc.) influenced the way in which people live.

_____Read *What's Up with Culture?* (a cultural training resource for study abroad) www.uop.edu/sis/culture

_____Get informed about US issues, foreign policy, and world affairs. Read major newspapers and books on the subject. Read *Great Decisions*, a 112-page briefing book prepared by the national, nonpartisan, not-for-profit Foreign Policy Association. See www.fpa.org for info.

_____Consider taking a basic self-defense course if you are willing and able. Self-defense training can heighten your awareness and understanding of how predators think and behave, and give you the street smarts to stay safe.

_____Consult Guidebooks, Social Networks, Blogs, etc.

Some Resources

- **Concierge.com** – Vacation ideas, travel guides and trip planning tools, with maps, photos, and videos.
- **Country-specific Handbooks** – Lots of information. www.studentsabroad.com/countries.html
- **GlobalScholar.us** – Online courses for study abroad (before, during, and after your trip).
- **Lonely Planet's Discussion Board** – A good source for travel trips. www.lonelyplanet.com
- **MSU Global Access** - A web portal to information about the world that contains a database of Websites

and other resources selected by experts at Michigan State University. www.msuglobalaccess.net
- **Students Abroad**. A new one-stop reference for college-age Americans concerning international travel. You can download checklists and flyers called *go! guides,* as well as a *Tips to Go Wallet Card.* studentsabroad.state.gov
- **World Fact Book** – A CIA publication with country profiles and maps https://www.cia.gov/library

Social Networks

- Bootsnall.com
- ExpatExchange.com
- Iagora.com
- IgoUgo.com
- Tripadvisor.com
- Triporama.com
- Triptie.com
- Planetware.com
- Realtravel.com
- Wayn.com

22. What about passport and visa?

Education is the passport to the future, for tomorrow belongs to those who prepare for it today. ~*Malcolm X*

A passport is a form of international identification that states your citizenship and other important information needed by immigration. If you don't already have a passport, then you should apply as soon as you know you'll be studying abroad. Processing can take four to eight weeks, although expedited service is available for an additional charge. A US passport is valid for 10 years (if you are 16 years of age or above). If you already have a passport, be sure it will be valid at least six months <u>after</u> you complete your travels abroad.

You can find applications and renewal forms at post offices, study abroad offices, courthouses, travel agencies, and online at http://travel.state.gov/passport. If you are applying for the first time, and you are at least 13 years old, or your passport was issued before you turned 16 years old, you must apply in person. You will need to bring two identical passport photos (2 by 2 in.), a photo ID, an original birth certificate (or a previous passport), and two blank checks.

Anytime you plan to stay in another country for longer than a week, you should register with the US Department of State, or your country's equivalent, in case you're studying in the US. Registration allows you to record information about your upcoming, international trip so that the Department of State can assist you in the event of an emergency. You can do this at https://travelregistration.state.gov.

Don't forget to sign your passport and fill in the emergency information. It is also wise for a parent or close friend have a valid passport while you're away, just in case an emergency comes up that requires immediate travel. If neither of your parents, nor your emergency contacts, have a valid passport, there is a one-day passport service available for a legitimate emergency and an additional fee, which is currently $60.

A visa is an official document, stamp, or seal affixed within your passport, which allows you to enter a foreign country for a particular purpose. A foreign government may issue a visa for tourism, study, or work. If you are a US citizen, you can determine whether or not you need a visa by visiting the website of your foreign embassy/consulate. If you determine you need a visa, apply as soon as possible (usually no earlier than 90 days prior to your program), for the period in which you'll be studying in the host country. The process can take anywhere from a few days to several months.

In most countries, you will need a visa only if you're staying more than 90 days; however, there are several countries that require a visa for any length of time, even a week. For most paperwork, you'll need to have a passport (valid for at least six months after your return date), your acceptance letter or enrollment certificate from the host institution, the address where you'll be staying/living, official verification of your international health insurance, and bank statements that show you have sufficient funds to pay for your entire stay.

You must have your passport before you can obtain the visa. Since both can take some time, you should start the process as soon as possible. Ideally, you should apply for a passport before you apply for your study abroad program. If you need a visa, then you can either use a visa agency or visit the host embassy's US website for instructions and forms. If you're running short on time, then use one of many agencies such as www.zvs.com, www.abriggs.com, or www.traveldocs.com to expedite processing. If you have time, and you would rather save money, then follow the list of instructions below:

1. Go to www.embassy.org/embassies and locate the embassy of your host country.
2. Usually visa information is located under "Consular Services." You may have to navigate the website.
3. Look for visa information, forms, and instructions for students, provided that you are *studying* abroad.
4. One you have your passport, your official acceptance letter, and other necessary documents (proof of funds, health insurance, etc.), you can start the paperwork.
5. Double-check your paperwork before finalizing it. Your application could be denied for missing data.
6. Make copies of all paperwork for your records, and provide copies of original documents if requested.

7. If your visa requires a visit, make an appointment as soon as possible and bring all required documents.
8. For security reasons, use certified mail when sending important documents.
9. When talking with consular officials in person or on the phone, always ask for their names.
10. When you get your visa, check the information carefully to make sure there are no errors.
11. Don't make travel plans until you have your passport and visa in hand, or until you are sure that you'll have the documents before your scheduled departure.
12. Know that you typically cannot *extend* a visa; you would have to return to the US and apply for another.

Other paperwork tips:

- Do not block out account numbers on bank statements unless the consulate gives you permission to do so.
- Staple where it says to staple and glue where it says to glue; keep your paperwork in the appropriate order.
- Do not submit scanned photographs; use official passport photos (Walgreens has a good deal).
- Follow payment requirements carefully. For example, many consulates will not accept personal checks.

23. What about my health?

The greatest wealth is health. ~*Virgil*

_____ Visit a doctor and develop a personal health strategy for the time that you will be away.

_____Update your medical records, including prescriptions

_____Get Immunized. Do this early; some vaccines (like Hepatitis A or B) require a series of two or more doses over a six-month period.

_____Get an *International Certificate of Vaccinations,* produced by WHO, if there are immunization restrictions in the countries you'll be visiting. See www.who.int.

_____Make arrangements to bring a complete supply of medications you take regularly. In addition, it's a smart idea to bring an extra pair of glasses or contacts in case of damage or loss. Obtain a letter from your physician if you need to use an inhaler (for some countries).

_____Check to see that your prescriptions and over-the-counter medications are legal in the countries you'll be visiting. You can usually find this information on the US embassy's website for any particular country. For example, it is illegal to bring into Japan some medications commonly used in the US (Sudafed, Pseudoephedrine, Vicks inhalers, and Codeine).

_____Obtain a copy of your prescriptions, and a doctor's statement for how they are supposed to be used, in case you're questioned by immigration.

_____Make sure your prescriptions are written for generic versions and not name brands (since name brands may not be available overseas).

_____Keep all your prescriptions in their original containers (for obvious reasons).

_____Document your blood type, allergies, and any medical conditions, and carry this documentation with you. Plan to wear a medical identification bracelet or necklace if you have any life-threatening allergies or serious medical conditions.

_____Plan to bring a starter supply of toiletries, a first aid kit, sunscreen, insect repellent, tissue paper, and a mosquito net (if going to a tropical area with malaria).

_____Pick out 2-3 doctors and a hospital in the area of your study abroad, in the event that you become ill or need to get medical attention and care.

_____Indicate your personal health needs on your medical and housing forms so that the program administrators can better assist you in terms of support. Don't forget to include important information that you take for granted in your current situation (allergies, dietary needs, challenges, phobias, etc.). For example, if you have a phobia of dogs, you shouldn't be placed with a family that owns one.

_____ Review relevant information on *Travelers Health* (http://wwwn.cdc.gov/travel), sponsored by the National Center for Infectious Diseases. This site provides up-to-date health information about specific travel destinations, including: recommended vaccinations, what to do to stay healthy, what to do to avoid getting sick, what to bring with you, and what to do after your trip when you get home. Another good site to check is the International Society of Travel Medicine at http://www.istm.org.

_____Review the consular information issued by other governments, to obtain a broader, worldwide perspective. Tripprep.com summarizes these varied perspectives.

- Australia: http://www.smartraveller.gov.au
- Canada: http://www.voyage.gc.ca
- Great Britain: http://www.fco.gov.uk

Take precautions to avoid getting sick. In areas where water is not potable, then consume only boiled water, bottled water, carbonated beverages, and beer/wine. Avoid unpasteurized milk and milk products, and only eat raw fruit or vegetables that are washed in treated water and peeled. As the doctors and nurses often put it, "Cook it, boil it, peel it, or forget it." People can get brain worms from eating strawberries that are contaminated with fecal matter! Carry with you appropriate medications and equipment for self-treatment, specific to the area(s) you are visiting. For instance, if you're heading for a remote area with poisonous snakes, bring a snakebite kit.

24. What about my safety?

A danger foreseen is half avoided. ~ *Unknown*

_____Review host country information through the US Department of State at http://travel.state.gov (click on International Travel > International Travel Information > *Country Specific Information* & *Country Background Notes*)

_____ Review relevant *Travel Warnings & Consular Information Sheets* issued by the US Department of State. (http://travel.state.gov/travel/warnings_consular.html). A Travel Warning is a notice recommending that Americans not travel to particular country while in effect. A Consular Information Sheet is a compilation of country-specific immigration practices, political disturbances, health conditions, crime and security, and unstable activities

_____Create an Emergency Card and Emergency Action Plan: www.studentsabroad.com/emergencycard.html

_____Understand the emergency protocols for your program and institution (home and host).

Both health and safety preparation involve pre-planning and a commitment to good decision-making. Although you may be prepared with lots of good information about how to be healthy and safe, it's easy to let down your guard, after you are familiar and comfortable with the territory. The euphoria you feel in a foreign country, combined with a newfounded sense of self, may also give you a false sense of invincibility.

Many crimes that occur are alcohol-related and/or have to do with poor decision-making. Some students drink beyond their ability to make good judgment; they sleep on park benches; they put their wallets in their back pockets; they trust anyone who smiles; they don't conceal their valuables, and the list goes on. Never let down your guard, and don't do things that you wouldn't do at home; take more protections, not less!

My intention is not to scare you, but to give you a dose of reality when you've been intoxicated by the beauty of travel. I, too, am guilty of not doing what I discern to be best, and have to continually remind myself that I'm not invincible; it *can* happen to me. When I was in Cameroon (Peace Corps), a young man who came and left before me was traveling after his two-year service. During his travels, he went to a bar and decided to stay rather than walk back to the hotel with his friends. Later, he turned up missing and was found murdered in an alley nearby. His glasses, boots, and wallet were gone. They caught the guy that killed him, but it was too late for the former volunteer. Heartbreaking!

Street Smarts for International Travel:

- Leave expensive or sentimental possessions at home. You can live without them for a while, so you don't have to worry about them getting lost or stolen.
- The less you carry, the more control you have over your possessions. The more you carry, the more you have to watch over, and subsequently worry about.
- Do what you can to look and act like the locals. When strangers start asking you for directions, then you're probably on the right track, in your appearance.

102

- Know where it is safe and not safe to go, especially if you are living and studying in an urban environment.
- Make sure that you have an emergency card with numbers you can contact when you need help.
- Be sure to carry the cell phone numbers of your leaders and fellow students, and not just on your phone. Have a list that you keep on elsewhere.
- Never leave without money and identification. Carry the addresses and phone numbers of your hotels, residences, program provider, and host institution.
- Know how to contact your local police and get to a hospital in the event of a medical emergency. While others often can and will help, you never know.
- Use a money belt under your clothing to carry your passport, credit cards, cash, and emergency card.
- Don't wear flashy, risqué, or expensive-looking clothing, unless you WANT to attract trouble. Also, don't broadcast "AMERICAN" by what you wear.
- Don't walk alone at night, only take secure and legal taxis, and never hitchhike. Stay in public, lighted areas where there are lots of other people around.
- Carry a small map and know how to find your way in the city/neighborhood. Understand how the public transportation system works and what is safe.
- Rather than whip out your map in the open street, try to be discreet… if you're lost, don't look lost, just stop for a coffee or something and get your bearings.
- Don't expose large sums of money for all to see.
- Lock your doors and windows when you're home and when you're away; thieves are more audacious in other countries.
- Limit your alcohol consumption so that it does not impair your awareness or judgment. Most trouble seems to occur when students are drinking to excess.

- Just as you wouldn't do at home, don't leave your drink unattended. Date rape drugs are popular all over the world, and are used to rob people also.
- When traveling on public transportation, don't go to sleep. You need to stay awake so that you can keep an eye on your possessions, etc.
- When traveling with a group, designate a primary and secondary meeting place for different emergencies that might happen. Remember, phones may go down.
- Consider a communication tree and buddy system for your group travel, with friends and associates.
- When traveling away from your host city, make sure that the right people know where you're going and how to contact you in the event of an emergency.
- When traveling away from your host city, don't let others handle your bags (esp. out of your sight), even if it seems like they're just being nice.
- Don't be a courier for someone, unless you know the person well, and the contents of the package.
- Avoid big crowds of people (markets, strikes, etc.) because the likelihood of theft and violence is higher.
- Avoid American hangouts and large, English-speaking groups of people walking around the city. It's better to split up into smaller groups.
- Stay away from strikes and other worker/political demonstrations, and stay away from tear gas.
- Don't share your political opinions with reporters. It is always best if you try to stay off the nightly news in the country you are visiting.
- Know the local laws and the traffic/pedestrian rules; never assume it is the same as it is back home. Also, don't forget to look both ways when crossing streets!
- Take a self-defense class before you leave. It should teach you how to be alert and trust your instincts, how to distance yourself when necessary or appropriate.

25. What should I know about flights?

A good traveler has no fixed plans, and is not intent on arriving. ~ *Lao Tzu*

How to find a deal

- Check a variety of sources (agencies, websites, newspapers, search engines, etc.)
- Purchase your ticket well in advance. Usually the more time in advance, the better the rate.
- If you purchase in advance, and then the price goes down, ask for a refund. See Yapta.com for help.
- Flying on a Tuesday-Wednesday-Thursday can be 25% to 50% cheaper than other days of the week.

105

- Avoid flying during busy holidays and weekends when fares are at a premium.
- Red-eye flights depart late in the evening or early in the morning, and can usually save you at least 25%.
- Putting up with more connections will allow you to get a better rate than flying direct.
- Include a Saturday overnight in your round-trip plans and check for rate differences at neighboring airports (both at home and abroad).
- If you're going to Europe, consider using London or another gateway city as a hub, and then a *Budget* airline to your final destination.
- If you're buying late, then look into agencies and sites that specialize in last minute travel for some real deals that could save you some serious cash.
- Consolidators are another way to go if you are flexible on your dates and live in or close to an international airport. They buy unsold tickets in bulk quantities, directly from airlines and then resell them to individuals at a discount. There are too many consolidators to name; check the Sunday travel sections of big newspapers like the *Chicago Tribune* or the *NY Times*.
- Air Courier is the way to go if your plans are very flexible. You are basically a freelance delivery person who is hired by a company to escort cargo by plane. You may have to carry paperwork for the shipment and make sure that the shipment is received in its destination. As payment, you get a discounted (and sometimes free) round-trip ticket.
- Always purchase airfare using a credit card, in case your travel agent or the airline goes bankrupt. Under the Fair Credit Billing Act (FCBA), Visa, Mastercard, and American Express purchases receive substantially more protections than cash, debits, and money orders. Check with your credit card company for more info.

Types of Tickets

- **One-way**: This is an option, but is ultimately more expensive than the cheapest round-trip tickets. An exception to this would be Aer Lingus, if you are going to Ireland or want to use Ireland as a hub.
- **Round-trip**: Usually the cheapest way of flying with fixed dates to and from the destination.
- **Flexible round-trip**: An international airline ticket with a flexible return date.
- **Multi-city**: Sometimes I fly into one destination and fly home from another, and it turns out to be cheaper than flying to and from the same destination. I use other forms of transportation in between.
- **Round-the-world**: A sequence of airplane tickets to take you to multiple destinations at a discount. You have to book everything in advance. Go westbound to avoid redeye flights; go eastbound for overnighters.

What to Know

- Does your visa require an onward or roundtrip ticket (i.e. China)? Sometimes consulates will not issue a visa, or border control won't let you through, without such evidence. Know before you go.
- Are you on a scholarship that requires you to use a US carrier? If so, you have to be careful.
- What is the fine print on your ticket (refundable or not, trip insurance, baggage limits, excess fees, etc.)?
- More airlines are adopting strict baggage limits and excess fees can be quite high. Know your weight limits and the number of bags you can check.

My Favorites

- **Airfare, General**: I always start my search for flights on sidestep.com or kayak.com to identify the cheaper fares. Since you're a student, you might want to check out STA Travel, Student Universe, and Travel CUTS.

- **Airfare, International**: I love FareCompare.com because you don't have to plug in dates. Put in your departure and destination airports, and it gives you the lowest fare by month, and then by day/airline.
- **Airfare Barometers**: Before you buy, check to see if rates might go up or down at farecast.com and get time-sensitive bargains at airfarewatchdog.com.
- **Airline Industry**: Read daily reports on airfare sales and the airline industry at RickSeaney.com.
- **Airports Abroad**: This site has information about world airports. www.hotelstravel.com/airports.html
- **Airport Sleeping:** See the budget traveler's guide to sleeping in airports at sleepinginairports.net.
- **Air Courier**: Visit the International Association of Air Travel Couriers at courier.org for information.
- **Baggage**: Go shopping for unclaimed baggage or look for lost items for sale at unclaimedbaggage.com.
- **Bidding for Travel**: Priceline.com usually has good rates on airfare and hotels if you can stand the bidding process. Use the message board biddingfortravel.com to get an idea of prices before you begin.
- **Budget Flights**: Find budget airlines and routes at flybudget.com, whichbudget.com, or flycheapo.com.
- **Driving Directions in Europe**: For roads, maps, pictures, and descriptions, try viamichelin.com
- **Frequent Flyer Miles**: A frequent flyer community with plenty of great information is flyertalk.com.
- **Hitchhiking**: If your travel plans are flexible and you live in a big city with lots of flights to the continent of your destination, check out airhitch.org to fly cheap.
- **Itinerary (customized for you)**: If you are planning a getaway with limited time, see homeandabroad.com for customized suggestions/advice about what to do.

- **Last Minute**: See the sites lastminutetravel.com and/or lastminute.com if you are buying your ticket late and don't want to pay an arm and a leg.
- **Meals**: For information about airline catering and meals, visit http://www.airlinemeals.net.
- **Seats**: Before you choose your airline seat, check out seatguru.com for detailed seating charts and details.
- **Security**: Official government site providing security and safety tips to travelers. www.faa.gov/safety
- **Taxis**: If you are tight on cash and want to share a cab from the airport, check out hitchsters.com.
- **Travel Advice**: There are lots of sites with good travel information, including budgettravel.com.

26. Do I need an International ID?

Half the fun of travel is the esthetic of lostness. ~ *Ray Bradbury*

Whether or not you buy an International ID card is a personal decision. Your decision should be based on your use for the card, and specifically its benefits. Most foreign universities will give you a student identification card for the institution. However, there are several commercial cards that come with other incentives, like insurance and discounts.

The *International Student Identification Card (ISIC)* can be purchased online at http://www.myisic.com, through various travel agencies, and in many study abroad offices. It provides valuable discounts in the US and abroad (100+ countries), including discounts on airfare and a mobile communications package. It also provides some basic health insurance as well as emergency evacuation and repatriation of remains. Finally, it carries travel insurance for lost documents, baggage and delays, as well as 24-hour assistance. The cost is $22 for a year, and it is produced by the International Student Travel Confederation (www.istc.org).

INext is a newer card that offers similar benefits to the ISIC. They don't seem to have the discounts of ISIC, but there are two levels of insurance coverage you can choose from (basic and premium). The basic level of coverage is almost the same as ISIC; the emergency medical evacuation is a bit better but there is nothing for travel delay and baggage/personal effects. The *premium* level of coverage is quite a bit better than ISIC for not a lot more money. The basic is $25 per year and the premium is $45 per year. If you are looking for discounts, then I'd go with the ISIC. However, if coverage is important, INext premium might be a better choice (although ISIC is now offering a premier option, too). Visit www.inext.com.

The *International Student Exchange Card (ISE)* offers lots of discounts, as a well as a guarantee on its discounts, $2000 medical, $5000 in evacuation fees (not enough for major medical), worldwide assistance service, $2000 of bankruptcy protection on your airline ticket, and a global phone card. Go to their website for information: http://www.isecard.com.

Decide carefully based on your unique situation and needs. Different cards have very different benefits. Always read the fine print, and try to get the most for your money. See the next chapter for a comparison of different types of insurance coverage. Note, the comparison is just an example; there are many more companies in which to choose.

27. What about insurance coverage?

Precaution is better than cure. ~ **Edward Coke**

You should make certain that you have adequate health and emergency insurance that will cover you internationally. In some cases, it may be provided by your home institution, and in other cases, it may be included with your fees to a third-party provider. Still in other circumstances, it may be covered by the government of the country you are visiting, after you register for classes and pay your fees. Whatever coverage is provided, look over it carefully because it may not be enough for your particular needs.

Medicare/Medicaid doesn't cover services outside of the US, and your regular health insurance company may not provide sufficient travel-specific coverage and limits. An emergency medical evacuation can cost over $100,000, far beyond what is *customary and reasonable* according to most insurance companies. In addition to coverage, you should look at your financial resources and whether or not you need a direct-pay service, rather than reimbursement after you submit receipts.

I once heard about a man whose appendix ruptured while he was in Europe. He was relying on the insurance provided by ISIC. Because ISIC does not pay hospitals directly, and he didn't have enough money to pay the bill at the hospital, they confiscated his passport and refused to treat him or let him leave after surgery. Luckily, a friend traveling with him was able to collect enough money to pay the hospital bill, get his passport back, and have him released. While he did get ISIC to reimburse him later on, the situation that he forwent in the hospital was dreadful. Moral of the story…if you don't have insurance that can pay hospitals directly for major medical issues, then make sure that you have a substantial emergency fund available and accessible by a third party.

There are lots of different insurance companies and policies with advantages and limitations. Before you start shopping, it's important that you know what you need. Major medical, medical evacuation, and repatriation insurance are necessary! You may consider trip interruption insurance to protect the investment you made, in case something prevents you from going or requires you to return early. It's also not a bad idea to consider security evacuation for natural disasters, outbreak of war, and terrorist attacks (otherwise, you will depend on your local US embassy). If you are traveling to an area where kidnapping or terrorism is common, then think about buying kidnapping and terrorism insurance.

You can shop for insurance online and compare rates through many websites (i.e. squaremouth.com and insuremytrip.com). However, purchase directly from the company that provides it, not from a third party. If you purchase from a third party that goes under, then you'll need to stand in line with all the creditors, which might prove difficult from across the ocean. Don't fall for a great price at the sacrifice of quality and reputation. Read the fine print, especially exclusion clauses. Many companies exclude pre-existing conditions, high-risk activities, care in the US (pre, post, or any stage in your trip), accidents involving alcohol or drugs, etc. Also, look closely at the amount of coverage. The following minimum coverage is recommended, but there's always room for more:

- Medical Expenses – 100K per incident
- Prescription Drugs – 80% to 100% coverage
- Emergency Medical Evacuation – 100K preferred, 75K acceptable (per occurrence, not per person) with flexibility in accommodating different needs, such as low altitude flight capacity for head injuries.
- Repatriation of Remains – 100K idea, 50K preferred, 25K acceptable (per person)
- 24-hour traveler assistance hotline
- Emergency Family Reunion – $2,500
- No pre-existing conditions clauses (if possible)
- Some mental health benefits (if possible)
- Coverage for your return to and care in the US

If there is a pre-existing conditions clause, then look at the period to which it pertains, because it may not be a problem. For example, if the period is six months in length, and you haven't had any consultations or treatments for your shoulder problem during the six months prior to purchasing coverage, then it's not a pre-existing condition according to their books. Think ahead when you plan your study abroad program, and act accordingly.

For travel insurance, you should try to secure coverage right after you purchase your trip. Some insurance companies will waive the pre-existing conditions exclusion, if you purchase within a certain number of days. I heard about a man who didn't do this; instead, he bought trip insurance at the last minute. He ended up having to cancel for medical reasons, and the insurance company refused to cover his loss because he had diagnostic tests prior to purchasing the insurance.

In most cases, the way non-emergency consultations work abroad is similar to the way they work in the States. If your provider is not *in-network* with your insurance company, and most are not, then you'll need to get an itemized receipt and present it to your insurance company for reimbursement upon return. Since medical consultations are more affordable in other countries, paying up front is usually not a problem for minor issues. It is the major medical and hospitalization that sometimes becomes an issue if you don't have a direct-pay arrangement. Most facilities also accept credit cards, unless you're in a remote location, but credit cards have low limits. Don't mess around when it comes to your health. Get the best coverage, and go with a company that has experience and a good reputation in international health care.

On the following pages are four charts comparing different types of insurance. These charts are provided only to give you a reference point and show you a few of the many, varied options available to students. Do not use this information, which could be inaccurate and out of date, to make decisions about your insurance policies and providers. Read the policy information and the fine print carefully, before you decide to purchase. Pay very close attention to benefits, coverage, and exclusions. Finally, make your decision wisely.

Note, many insurance policies will overlap (i.e. emergency evacuation with health insurance). If you have more than one insurer, know which is *primary* and *secondary* (see glossary).

Student Card

	ISIC (Basic)	iNext (Basic)	iNext (Premium)
Website	Myisic.com	iNext.com	iNext.com
Approximate Cost	$22 per year	$25 per year	$45 per year
Deductible	None	None	None
Emergency Medical Transportation	300K	250K	500K
Major Medical	25K	25K	50K
Basic Medical	$165 per day (up to 61 days)	$165 per day	$250 per day
Accidental Death	1K to 5K	5K	10K
Repatriation	25K	25K	50K
Lost Document	$500	$500	$1,000
Travel Delay	$100	No	$200
Baggage Delay	$100	$100	$200
Lost, Stolen, or Damaged Baggage	No	No	$500
24-hr Hotline	Yes	Yes	Yes
Emergency Reunion	No	No	No
Direct Pay	No	No	No
Other Benefits	Yes	No	No

Emergency Evacuation

	MedjetAssist	Intl SOS
Website	Medjetassist.com	Internationalsos.com
Cost	$225 per year	About $413 per year but varies
24-hr line	Yes	Yes
Triage	Yes	Yes
Medical Evacuation and Repatriation	Yes – but you decide where you want to go. If hospitalized, no cost limitations.	Yes – but they decide on the nearest medical facility, capable of required treatment.
Evacuation for Security Reasons	Optional	Yes

Health Insurance

	HTH Worldwide	CISI (Upgrade)
Website	Hthworldwide.com	Culturalinsurance.com
Approximate Cost	$34 to $90 per month	$31 to $261 per month plus $100 to $200
Deductible	$50 per incident	$100 per incident
Emergency Medical Transportation	50K	50K limit combined
Major Medical	100K/yr to 250K	50K
Basic Medical	10K after deductible	Above
Accidental Death	10K	10K
Repatriation	15K	Included above
Lost Document	No	No
Travel Delay	No	No
Baggage Delay	No	No
24-hr Hotline	Yes	Yes
Emergency Reunion	$1,500	$1,500
Direct Pay	Yes	Yes

Travel Insurance

	AIG Travel Guard	Travelex Travel Plus
Website	Travelguard.com	travelex-insurance.com
Approximate Cost	5-7% of total trip cost	6-7% of total trip cost
Trip Cancellation	Up to 100K	Up to 100K
Notes	Option can be added to cancel for any reason	Option can be added to cancel for any reason
Itinerary Change	n/a	$250
Trip Interruption	Up to 150% of trip cost	Included in Medical Expenses
Travel Delay	$750	$1000
Missed Connection	$250	Included in Trip Delay
Medical Expenses	Up to 50K	500K for emergency
Emergency Medical Transportation	Up to 1 million	Included in Medical Expenses
Evacuation	Home or Hospital of Choice	Included in Medical Expenses
Lost, Stolen, or Damaged Baggage	$1000	$2500

Baggage Delay	$300	$600
Accident Death Dismemberment	25K	50K
Flight Accident	Up to 500K	Optional, different levels
Car Rental Collision	35K	50K

Other major companies include:

AssessAmerica – www.accessamerica.com
Assist America - www.assistamerica.com
Chickering Group – www.chickering.com
CMI Insurance Specialists – www.cmi-insurance.com
Compass Benefits Group – www.compassbenefit.com
CSA – www.csatravelprotection.com
Harbour Group – www.hginsurance.com
Lewer Agency – www.lewer.com
Marsh Affinity Group – www.gatewayplans.com
MedAire - www.medaire.com
Multinacional Underwriters – www.mnui.com
RustInternationalAssociates – www.rustassoc.com
Summit Insurance – www.summitamerica-ins.com
Travel Insured – www.travelinsured.com
Universal Travel Protection (UTP) – www.utravelpro.com

28. What and how should I pack?

When preparing to travel, lay out all your clothes and all your money. Then take half the clothes and twice the money. ~*Susan Heller*

What and how to pack isn't as easy as it looks. It takes a lot of planning. The best way to tackle it is to prepare a checklist of items you think you'll need and then narrow it down to no more than you can carry (usually not more than one or two pieces of checked luggage, 50 lbs combined or less, and a small carry-on bag). Pack light! Remember, you'll probably be bringing home more than you take. It's always a good idea to bring an extra nylon bag or backpack that you can shape into a ball, pack in one of your other bags when you leave, and fill up with souvenirs, and other items when you return.

One small suitcase (with wheels), a large travel backpack, and a daypack should be sufficient for everything you need. Unless you have a really nice *significant other* who is going also, then you will most likely be carrying your luggage. In general, people do a lot more walking in other countries than they do in the US, and there aren't as many elevators either. After you've packed, carry your luggage around the block to see if it's too heavy. If you can't endure long, then repack. Don't bring more than you can carry. Mark items off your checklist so you don't forget anything.

Pack your carry-on bag as if you were living out of it for at least two or three nights. If your luggage is lost or flights are delayed, you should be able to brush your teeth and change your socks and underwear. Many airlines have become quite strict on baggage limits, permitting you to carry on a small bag or briefcase. Be sure to carry on anything that you can't live without, as well as valuable items such as plane tickets, your passport, plastic cards, birth certificates, health records, host letters/certifications, etc. Don't carry the copies of your passport in the same bag as your original passport.

In order to avoid problems with your luggage, don't pack valuables in your checked bags. Since you cannot use locks any longer, safety-pin your zippers shut. Use ugly, weird, or worn (but durable) bags that can be easily distinguished from the luggage of others. Put identification tags on your luggage inside and out. Keep in mind that most fruits, vegetables and animal products are not transportable across international borders. Consider mailing some items so you will not have to carry as much, especially if you will be staying in the same location for an extended period of time.

Some other things to keep in mind...don't pack your film in checked luggage (as the screening equipment may destroy it). Don't pack seemingly harmless items that could be used as weapons (ex. curling iron, corkscrews) in your carry-on bag. Don't over-pack bags as to prevent items from spilling out. I once packed a bag so full that it split in half. When it came across the conveyer belt, it arrived in two pieces instead of one. Don't wrap your gifts, unless you don't mind if airport security unwraps them. Carry all medications in their original containers; mixing them in one container will likely confuse customs and cause unwanted headaches for you.

Ultimately, you have to decide what you need and what you don't need. In terms of your clothing, plan for all possible weather conditions and various activities. I tend to bring what I can wear in layers. I also bring dark-colored clothing that doesn't show dirt or require any ironing. Sometimes, I bring old clothes (to sleep in) and old shoes (to walk around in) and then I give them to the homeless or leave them in my hotel room upon departure. This frees up space in my luggage for souvenirs and gifts on the return trip. Usually, I don't bring things that I can easily purchase abroad, such as toiletries. It's a lot more fun to pack light than it is to pack heavy.

I often get questions from students about whether they should bring their laptops or not. Personally, I think a laptop is a wonderful tool to have while you're studying abroad, for lots of excellent reasons (accessing the Internet, chatting with family/friends, doing your homework, listening to music, calling home for free on Skype, storing your digital pictures, watching movies, etc.). However, laptops are easily stolen and should be insured before you leave. Check with your homeowner's insurance about coverage. Also, see *Roadnews* at http://www.roadnews.com (tricks/tips for laptop travelers).

Note, there are many items that are illegal to take on a plane, and the rules change frequently. Currently, you can't even carry on a tube of toothpaste unless it's three ounces or less and in a one-quart clear plastic bag. Even worse, you can't carry a bottle of water through airport security. Consult the Transportation Security Administration (www.tsa.gov/public) for current information about restricted and prohibited items. Be prepared to take a lot of stuff out of your bag and take off loose clothing and shoes when you go through security.

Besides cameras and laptops, I've always preferred to leave my valuables at home, even my wedding ring! The less you have, the less you have to worry about. The less you have to carry around, the less you have to be stolen. The more you have to give away, the less you have to deal with. It's not so bad to travel light because you learn to manage with less. In some places, I've heard of thieves cutting off fingers to get to diamond rings. If you're not going to use it, and/or it's not going to benefit your trip, then don't bring it. Most electronic devices like hair dryers and curling irons you can buy over there and keep for your future trips, after study abroad.

If you insist on bringing electrical appliances, determine the voltage and outlets, and purchase an adapter or converter if needed. An adapter is just a small device that fits over your plug and into the different outlet. It doesn't change voltage, so if you use it without a converter, it can fry things such as radios, alarm clocks, hairdryers, and other voltage-dependent devices. A converter actually changes the voltage, but don't forget to flip the switch on your appliance (see instructions before doing anything). In the US, most equipment operates with 110 volts, but in Europe, it typically operates with 220 volts. Many laptops are now made with build-in converters.

For what it's worth, here's my *Smart List* for traveling, and you probably shouldn't bring all of the items listed. You can go to dontforgetyourtoothbrush.com to create your personal checklist of things to pack and do before you leave. If you're having trouble with too much stuff, then learn the art and science of traveling light at <u>onebag.com</u>. <u>Travelsense.org</u> is another site you might want to see for packing tips, advice, and news (such as the most recent scams and how to avoid them). Sometimes you can buy items that help you preserve space. Visit <u>practicaltravelgear.blogspot.com</u> for cool ideas.

Carry-On Bag

<u>Must Have</u>
_____Passport/Visa and Plane Tickets
_____Photocopies of your Passport and Plane Tickets (put a few copies in different bags, and leave a copy at home)
_____International Certificate of Vaccinations (if applicable)
_____Health Insurance Card and Benefits Information
_____Home University ID Card (unless you're getting ISIC)
_____1 to 2 ATM Cards (must be numeric for checking accounts, not savings; most popular are PLUS and CIRRUS)
_____1 to 2 Credit Cards (Visa, MasterCard, AMEX)
_____$100 Cash for emergency purposes
_____Phone numbers, addresses, directions, and maps to where you're going, from your point of arrival
_____A *Getting Help from Home* list with the contact and tracking information below. If you can code this information, it's always a good thing in case your list is lost or stolen. You can put the numbers backwards, out of order, etc. Just don't forget how to decode it! 800 & toll-free numbers won't work.

- All the plastic cards you are taking abroad (keep photocopies of the cards at home in a safe place)
- Banking and serial numbers for traveler's checks you are taking abroad (if applicable)
- Health Insurance Company & 24-hour Assistance
- Parents/Guardians & Emergency Contacts
- Your study abroad office
- Your academic advisors
- Your doctors and hospitals at home

_____A *Getting Help Abroad* list for each location you'll be studying with contact information.

- Host institution program/provider contacts
- Local US Embassy and local 911 numbers
- Your choice of doctor and hospital on-site
- Your blood type, allergies, and medical conditions

_____ A list of what is in all your suitcases in case lost or stolen, so you can make an insurance claim

_____ Extra Passport Photos (for IDs and Emergencies)

_____ A Watch, to keep track of time (waterproof)

_____ Money Belt or Carrier (to put under your clothing and carry around your credit card, ATM card, phone numbers, cash, and a copy of your passport)

_____ Waist Pack or Fanny Pack (to carry like a purse)

_____ If you're checking your other bag, then you need enough Essentials for two to three nights of lost luggage.

_____ Prescriptions and Over-the-Counter medications for at least a month (if applicable), including eyeglasses or contacts

_____ Extra pair of Eyeglasses or Contact Lenses

Optional (to bring and/or pack in your carry-on)

_____ A good Travel Guide for the area with maps. Pick out one or two of the following:
- Europe Backpack: http://www.europebackpack.com
- Let's Go Guidebooks: http://www.letsgo.com
- Lonely Planet: http://www.lonelyplanet.com
- Fodors: http://www.fodors.com
- Frommers: http://www.frommers.com
- Rick Steve's Europe: http://www.ricksteves.com
- Rough Guides: http://www.roughguides.com
- Tourism Offices Worldwide: http://www.towd.com
- Visit Europe: http://www.visiteurope.com
- wGuides: http://www.wguides.com

_____ A small Bilingual Dictionary with phrases

_____ Traveler's Checks (for emergencies)

_____ Rail Passes, ISIC, Hostel Card, etc.

_____ Laptop, Camera, etc. (any expensive equipment)

_____ Skype Headset or alternative Microphone/Headset

_____iPod or another music player
_____USB Flash Drive (nice to save work to print in the lab)
_____Batteries and Chargers for any equipment you have
_____Electrical Adapter if needed (to fit electrical outlet)
_____Electrical Converter if needed (to convert electrical voltage, usually from 110 to 220)
_____Address Book, Photos of Family and Friends

Checked Luggage

_____7 Socks (pairs)
_____7 Underwear
_____1 Bathing Suit
_____3 T-Shirts
_____3 Shorts
_____3 School Pants
_____5 School Shirts
_____1 Sweater
_____1 Dressier Outfit
_____1 Coat (waterproof/wind-resistant)
_____1 Travel Umbrella
_____2 Pajamas (take old ones you can part with)
_____Rainproof Shoes (1 for walking/dress, 1 for exercise, 1 flip flop for showers)
_____2-3 Plastic Bags for wet/dirty clothes
_____A starter supply of regular Toiletries (toothbrush, toothpaste, bath sponge, fast-drying thin towel, dental floss, cream, makeup)
_____Sufficient *hard-to-find* Toiletries (tampons, name-brand pads, special razors, double/triple blades, deodorant)
_____Tweezers and a Nail Kit (file, cutter, etc.)
_____Hair Brush and Comb
_____Pocket Knife with a Bottle Opener, Corkscrew, and Can Opener (all-in-one, don't put in carry-on bag)
_____Small Flashlight
_____First Aid/Medical Kit for your particular needs
_____Sewing Kit

_____Insect Repellent
_____Sunscreen
_____Multivitamins (Vitamin B is good for jetlag)
_____Your preferred Headache/Pain Formula
_____Sun Glasses and a Hat (to protect from sun or cold)
_____Travel Alarm Clock (great for overnight train rides)
_____1 Hostel Sleep Sack (a sheet folded and hemmed)
_____Notebook, Weekly/Daily Planner, Pens/Pencils
_____Mosquito Net (if going to Malaria-prone area)
_____Small Gifts (for host family, friends)—music CDs,
DVDs, candy, jewelry, or something else typical in your area
_____Pack of Cards, this Book, a Journal, blank CDs
_____An *extra* Bag or Backpack for school and light travel
_____Water Filter (in undeveloped countries where water
isn't potable, or if you're doing a lot of outdoor excursions
where you cannot or don't want to boil water)

29. How much money should I bring?

Yesterday is a canceled check; tomorrow is a promissory note; today is the only cash you have - so spend it wisely. ~ Kay Lyon

Bring some cash with you for incidental expenses when you arrive (buses, taxis, phone calls, etc.). Exchange it at the airport, or outside of the airport for a better rate. You may want to have some traveler's checks in case of an emergency. They don't cost much and can be purchased in a variety of currencies (if you want to avoid currency fluctuations). You buy can buy them for face value from an American Express office (AMEX), AAA, or your bank. Your bank may charge a modest fee. AMEX and AAA members can purchase and redeem them, minus the usual 1% to 4% commissions.

If you choose to purchase traveler's checks, then keep them in a safe place. Create a record of the serial numbers on the checks and cross off those that you redeem. Also, leave a copy of your serial numbers at home with someone you can call in case you lose your list. For most of your visit, plan to either open up a bank account or use ATMs (CIRRUS and PLUS are popular and accessible) to withdraw your cash from home. Many students opt to use an ATM, when it offers the most favorable exchange rates.

If you plan to use your ATM card in conjunction with your bank at home, check with your bank to make sure that your pin is valid, and verify the amount of service charge invoked for each transaction. Also, check to make your ATM card is working and is not going to expire while you're overseas. Have a backup plan in case your ATM card stops working, is damaged, or gets lost or stolen. You don't want to be left with nothing but the clothes on your back. You can use credit cards, too, but not as often as in the US.

Credit cards also have favorable exchange rates; on the other hand, not all credit cards are accepted. Discover, for example, is accepted only on a limited basis outside of North America. American Express, MasterCard, and Visa are most prevalent, and are therefore, your safest options. Look into banking fees before you commit to a credit card. Capital One boasts a zero percent transaction fee on all international transactions, while Chase and Citibank charge three percent. Depending on the card type, HSBC charges between one and three percent.

If you are thinking about opening a bank account, then think also about the exchange rates and whether or not it might be to your advantage or disadvantage to deposit a large amount of money when you arrive. Obviously, if the US dollar is getting weaker, then it would probably be to your advantage, guaranteeing your money will stretch as you planned, but if the dollar is getting stronger, then it might serve you better to withdraw cash, as you need it, using your ATM card. This is a personal decision, but obviously a very important one.

If you're planning to withdraw large sums of cash to pay rent or something else, then consider getting a local bankcard. You can open a local account and arrange for lump sums to be transferred from home. Rather than paying ATM fees to withdraw your money from home, you'll just pay a small fee for each transfer. Try to limit your transfers in order to better monitor your cash flow, and save on fees. Use the *Automated Clearinghouse* (ACH) system if you can wait at least two or three days; they are cheaper than same-day wire transfers.

International banking is yet another service that students are taking advantage of when they study abroad. Some examples consist of HTH Worldwide (www.hthworldwidebank.com), Barclays (barclays.com/international/ibs_ibank_student.html) and HSBC Offshore Bank International (offshore.hsbc.com). Whether you choose Internet banking or not, make sure that you have Internet access for your bank accounts and credit cards. It is easier to pay bills, make transfers, and monitor your account online, than it is via phone or fax.

Weekly Budget Worksheet

Category		Amounts
How much money do you have to spend?	1	
One-time Expenses (i.e. books, supplies, etc.)	2	
Subtract box 2 from box 1 and record in box 3	3	
Weekly Rent	4	
Weekly Utilities	5	
Weekly Food	6	
Weekly Transportation	7	
Weekly Entertainment	8	
Add box 4 thru box 8 and record in box 9	9	
Number of weeks you'll have these weekly expenses	10	
Multiply box 9 by box 10 and record in box 11	11	
Subtract box 11 from box 3 and record in box 12	12	
How much from box 12 will go to other travel?	13	
How much from box 12 will go to souvenirs?	14	
Subtract box 13 and box 14 from box 12 and this is how much money you have left, which should be zero	15	

30. What else should I know?

Live as if you were to die tomorrow. Learn as if you were to live forever.
~ Mahatma Gandhi

You should prepare for your international experience as if you were studying for a final exam. Learn as much as you can about your host and home countries. Use the following categories if you're not sure where to start.

Customs and Culture – There are lots of sources where you can gather this information. You're looking for culture and customs that surround food, drink, family, friends, marriage, work, play, sports, languages, health, religion, education, etc. Whatever you learn may not portray everyone you encounter; leave room for individuality and expression.

Politics and Economics – There are plenty of resources with this information. Start with the US embassy's website in your host country. If you're traveling to Europe, then spend some time at the European Union's website (europa.eu). This is an outstanding resource with lots of information about the laws, structure, countries, history, and much more.

Geography and History – You should have a general idea of where major cities are located and what they represent to the people. Know the geography and history of the city you'll be visiting and how it differs from other cities in the region and country. Know the neighboring countries. Look at photos and videos online at Travelistic.com and Travelervideos.com.

International Affairs – People from other countries tend to follow world events more closely than people from the US. People also have a tendency to know more than we do about many countries, including our own. If you don't know much about your country and the world, then you won't have much to contribute to frequent conversations, and you may appear to be another *uninformed* American. Follow international and host-country news in English through world newspapers and magazines: www.world-newspapers.com. Watch CNN, BBC, and other international news channels.

International Etiquette – If you're going to be living with a family, then you may want to present them a gift when you arrive. First, find out if gifts are appropriate, and how they should be presented. Then, pick something that represents your university or hometown, something not easily obtained in your host country. Know weather or not it is appropriate to ask questions during lectures, rest your feet on another table or chair, eat during class time, arrive late or leave early, chew gum, send text messages, etc. Learn etiquette and protocol: www.cyborlink.com and/or www.mannersinternational.com.

Quick Country Facts

Fill in this worksheet to categorize and remember what you learn. Bring it with you when you go abroad.

	Host Country	**Home Country**
Government		
Political Parties		

Name of President		
Name of the Prime Minister		
Names of the Royal Family		
Other Political Figures, Leaders		
Legal System		
Military Power		
Current Political State and Situation		
Significant Historical and Political Events		

Major Religions		
Economic System		
Health System		
Day/Year of Independence (and the country from which it was liberated/freed)		
Other Holidays		
Geography		
Climate		
Population		

Life Expectancy		
Fertility Rate		
Mortality Rate		
Languages (official and non, popularity of each)		
Ethnic Groups (percentages)		
Socioeconomic Classes		
Unemployment Rate		
Average Education		

Average Income		
Poverty Line (and the percentage beneath it)		
Literacy Rates and Percentages		
Transnational Issues		
Continent		
Neighboring Countries		
Capital City		
Size (in sq. km/sq. miles)		

Other Important Cities		
Major Exports		
Major Imports		
Gross Domestic Product (GDP)		
Currency and Exchange Rate		
Modern Tech (TV, cell, Internet use)		
Major Radio, Television, Newspapers, Magazines		
Hot Topics/News		

Favorite Sport (and other sports played/admired)		
Great Musicians (both present and historical)		
Traditional Music and Instruments		
Entertainment and Games in Country		
Great Artists (both present and historical)		
Favorite Foods and Drinks		
Tourist Attractions		
Natural Disasters		

Natural Resources		
Country Issues and Other Problems		

31. What should I do before takeoff?

Motivation is what gets you started. Habit is what keeps you going. ~ *Jim Rohn*

____Wear comfortable clothing for your trip. Dress in layers in case you get too hot or cold on the flight. Bring a cardigan if you're not wearing one. Don't wear jewelry and don't carry metal in your pockets, to prevent having to take it off and out during airport screening.

____Put all official documentation, personal information, and valuables with your carry-on items. In addition to what's on your carry-on packing list (section #28), think about adding enough clothing and toiletries for two to three days, in case your checked luggage is lost or stolen.

____Map your final destination (i.e. a hotel, a school, a family), and figure out how you're going to get there, before you get on the plane. Have a backup plan if this fails.

____Have the map, address, and phone number of school and family accessible in your carry-on bag.

____Tag all of your luggage inside and out, in case of loss.

____Bring enough cash for a few days, in case of a problem.

____Bring something to do on the plane and during layovers (book, magazine, music player, etc.).

____Bring snacks, especially if you tend to get hungry between meals.

_____Double-check your departure dates and times, paying careful attention to AM and PM. One student I know missed her flight because she thought it was PM when it was AM.
_____Call at least 72 hours in advance to confirm your flights. Sometimes there are cancellations and changes.
_____Check in early to avoid long lines and last-minute crowds, and subsequently *missed* flights.
_____Never leave your bags unattended and don't carry or transport items for others. Keep a careful watch on your bags.
_____Register valuables with the US Customs station at your international airport of departure. Keep the certificates.
_____Leave your itinerary with someone. Say goodbye to people you love and be sure to have their email and phone.
_____Get up, walk around, and stretch on the plane.
_____Say your goodbyes and don't forget your passport!

32. What should I expect on the way?

Most travel is best of all in the anticipation or the remembering; the reality has more to do with losing your luggage. ~ **Regina Nadelson**

Once you get to the airport, you can expect to check in, to check your luggage, and go through a screening process with your carry-on bags and personal items. Anything that can be removed (except for the clothing that you are wearing) must be placed on the conveyor belt and you'll be asked to walk through a metal detector, or some other weird machine that blows air at you. If there's a detection, you'll get a secondary screening with a handheld device and possibly a pat-down.

Once you're on the plane, sit back, relax, and enjoy the trip. If you have a layover, then you'll need to change planes in the airport. If you end up missing a flight because one of the planes didn't make it on time, then the airline representative will put you on the next available flight. If you have to spend the night, ask about hotel/food vouchers. Oftentimes, airlines will pay if it is their fault. They will not pay for bad weather or other acts of God that are out of their control.

You should be able to get a meal or two on most international flights. You may also have the opportunity to watch a movie. Unless you're in *first class*, you won't get a good night sleep. You can buy a neck pillow that allows you to sleep without your head flopping all over the place; it looks like a mini-nursing pillow. You will be given immigration paperwork to fill out. Be sure to have a pen, your passport number, and the address of your final destination ready.

When you arrive, you will have to go through customs with your passport and paperwork in hand. If you don't have a student/work visa, and you aren't planning to get one at the airport, then you should keep the words "study" and "work" out of your vocabulary. When asked why you are visiting, just say it's for tourism. Customs officials are paid to police visits. For example, if you say you're in Italy to work (and you mean a study internship), then they'll stop you and want to see your work visa. Keep any immigration papers that are returned to you in a safe place for your return trip.

After you exit customs, there will be a place where you can pick up your baggage. If your baggage doesn't arrive, then talk to an airline representative for guidance on what you should do next. All airlines have procedures to search for lost baggage, and when found, your bags are usually delivered to you at wherever it is you're staying. If you don't have an address or phone yet, you can always provide your hotel or your host's information, such as the local international office. Most bags are found, and it turns out to be an inconvenience rather than a loss. So try not to worry too much.

IV.

Be Healthy and Safe

33. What is jet lag and how do I cope?

I refer to jet lag as 'jet-psychosis' — there's an old saying that the spirit cannot move faster than a camel. ~ *Spalding Gray*

Jet lag is a disruption of the circadian rhythm (the body's 24-hour inner clock) and is caused by time-zone changes. If you fly from Michigan to France, you've probably missed a night. Although midnight registers on your inner clock, your outer clock reads 7am. At night, when the country is asleep, you may feel hungry and energetic. In the day, when the country is awake, you may feel exhausted.

What are the Symptoms?

Physically, you may experience fatigue, insomnia, irritation of the eyes/nose/ears, swollen limbs, headaches, dehydration, lightheadedness, and bowel irregularity.

Mentally, you may be tired, irritable, aloof, and disoriented.

How do you Overcome?

a   Get lots of rest before you leave.
b. Eat well and take vitamins (esp. Vitamin B, which is another item to put in your carry-on bag).
c. Set your watch to the time of your destination.
d. Avoid alcohol before and during the flight.
e. Drink lots of water to avoid dehydration.
f. Dress comfortably on the flight so you can relax.
g. Stretch and walk around on the plane, hourly.
h. Avoid crossing your legs at the knees and ankles.
i. Yawn or chew gum to pop pressure in the ears.
j. Start operating on local time right away.
k. Exercise to increase your energy levels.
l. Be patient with yourself and you'll adjust.

34. Where do I get medical assistance?

Never go to a doctor whose office plants have died. ~ **Erma Bombeck**

Doctors in other countries do not undergo the same type of education that they do in the US. Therefore, it is important to think about whom you might want to see for your minor and major medical needs. Make a list of recommended physicians and hospitals before you leave, or get a list from the embassy after you arrive in the host country. Then decide where you would you go for a minor injury vs. where you would go for something major. If you become seriously ill or injured, a US consular officer can help you locate medical services, as well as contact family and friends.

When I was in the Peace Corps, I often had to treat myself for illnesses that in the US I would normally see a doctor about. This is because I wasn't able to obtain optimal health care in my remote African village. As a volunteer, I received a book, *Where There is No Doctor: A Village Health Care Handbook* by David Werner, Carol Thuman, and Jane Maxwell. It is an excellent source of information for identifying and treating both common and rare illnesses. For example, papaya seeds can cure parasites, and natural yogurt (without sugar) can take care of a yeast infection when applied like cream.

Before you leave, you should get enough prescription drugs to last your entire trip. Leave them in their original containers and keep a copy of the prescription on hand. Put these drugs (and the prescriptions) in your carry-on bag, not your checked luggage. Possession of certain drugs without a prescription may violate local laws. Also, bring syringes or other types of instruments that you use to administer your drugs (with a note from your physician of course). In some countries, medical personnel still reuse needles and syringes, which is a cause of HIV infection and other viruses/diseases.

If you get sick abroad and have to go to a medical doctor, he/she may prescribe something for you to take. You should stick with major in-country pharmacies for these needs. Try to avoid small kiosks that may acquire the drugs suspiciously. Call the embassy for advice. Find out which pharmacies they use. The Food and Drug Administration (FDA) cannot assure the content or quality of pharmaceuticals sold outside of the US. Medications approved for the pharmaceutical market in the US undergo review and rigorous testing that assures they are not only safe, but also effective for a proposed use.

Wherever you decide to study abroad, it's important that you understand the health care system. In addition to helping you navigate the culture, this information will also help you to make better decisions about the insurance you purchase. The World Health Organization ranks the world's health systems (http://www.photius.com/rankings/healthranks.html). France is #1, Italy is #2, Canada is #30, and the US is #37. Another study conducted by Ellen Nolte and Martin McKee of the London School of Hygiene and Tropical Medicine compared the trends in preventable deaths among industrialized nations. They rated France, Japan and Australia best and the US worst in preventable deaths due to treatable conditions.

You may receive better care abroad than you otherwise would in the US. Some countries even offer free emergency services to visitors. Italy's national health system provides low or no-cost health care to all EU citizens, and free emergency health care to all visitors (both EU and non). One of our professors took a very serious fall in Italy while she was leading a study abroad program. Her hospitalization was immediate and high quality, and it was completely free. This doesn't happen in most countries of the world.

Don't underestimate the fact that you could become seriously ill or injured while abroad. Especially if you're studying in a rural location, it is important that you have a good medical evacuation provider. Imagine yourself in a remote area of Costa Rica when you start having severe stomach pain and need to have your appendix removed promptly. Time is your only hope, and if you can't get someone who can perform a safe surgery for you, then you could lose your life and die. If you allow an unqualified doctor and facility to perform your surgery (such as a primitive health center), then you also run a risk of infection and possible death.

Medical practices vary widely in other countries. My dentist in Africa gave me vodka to swish around in my mouth before he checked my aching wisdom teeth. When I sprained my ankle, I happened to stumble upon a traditional healer and he asked if he could perform a demonstration on me. I unwisely allowed him to rub the fat of a boa constrictor on my joint and squeeze it fiercely. He claimed that by massaging my ankle with the boa fat, it would swell up and therefore heal faster. It still took me more than a month to heal, and I'm not convinced that the boa fat or the massage aided the process. The Peace Corps nurse later reprimanded me for this mistake.

The most important thing to remember is that you maintain access to the highest level of medical care, should you happen to need it. If you're in a remote village and a health center can treat your minor ailments, that is okay, but if something goes wrong and you need to have specialized treatment or surgery, you should be able to get it. Visit the following websites for more information:

- **International Association of Medical Assistance to Travelers** – Join free: http://www.iamat.org
- **International SOS** – www.internationalsos.com
- **List of Doctors and Hospitals by Country** http://travel.state.gov/law/acs.html
- **Medical Information for Americans Abroad**: http://travel.state.gov/travel/abroad_health.html
- **Med Help International** – http://www.medhelp.org

35. What about road safety?

According to the US Department of State, the number one cause of death among US citizens abroad is auto accidents. While motor vehicle accidents can and do happen all over the world, there is greater risk for them to happen in developing nations, with deteriorating road infrastructure and regulatory systems, as well as irregular or corrupt law enforcement. In these countries, drivers are not motivated by law, but rather by how many trips they can make, and thus how much money they can earn in a day. Vehicles are old and not maintained to US standards, and emergency medical care may not exist.

Regardless of where you are going to study, but especially if you are going to a developing country, you need to be careful about the transportation you choose to take. According to the Association of Safe International Road Travel (asirt.org), the rate of road deaths has fallen in industrialized nations such as the US, Canada, Australia, and Europe. Conversely, the rate of road deaths has increased in developing nations, especially in the areas of Asia, Africa, and Latin America. These rates can be up to 80 times as high as they are in the industrialized world. Therefore, it is important to be very careful.

Educate yourself about road safety in the countries you'll be visiting. Not only do you need to be aware of driving/riding in vehicles, but being around vehicles also. According to the US Department of State, the majority of deaths and injuries in developing countries are not the occupants of cars, but rather the pedestrians, motorcyclists, and bicyclists that ride beside them. This is because there are no consequences for driving without a license or insurance, or for driving erratically. Walk and ride defensively at all times. For more information from the State Department, go to travel.state.gov and type "Road Safety" in the search box.

When I was living in Quito, my landlord was hit by a car and killed. She was about 70 years old and she was walking home after paying the electric bill when it happened. I'm not sure exactly what happened, but a driver hit her and crushed her head. It was a very difficult and sad moment for me as I had to move my stuff out of the house, find another place to live, attend her funeral, and offer my condolences, all with very little Spanish language skills. Today, you can find blue hearts all over the streets of Quito. This marks where somebody has died in an accident. The local government paints the hearts in an attempt to raise awareness on safe driving. Accidents don't just happen to foreigners but to locals, too!

36. What about emergencies?

One of the true tests of leadership is the ability to recognize a problem before it becomes an emergency. ~ **Arnold H. Glasgow**

Register with the US Embassy either shortly before or after you arrive in country. This will help you and your family in the event of a personal or national emergency. The *Overseas Citizens Services* (OCS) of the Bureau of Consular Affairs is responsible for the whereabouts and general welfare of US citizens who are overseas. *American Citizens Services and Crisis Management* (ACS), is a branch of the OCS that assists Americans with many kinds of medical, financial, and legal emergencies. During business hours, call 1-888-407-4747 or 317-472-2328. For after-hour emergencies, call 202-647-4000. Website: http://travel.state.gov/travel/overseas.html.

A crisis is an unstable situation, an immensely stressful event, and/or a traumatic change in someone's life. A crisis may be an accident, illness, hospitalization, protest/civil unrest, war, earthquake, volcano eruption, military coup, widespread riot, sexual assault, strike, terrorist attack, etc. It may involve you or someone you know. It may stem from a particular area of the world, like an epidemic flu or a natural disaster. It may affect different countries, or it may impact the entire world. While it is impossible to foresee many of the crises we may encounter, it is important to be mindful of the possibilities. Nowadays, what you'd least expect can happen and does.

The way to manage crises in your life is to be informed and ready to respond to a variety of foreseeable emergencies. This is called an *Emergency Action Plan* (EAP). First, write down your support mechanisms: home, host, health insurance, 24/7 emergency numbers, etc. Record this contact information on a small card that you carry on your person at all times (in your money belt). Second, you should walk through, write down, and memorize the possible scenarios and your pre-planned responses to an (a) medical emergency, (b) political situation, (c) terrorism, (d) natural disaster, (e) legal situation, (f) theft of money or important documents, (g) sexual or other type of assault, and (h) accident-illness-death of people at home.

For example, if you're a student in Ecuador, then you should be aware of the active volcanoes and how they would impact your city if they were to erupt. You should know what to do in the event of a volcanic eruption, or earthquake, since both are possible in the country. Planning shouldn't take too much of your time and will help you to be less vulnerable and more capable if happens. Many emergencies require swift response, and in some cases, this response time is a matter of life and death (all the more reason to have an EAP).

Develop awareness. Pay attention to your body. Stay alert to your surroundings. Read the news on a daily basis and know what's happening in the city, country, and world around you. These things not only increase the odds of your identifying a potential crisis before it hits you, but of possibly terminating it as well. Don't forget, you can only be aware to the extent of your knowledge. Knowledge is power; so seek it diligently. It reduces fear and builds confidence. It helps us to manage our behavior toward a positive outcome. Know the emergencies that can happen, pay attention to signs and signals, and learn what you should do. Stay calm and RESPOND appropriately, rather than REACT spontaneously.

If there's an emergency, try very hard to communicate your personal situation to loved ones, as well as to your college or university, so that they know you are okay and in safe hands. If anything newsworthy happens in your host country, then you should quickly get in touch with people at home. When an earthquake hit China, we had a group of students on tour, scheduled to be in Beijing. They did not communicate their safety to anyone at home because they figured that everyone realized they were 960 miles from the epicenter. Meanwhile, frantic parents were calling our office because the media had already announced 10,000 people dead. More communication would have saved a lot worry and concern.

The following resources will help you develop a personalized EAP. Before you write down step by step, and memorize how you would respond to the possible scenarios, ask yourself if your plan is realistic. For example, if your plan relies on the use of telecommunications devices and electricity in the event of an earthquake, then it may not work for you. Your EAP should get you out of danger, help you find people, and help people find you. You should include primary and secondary meeting places, maps, and much more. After you create your EAP, give copies to your contacts at home and abroad.

- **Crisis Awareness and Preparedness** – travel.state. gov/travel/tips/emergencies/emergencies_1187.html
- **Citizen Services** – http://travel.state.gov/law/acs.html
- **Emergency Planning, Study Abroad Handbook** http://www.studentsabroad.com/planning.html
- **Help for Americans Abroad from A to Z** http://www.travel.state.gov/law/info/info_2242.html
- **Homeland Security** – http://www.ready.gov

37. What if I get robbed?

Poverty is the mother of crime. ~*Marcus Aurelius*

If you get robbed while abroad, don't panic…just know how to respond. First, contact your financial institutions; you may have to cancel your cards. Also call the major credit-reporting organizations to place a fraud alert on your name and social security number. This will prevent thieves from successfully opening bank accounts and credit cards in your name, which they often try to do through liaisons in the US.

Your next step should be to go to the local police station to file a *police report*. You will have to present the report if you need to get your passport replaced and/or if you need to file a claim with your insurance company for stolen goods. Filing a police report also proves to creditors that you were diligent if there is ever an investigation.

After you receive the police report, contact your banks and credit companies again. They should be able to inform you if any withdrawals or charges were made by the crooks. If so, you may only be held responsible for a small amount; the rest will be returned to you. It's imperative however that you do all of these things within two or three business days.

- If your passport is stolen, then see the following site: http://studentsabroad.state.gov > Travel Docs > Lost or Stolen Passports
- Numbers of the three national credit bureaus:
  o Equifax: 1-800 525-6285*
  o Experian (formerly TRW): 1-888-397-3742*
  o Trans Union: 1-800-680-7289*
- Social Security fraud line: 1-800-269-0271*

*Have Mom, Dad, or someone else call these 800 numbers from home, as you won't be able to use them outside of the US

38. What about STDs and HIV/AIDS?

No war on the face of the Earth is more destructive than the AIDS pandemic.
~ *Colin Powell*

STDs and HIV/AIDS are ubiquitous. Many of them are viral, and therefore incurable. While they can be acquired in other ways (i.e. sharing syringes, having a blood transfusion), these diseases are generally contracted through sexual activity, and the exchange of bodily fluids. I don't particularly like giving advice about sexual relations, but it is best to abstain until a serious monogamous commitment is made. The only method proven to be 100% effective against STDs is abstinence.

Certainly, you can reduce the risks by using a condom, but a condom isn't foolproof. Is it wise to rely on a piece of rubber to protect you from a long-long or life-threatening disease? I know of one young woman who was following all 'the rules' and still got sick. Her boyfriend was wearing a condom, but it came off inside of her during sex. Prior medical testing of your partner is no guarantee of present or future disease. Even in a monogamous relationship, you can never be certain.

Some students acquire these diseases while they are studying and/or working abroad, others are infected before they go. It is hard to comprehend these diseases until you meet people who are infected with them. I know people just like you and me who are infected. It is estimated that 33.2 million people are living with HIV or AIDS and 2.1 million people die from it every year (2007 UNAIDS/WHO). Since 1981, more than 25 million people have died of AIDS.

- **AIDS.org** – http://www.aids.org
- **Health Awareness Connection**
  http://www.healthac.org

- **Sexually Transmitted Diseases** (for prevention)
  http://www2.ncid.cdc.gov/travel/yb/utils/ybGet.asp?se
  ction=dis&obj=stds.htm
- **HIV, AIDS, STD epidemiological facts by country**
  http://www.who.int/hiv/countries/en
- **Travel's Health Yellow Book**
  http://wwwn.cdc.gov/travel/contentYellowBook.aspx

39. Is sexual harassment a concern?

*Of the delights of this world, man cares most for sexual intercourse. He will go
to any length for it-risk fortune, character, reputation, life itself.*

~ Mark Twain

There is a line, a very thick line, between *cultural sensitivity*
and *maintaining your personal boundaries*. For some people,
identifying that line is simple, but for most of us, it takes
some self-awareness and practice. In some parts of the world,
women are socialized to view sexual harassment as a normal
behavior of men. They see harassment as harmless, unless it
escalates to unconsenting sex, and that's a whole different can
of worms. When it comes to tolerating sexual harassment,
you should NOT do as the Romans do when in Rome. Never
risk or sacrifice your safety in order to be culturally sensitive!

No matter who you are or where you come from, you have a
right and responsibility to protect your own body, to patrol
your surroundings for anything that may be harmful, or fatal.
Your body has many built-in mechanisms to do this, one of
which is called *reflexes*. Have you ever heard a loud noise
and jumped out of your chair? That was your body preparing
to protect itself from danger. Your heart was beating a million
miles per minute and your arms and legs probably flew up to
protect your head and chest. Similarly, have you ever just had
a strange feeling about somebody? Maybe you didn't want to

be around him, or he was getting a little too close for your comfort? Well, that is one of your body's reflexes, too!

When the wrong person gets too close, your body triggers an internal alarm. The key is to know what to do when the alarm goes off. You wouldn't want to hide under your bed if a fire alarm went off in your house and you wouldn't want to run outside in the event of a tornado. Dealing with harassment in another country is a *learned* response and it takes practice. It doesn't come naturally, because we are taught to respond to people unnaturally, not to mention the same response in two different cultures can mean two completely different things. Sometimes your internal alarm fails to go off when it should, which is why it's good to use your common sense in addition to your body to make decisions based on your surroundings.

In America, you may be used to inviting guys over to your house, and the guys don't think anything of it, except that you're good friends. However, in other cultures, an invitation to your house also means an invitation to your bed. Not only do the guys think this way, but the gals do, too. If you don't see the women in another culture inviting men to their homes, then don't do it yourself. Don't escalate the situation... *I love you*, from some stranger shouldn't beget, *How could you love me, you don't even know me?* If you're being harassed, just say *no*, (assertively) and get away. Lots of dogs bark, but few bite. Acknowledge a dog and it'll keep on barking. Ignore a dog and it'll probably find something else to do.

Rape is something altogether different from harassment. Rape isn't about sex; it's about power. Men who rape take pleasure in hurting other people. It makes them feel powerful and in control. Men who rape are like ravaging wolves that carefully select their victims (prey), wait for an opportunity, and then strike. They don't want to get hurt in the process, so they hunt down people that they think are easy to overpower or won't put up a fight. They don't want to get caught, so they wait for

150

or set-up the right opportunity. If a rapist thinks you might overpower him, or hurt him in the process of trying, then he is not prone to attack. Likewise, if the right opportunity never presents itself, then he cannot attack. Remember, most rapes occur with someone you know; listen to your internal alarm.

Portray yourself as strong and confident, with boundaries. Be assertive not only with words, but with your body language and behaviors, too. Show the ravaging dogs that you can hold your own. Don't allow any opportunities for an attack. Do not jog alone with earphones; don't go out at night by yourself, keep your doors locked whether you're inside and out. Even if you look vulnerable to an attacker, you can take away his opportunity and he'll never be able to assault you. If you can take away an attacker's confidence about overcoming you or the occasion by which he is able, then you've won the battle. Once again, listen to your internal alarm system. When your body tells you to get out, then go!

Take a self-defense course before you go. While you may not remember all the techniques, you will garner awareness and confidence about self-protection. In addition, you'll acquire some useful skills. Also, don't forget to protect yourself from the often colorless, tasteless, and odorless date-rape drugs like rohypnol and GHB (BKA Roofies); never accept an open drink or never let your drink out of sight. These drugs depress the central nervous system. Rapists can slip them into your drink and within a half-hour they begin to take effect. Victims are unable to refuse sex due to physical helplessness and can't remember what happened. If you think you've been drugged, get to a safe place immediately, ask for help from a trusted friend, and file a report with the police.

- **Crime Library** – www.crimelibrary.com
- **Protective Strategies** – www.protectivestrategies.com
- **The Roofie Foundation** – www.roofie.com
- **Self-Defense** – www.nononsenseselfdefense.com

40. What if I run into legal problems?

Liberty is the right of doing whatever the laws permit. ~*Charles Montesquieu*

As a US citizen in a foreign country, you are subject to the laws of that country. One of the biggest legal problems that students face abroad is drugs. Other problems are alcohol and disorderly behavior. More than 2,000 Americans are arrested every year, and half of the arrests are on drug-related charges. What you need to know is that there is very little that the US government can do for you if you're arrested for drug use or possession in another country. No magic wands, no special deals, no signing on the dotted line and you're out.

Once you step in another country, you are subject to the laws and regulations of that country. The system and penalties are different from in the US, and they may not offer the same or similar protections. If you're arrested, you can expect a visit from a US consular officer. He/she can notify your family or friends, give you a list of attorneys, and help you obtain legal representation, among other things. You can also expect the officer to intercede with local authorities to help assure your rights under the country's legal system, by protesting abuse to the authorities in line with internationally accepted standards. The officer cannot demand your release, represent you in a trial, give you legal advice, or pay your legal fees.

It is your responsibility to know and obey the laws of the land you are visiting. You don't have to do something really bad to break the law and go to jail. Students have been arrested for carrying medications that are considered illegal narcotics; for inadvertently trying to make a purchase on a credit card that will exceed the limit; for taking photographs of a government, police, or military building; for purchasing or trying to leave the country with souvenirs that customs authorities believe are national treasures; for carrying a package for someone, which unknowingly contains illegal drugs; for participating in demonstrations or strikes, and more. Don't make assumptions about the law; learn the law and how to be safe within it!

- **Assistance to US Citizens Arrested Abroad**
  http://travel.state.gov/law/info/info_639.html
- **International Constitutional Law Country Index**
  http://www.oefre.unibe.ch/law/icl/index.html
- **International Judicial Assistance**
  travel.state.gov/law/info/judicial/judicial_702.html
- **International Law Library of Congress**
  http://www.loc.gov/law/help/guide/international.html
- **World Law Index** – http://www.worldlii.org/catalog

41. How can I use my embassy/consulate?

An ambassador is an honest man sent abroad to lie for his country.
~Henry Wotton, Sr.

Both embassies and consulates represent their governments and are exclusively located in foreign countries. Embassies speak for their national governments in foreign countries, and consulates provide diplomatic services to individuals and businesses, such as visas and trade, but both work together in various ways. They provide emergency and non-emergency assistance for all types of situations. They also provide safety, security, and other useful information. Review the consulate's website before you go abroad, and gather needed information. Also, don't forget to register your trip!

Emergency	Non-Emergency	No Service
Some assistance for serious legal, medical, and/or financial trouble. Evacuation plan in case of a disaster.	Absentee voting, visas, permits, tax forms, notarizing documents, local information for travelers, etc.	Tourism, missing luggage, obtaining foreign documents on your behalf, translations, legal advice/services.

Embassies are always located in the capital city (near the seat of foreign government), and consulates are located in one or more other major cities with a large population. In Ecuador, the US embassy is located in Quito, while the consulate is in Guayaquil. Depending on the nature of your inquiry, you may be directed to one or the other. In some countries, there may be a consular section of the embassy, which would be in the Capital city. In other countries, there may be a consulate but no embassy (usually to preserve our diplomatic relations with a third country w/o sacrificing services for citizens abroad).

In any emergency affecting US citizens, the Embassy will usually broadcast information via their web site, email lists, phone trees, warden network, and local media channels. The best way to ensure you receive this information is to register with the Embassy. If the disaster is of a large-enough scale and if the situation warrants it, the Embassy may advise all Americans to evacuate the country, and may even provide the means to do so, with the assistance of the US Department of State and the US Military. Plans usually place responsibility on US citizens to take an active role in their own evacuation.

The Embassy's evacuation plan has one objective: to help you to move away from an area of possible danger as safely and quickly as possible. In some countries, you must get yourself to the closest *Evacuation Control Center*. When you create your EAP (section #36), go to your embassy's website, and look up their evacuation plan or procedures. Build these into your EAP. If there are Evacuation Control Centers, map them out and know how to get there in an emergency. Bring your passport, birth/naturalization certificate, or other primary evidence of your US citizenship.

- **Register your trip** – https://travelregistration.state.gov
- **US Embassies & Consulates** – www.usembassy.gov
- **All the World's Embassies** – www.embassyworld.com
- **OSAC (Security Advisory Council)**– www.osac.gov

$$

Part V.

Manage your
Money and Life

$$

42. How can I save money?

A penny saved is a dollar earned. ~ *Benjamin Franklin*

One of the best ways to cut corners and save money is to start the process early enough to apply for grants and scholarships. My college roommate wanted to study abroad, but her parents wouldn't help her with costs. Because she was so determined, she didn't let anything get in her way. She applied for several scholarships, ended up getting two big ones, studied abroad for a semester in Italy, and came back with not only a study abroad experience, but also a profit from all the scholarship money she received to go! Yes, anything is possible if you put your mind and heart into it.

Whether or not you're fortunate enough to get a scholarship, there are other ways to save money. The more careful you are about spending money here and there, the more you will have in your pockets to spend on what you really want and need. I think what convinced me of this fact was a demonstration I saw in the third grade. While I don't remember the amounts, the presenter showed how much money we could save over the course of a year, if we decided NOT to buy cigarettes. In that time, it was enough to purchase a new bicycle, and much more. This truth that I assimilated at a very young age, taught me how to use money to advance my goals.

Saving money is both religious and innovative. It's religious in the sense that it involves organizing priorities, exercising self-discipline, and making sacrifices. It's innovative because it takes time, planning, and *know-how* to get the same thing you otherwise would, for less. You won't be able to save if you don't believe that every little bit counts. I know people who bring in twice as much income as I, but live at the same standard or lower because they don't know how to save. On the next page are some tips for saving money abroad. Don't underestimate their value; it's the little things that add up.

Tips for Saving Money Abroad

- Always research and compare to find the best deals.
- Understand the local currency and familiarize yourself with coins, so you don't overpay.
- Know the prices for different items you commonly buy and know where to buy them for less.
- Look for special student rates and discounts, and consider buying an International Student ID Card.
- Shop where locals shop. Outdoor markets are exciting and fun, and usually offer the freshest produce.
- Use debit cards at ATMs for favorable exchange rates.
- Buy your guidebooks in the US before you leave, for the best prices; check out www.allbookstores.com.
- Use a calling card, cyber café, or an online phone service like Skype to make international calls. Don't use your cell phone unless it's low or no cost.
- Look at the different ways in which you can use public transportation (day passes, weekly passes, monthly passes, student passes) and choose the one that will *most benefit* your particular needs.
- Bring your lunch to school everyday, if it costs less than it would to buy something at the cafeteria.
- Buy your train tickets and/or rail passes ahead of time; this requires pre-planning and arrangements.
- Take overnight trains en lieu of paying for hotels.
- Consider hostels en lieu of hotels or motels.
- Eat in outdoor markets, grocery stores, or small cafes as opposed to expensive, fancy restaurants.
- Check menu prices before you decide on a restaurant.
- Know the *tipping* customs. In many parts of the world, tips are added into the bill or you don't tip.
- Buy generic instead of name brand products, if you're not sacrificing much or any quality.
- Don't be afraid to buy second-hand and used items.
- Don't be wasteful of anything (food or belongings).

43. How should I access my money?

Money is like a sixth sense - and you can't make use of the other five without it
~ William Somerset Maugham

Don't exchange money in hotels, restaurants, or shops if you want to get the best rates. Don't exchange money on the street because it's illegal, but also because of many scams. In some countries, crooks give you worthless currency from another nation that looks like the currency you need, or they give you counterfeit bills. By the time you figure it out, they're gone, along with your cash.

ATMs usually offer the best rates; an ATM card may be all you need, but have a backup plan. Traveler's checks are nice to have if your ATM cards are lost, stolen, or eaten by the machines. They are insured and can be replaced by the issuer, free of charge. However, fees may be high to redeem, not to mention the pain-in-the-butt process, so use sparingly. If you are an AMEX member, you can cash them at any American Express location (worldwide), without paying commissions.

If you choose to use traveler's checks frequently, then be sure you record the serial numbers on a separate piece of paper, and cross off the checks you redeem. In certain parts of the world, traveler's checks issued in US dollars are the easiest to exchange. You can buy them for $20, $50, or $100. Use them to get cash from a bank or American Express office, but don't use them in restaurants, stores, and hotels, unless you're okay with a really lousy exchange rate.

Paying with a credit card is an excellent option, too. Visa, MasterCard, and AMEX offer competitive exchange rates and are commonly accepted in Europe, Latin America, and Asia. For the sake of convenience, I use a credit card as much as possible, and make an effort to pay it off every month (so it's interest-free). Don't forget to bring your credit card pins, too. While you wouldn't want to make a habit of drawing cash on credit, it may be invaluable in the event of an emergency.

- **AAA**: www.aaa.com
- **AMEX**: www.americanexpress.com
- **MasterCard ATM Locator**
  http://www.mastercard.com/atmlocator/index.jsp
- **Visa ATM Locator**
  visa.via.infonow.net/locator/global/jsp/SearchPage.jsp

44. Where should I keep my money?

A bank is a place where they lend you an umbrella in fair weather and ask for it back when it begins to rain. ~ Robert Frost

In order to avoid theft, you should never carry or store large sums of cash. However, if you need to do so from time to time, then be extremely careful and don't tell anyone about it. When out and about, keep your money in a money belt or flat pouch tied snuggly around your waist, under your clothing. Small purses that hang around the neck from a cord and fall under the shirt can be easily slit and stolen. You can also put money in a bandana tied snuggly around your ankle.

When you're not out and about and just want a good place to store extra cash, think about the layout of your living area or hotel room and where a thief would be least likely to look. Some apartments, schools, and hotels have safes. However, it is harder to access your protected goods when they are in a safe; safes are easily stolen, too. Here are a few ideas about storing cash temporarily. While they may be theft-resistant, they probably aren't safe from natural disasters, such as fires.

- Wrap money in a piece of newspaper and tape it to the bottom of a drawer or piece of furniture.

160

- Put money in a clean sock, in a bag of dirty clothes; just don't forget it's there. Depending on how strong the smell is, this method may even keep bugs away.
- Put money in a plastic container in your refrigerator, making it look like old leftovers that nobody wants.
- Put money in the fireplace, as long as nobody lights a fire and you don't forget that it's there.
- Put money in a book on a shelf, only if you have lots of books. Also, tape it so it doesn't fall out.
- Put money in the bathroom, in the middle of a roll of toilet paper or in a tampon holder.
- Put money in a vitamin container in the medicine cabinet or in a bag of personal toiletries.
- Put money in a photo album, behind some pictures, inside a couch cushion.
- Put money in a pile of graded papers and notes, where someone would never find it.

45. How can I protect my money?

The art is not in making money, but in keeping it. ~ **Proverb**

Prevent pickpocketing by keeping your money out of sight and carefully watching your possessions when out and about. Put most of your cash, plastic cards, and passport (or copy) in a small plastic bag, inside of a money belt or a flat pouch; this is tied snuggly around your waist, under your clothing. Put the day's spending money in a zipped pocket of your daypack or purse. Don't lift up your shirt to get money out in order to pay a cashier. You shouldn't ever expose your money belt in public. When you need more money, go to a restroom, take some out of your money belt, and place it in your daypack or purse. This way if someone steals your daypack or purse, then he/she hasn't gotten away with much.

In order to prevent pickpocketing or theft of your daypack or purse, wear it in a way that people can't grab it and run away. As stupid as it looks, wear your daypack, purse, and wallet in front, when in crowded places and spaces. Keep valuables in zipped pockets, which you can lock with a safety pin. Don't hang your purse over your shoulder, but rather crisscross it over your chest. In order for a thief to get it, he/she would have to cut the strap or cleverly pull it over your head, faster than you can grab it. It's easier to select another target than taking his chances with you. Most criminals are more content with the path of least resistance than a challenge.

Know about the strategies of criminals. Thieves often attack from behind. My boyfriend and I were in an overly crowded market when someone managed to slip in between he and I, meanwhile his partner pushed everybody in the crowd from behind. We all fell forward like dominos, and when we exited the crowd, my boyfriend's wallet was gone. There was only about a dollar in his wallet, but all his identification cards and other important items were lost, too. Because he had to spend so much time and money getting replacements, he really lost a lot more than he thought he did.

Be careful about children and beggars asking for money. See the potential for scams. Generally speaking, it's never a good idea to pull out your wallet, and look for money to give to children. First, they see where you are keeping your cash, and it makes following you and stealing it a lot easier for them when your guard is down. Second, if they see lots of bills or credit cards when you open your wallet, they might just grab it and run, or plan to assault you later. If you want to give to beggars, then be smart about it. Clothing and food are just as good as money!

Not only do you have to worry about protecting your money outside, but also inside if you are staying in hotels or living with other people. While it may be easy to blame the cleaning staff, most cases of theft inside of hotels or apartments can be linked back to your peers, roommates, or the friends/partners of your roommates. Yes, as disheartening as it is, your peers may steal from you, especially if it is easy to get the money while shifting the blame. Don't leave your cash lying around, and keep it hidden, even from the unsuspecting! You cannot be too safe with your hard-earned cash, because it is so fluid and hard to reclaim.

Know the local ATM scams. Thieves can attach scanning devices and fake keypads over the originals. This equipment is cleverly disguised and looks like normal ATM equipment. A skimmer is mounted to the front of the card slot, reads the ATM card number, and transmits it to the criminals. A fake keypad or a hidden wireless camera, which look like a leaflet holder, can record your pin. Avoid this scam and more, by carefully screening the machine before you use it; card slots and key pads shouldn't protrude outwards. Shield your hand when entering your pin, so that cameras can't catch it on tape. These highly skilled thieves can copy cards and use your pin numbers to quickly withdraw large amounts of cash.

- If you're carrying a wallet, carry it in a front pocket that zips, where you can keep an eye/hand on it.
- Carry your bag or purse on the opposite side of bicycles and vehicles, so they can't snatch it.
- NEVER put your purse or bag down in a restaurant or anywhere in public or you'll likely find it vanished.
- Consider not carrying around a purse or bag, but rather a waist pouch that is fastened to your body.
- Know that petty theft is more sophisticated in countries typically visited by US students. It's important to know the scams that are used.
- Pickpockets and bag-snatchers work in pairs. One distracts and the other discretely steals, while all eyes are on the distraction. This is common and easy for thieves to pull off, especially in airports/train stations.

46. Can I work while studying abroad?

The world is full of willing people, some willing to work, the rest willing to let them. ~ **Robert Frost**

Whether or not you can work really depends on the flexibility of your visa. Check with the consulate that issued your visa for restrictions. If there are no restrictions, then check with the host institution about where you can locate job openings. Don't study abroad unless you know that you can pay for it, because there are no guarantees. It's better to get a loan and not end up using it, than it is to depend on a job that you don't have, and find yourself between a rock and a hard place.

There are advantages and disadvantages to working while you study abroad. Working can give you some extra cash and help you get to know the locals. On the other hand, it takes time away from your studies and travel. Coursework abroad can be more difficult than in the US, so you may need extra time just to keep up in class. Only you can gauge what's best for you. Whatever you decide, base it on what you hope to get out of the experience.

If you're not allowed to work in the host country, there are other ways to earn money without getting a job. I know of one student who decided to play music on the street for loose change and donations; believe it or not, he ended up bringing in a lot of extra cash. Other students babysit, teach English, or do odd jobs for local people that need help.

Teaching English can be fun, but it isn't as easy as it looks. It takes a great deal of time and patience to teach languages. Contact some US companies that might need help and can benefit from your location abroad. Maybe a publisher would be willing to pay you to try out different hotels, cafes, etc. and write up a section in their upcoming book.

Examples of Work Restrictions

Country	Can they work?	Under what conditions?
Australia	Yes, with a student visa	Twenty hours per week during the academic year. Forty hours during summer break and holidays.
China	No, not with a student visa	Students tend to offer English lessons for cash.
Ecuador	No, not with a student visa	It is not permitted to work on a student or tourist visa.
France	Only with a special permit	Students can generally work up to 20 hours per week during the school year. Must present a student ID and offer of employment.
Germany	Yes, with a student visa	Up to 90 days.
Ireland	No	Students are not allowed to work while in Ireland.
Italy	Only with a special permit	A work permit is very difficult to obtain. It isn't impossible, but it would take planning and preparation.
Japan	No	It is not permitted to work on a student or tourist visa.
New Zealand	No	A study tour of two years or longer for work eligibility.
South Africa	Yes	Twenty hours per week.
Spain	Only with a special permit	Proof of employment contract and work permit before departure. This is very difficult to obtain.
United Kingdom	Yes, with a student visa	Advise the immigration officers of your intent before entry. Twenty hrs/wk, and less than six months.

Another option for work is through the Internet, if you have some talent or skill. Are you a good writer? Are your foreign language skills competent enough to translate? Do you know how to design web pages and do you have the ability to do so from your overseas location? If so, market your services as a freelancer. You can do the work from wherever you are and have the payments deposited into your checking account at home, which you can then withdraw abroad using an ATM card. It's easy to accept credit cards, e-checks, etc. through PayPal (www.paypal.com). The following companies connect businesses with freelancers for all sorts of creative projects.

- **All Freelance Directory** – www.allfreelance.com
- **Freelance Designers** – www.freelancedesigners.com
- **Elance** – www.elance.com
- **Gofreelance** – www.gofreelance.com
- **Guru.com** – www.guru.com
- **iFreelance** – www.ifreelance.com
- **ProZ** – www.proz.com
- **Sologig** – www.sologig.com

This is just a short list. There are lots of companies out there, so take an inventory of your talents and skills, and see what's available for you to do. A laptop and access to the Internet is all you need. Be careful about companies and services you go through and make sure they are legitimate before you render your services. Check www.consumerfraudreporting.org if you suspect a fake company or other Internet scam.

47. What if I run out of money?

Beware of little expenses; a small leak will sink a great ship
~ Benjamin Franklin

If your bank is dry or will be going dry soon, ask someone for help. If someone is willing to help you, there are many ways to get the money into your hands. The free and easy way is to have the money deposited into your checking account from home. You can withdraw it overseas using your ATM card. If this is not an option for you, then there are many other ways to send money, depending on the level of security that you need and the time in which you have to work with.

American Express money orders can be initiated in the US and completed at an office branch abroad. Another option is PayPal or similar operations like Neteller and Moneybookers. If you have a bank account at home or in one of the countries on their list, someone can pay you by credit card or e-check, and it will show up in your account. Transfers usually take two to three days, and sometimes longer. If you have a pin number, you can use your credit card to take out a loan from an ATM. Unsecured cash loans start accruing high interest immediately, and it's wise to pay it off right away.

Time/Cost Comparison
Moving $300 from the US to the UK

Method	Time it Takes	Approx. Cost
Paypal	2 to 3 days, or longer	$15
Western Union	varies	$16
MoneyGram	varies	$10
Xoom	varies	$7 to $14
Intl. Money Order	1 to 5 days	$3 to $10
Wire Transfer	Same day	$40 to $60

- **Western Union** – Must find a sending/receiving agent (80,000 in 170 countries) or transfer money online. http://www.westernunion.com
- **MoneyGram** – Must find sending/receiving agent, no online transfers. http://www.moneygram.com
- **Xoom** – Similar to Western Union and MoneyGram. http://www.xoom.com
- **Oanda.com** – The site for calculating your money in another currency. http://www.oanda.com

48. What about income or sales taxes?

The hardest thing in the world to understand is the income tax.
~Albert Einstein

You may have questions about foreign income and sales tax, so let's just jump right in. There are lots of different taxes in other countries. In fact, the UN is discussing *global* taxation on such things as email, fossil fuels, currency exchange, avian fuel tax, and international air travel. The thought is that global tax can help with global warming and other global issues. In fact, the *Global Poverty Act* (H.R. 1302 and S. 2433), which is now before Congress, would make it official US policy to implement a US tax that reduces global poverty, toward the realization of the UN's Millennium Development Goal (see section #86). For international tax information and resources, visit http://www.taxsites.com/international.html.

Value Added Tax (VAT) is a regressive tax in the EU on the *added* value that results from exchanges. It is different from sales tax, which is levied on the *total* value. As a visitor who resides outside of the EU, you can get a refund on purchases you take home. Look for stores with a "Tax-Free Shopping" logo in the window. When purchasing something for export, just present your passport and ask for a *Global Refund Check*. When you exit the country, the check should be stamped by customs officials and taken to a Global Refund Office in the airport for cash, check, direct crediting of a credit/debit card, or transfer to a bank account. For more information, visit the following website: www.globalrefund.com.

Watch out for scams with the VAT. Some stores tell you that you can get a refund at the airport, but your purchase receipt reads that you have already received the refund directly from the shop, and worse of all, you signed the receipt, stating that you received it! If you sign unfamiliar forms without reading them, then please consider breaking this bad habit. One thing you can do to avoid this scam and others is not to sign what you have not read or have not completely understood in the foreign language. The only thing you should be signing in a store is a credit card slip that authorizes payment (if you're paying by credit card). If you don't read the language, and the clerk insists that you sign, then kindly ask a third party (not employed by the store) to translate the document.

Don't forget to file your income tax return or an extension if you need more time. As a US student residing abroad, you are still obligated to pay income tax under US tax laws and must file a state and federal return if your gross income is over a certain amount. In 2007, if you were single and your gross income from worldwide sources was $8,750 or higher, you must have filed a federal tax return. Gross income is all your earnings in any given tax year (wages, overseas income, self-employment income, interest, dividends, etc.). It may also include scholarships. Pell Grants, Supplemental Educational Opportunity Grants, and Grants to States for State Student Incentives are nontaxable scholarships to the extent used for tuition and course-related expenses during the grant period. If the host country takes out income taxes, then you may be eligible for a deduction or refund. Check with the IRS.

The US now has income tax treaties with more than 35 other countries, which means that international taxing authorities can exchange financial information. You can look up most of these in TaxAlmanac (www.taxalmanac.org). So, don't fudge on your tax return. Even the interest you have earned through a foreign bank account is taxable. Publication 54, *The Tax Guide for US Citizens Abroad* will answer most of your questions: www.irs.gov/publications/p54/index.html. See *Tax Information for Students* for further information and advice: http://www.irs.ustreas.gov/individuals/students.

49. Can I travel without much money?

Frugality may be termed the daughter of Prudence, the sister of Temperance, and the parent of Liberty ~ **Samuel Johnson**

If you're willing to sacrifice some time, and do some careful planning, then there's no reason why you can't travel around on less. You'll be amazed at how far your budget can stretch.

Accommodations
Your money will go a lot further if you choose hostels instead of motels. However, you must be willing to sacrifice privacy and service. While there are many different types of hostels, typically you provide your own bath towel and sleep sack (a sheet folded and hemmed). Bedrooms (or dormitories) and bathrooms are often shared by guests; however, single rooms may be possible for an additional cost. More than having a bed/bath, you will probably have self-serve kitchen facilities.

Hostelling (living out of hostels) is a culture unto itself for those who are adventurous, independent, and frugal. While people from all walks of life use hostels, they are especially popular among backpackers and those who are traveling for long periods of time (ex. a twelve-week trip around Australia and New Zealand). Hostelling is an excellent way to see and do more, meet people from everywhere, and learn about the culture and country, as they are located around people.

If you're interested and want to learn more about hostels, see *The Hostel Handbook* (www.hostelhandbook.com). *Backpack Europe* (www.backpackeurope.com) is another good website. If you're looking for some information about budget travel in Europe, visit www.eurotrip.com. To get additional discounts from 10-15%, purchase a hostel membership card from one of many providers. You can also buy a VIP Backpackers card at www.vipbackpackers.com.

- **Hostels.net** – http://www.hostels.net
- **Hostels.com** – http://www.hostels.com
- **Hostelling International** – http://www.hihostels.com
- **Hostelling International USA** – http://www.hiusa.org
- **Hostels of Europe** – http://www.hostelseurope.com
- **Hostel World** – http://www.hostelworld.com
- **Hostel Z** – http://www.hostelz.com

An alternative to staying in hostels is staying with people you know or contact in other areas of the world. This guy named Ramon Stoppelenburg set up a website and traveled the world for over two years, without any money. He found people who were willing to help him out with food and shelter, as well as other essentials. Basically, he asked strangers to let him stay at their homes for a day, and in return, he posted daily reports on his website: letmestayforaday.com. If you have a desire to stay in people's homes, then also visit *SERVAS International* at http://joomla.servas.org.

Food
When I travel, I have to eat cheap due a restrictive budget. If I don't have cooking facilities, then I still manage on just one restaurant a day. For the other meals, I go to the grocery store or outdoor market and buy food that doesn't require cooking and is easy to eat. Breads are delicious and cheap, and go well with lots of other foods like cheese, spreads, meats, olives, etc. Pastries are also good and cheap. Fruits are great to throw in your backpack and eat when you get hungry. Eating out of your backpack may not be as satisfying, but it is definitely better for your health than restaurants. If you buy cans, make sure you have a cap opener, and don't forget to bring some silverware to keep you from having to eat with your hands. Now, here's the mom in me… wash your hands before eating so you don't get sick on your journeys abroad.

If you feel like eating something with a little more flavor and pizzazz, then try some of foods you find in street stands and cafes like crepes, sandwiches, pretzels, nuts, etc. Avoid meat and other items that may spoil easily outside and make sure your attendant is wearing gloves and not touching the food with his/her hands. These items are never very expensive and usually fill me up when I'm out and about. Don't worry about consuming too much grease or fat because chances are your body needs it to accommodate the many long walks and other activities abroad. Buy yummy juices in the grocery stores, made with fruits that you can't find at home. They usually come in a box and are less costly than soda pop.

50. How should I plan my time?

When we are doing what we love, we don't care about time. For at least at that moment, time doesn't exist and we are truly free. ~*Marcia Wieder*

In addition to managing your money, it's important that you know how to manage your time. People who know how to manage their time get more done and accomplish their goals. If you know why you're studying abroad and you know what you want to accomplish, then good time management skills will benefit you, throughout your entire stay. People who let time manage them, instead managing time, don't make the same progress, and oftentimes don't accomplish their goals to a level in which they can be satisfied. Time management is one of my strong American values, so bear with me while I drag you through my approach.

There are three kinds of time: *scheduled* time, *down* time, and *wait* time. If you have goals to accomplish, then no time need be wasted. By virtue of the fact that you voluntarily chose to study abroad, one of your big goals should be to successfully complete your classes. Use a weekly/daily planner to keep track of all your meetings, due dates, exams, field trips, etc. You should also use your planner to break down projects and assignments into smaller tasks. For a paper, write down steps in the form of *tasks* that will need to be completed several weeks in advance (i.e. selecting a topic, conducting research, and preparing an outline). After you add your academic goals, add your personal goals and the many activities necessary to accomplish them along the way.

Now that you have weekly goals laid out, you should also use your planner to organize your daily activities with *to do lists*. As you complete items on this list, you can cross them out. If you've managed your time well, you should have some *down time* each day in which you can schedule other activities (if they are not already scheduled) like working out at the gym, reading, or socializing with friends. You may have a set time every day in which you simply designate as *fun*, but only if you are sure you can get everything else finished on your list. This will give you a point of reference and help you stay on track with your study abroad experience. It will also help you know that you are accomplishing your goals (a great feeling)!

Wait time is the time you spend *waiting for* or *on your way to* your scheduled activities and events (both work and play). The nice thing about wait time is that you can also use it for something else other than simply waiting. You can choose to read, write, finish homework, or whatever else you like to do. Really though, you have only two choices for wait time; you can use it productively towards your goals or you can use it for whatever you like to do for fun. I have many goals, so I prefer to spend my wait time doing productive things so that I can have more down time to spend enjoyably. I've used my wait time to write this book (in airports, on trains, in the car when I'm not driving). It's amazing how much I've been able to accomplish by effectively using this time toward my goals.

My long and bewildering advice is to *align your time with your goals*, whatever those goals may be. If your goal is to learn the culture and language, then you should spend your time doing things that help you along in this process. If your goal is to see ten major cities in Europe, then you had better start scheduling your flights. Wait a minute…what if both of these things are goals? Learning the culture and language requires that you stay put, and seeing ten major cities in Europe means you'll need to be gone much of the time. Two conflicting goals will only frustrate and set you up for failure, so you'll need to make a choice or a compromise.

If you want to do some of both, then think carefully about which one of these goals is more important and how you can compromise your time. Maybe staying home seventy percent of the time is sufficient for culture and language learning, and you can plan two or three (instead of ten) trips to other major European cities. This makes a lot of sense for a study abroad experience, since it's an important part of your education to learn the customs and culture of your host country. You can always go back to Europe or any other area of the world and travel for fun. What you have now is a unique opportunity to study in the same place for an extended period of time.

Imagine this scenario. You are studying abroad in Spain and you want to learn the culture and language well. You have a choice of spending the weekend with your host family at a festival or traveling to Rome with some US friends. What do you do? Ahh, tough question…I guess what it comes down to is will you do what it takes to reach your goal a year from now or will you give in to your desire to be with friends? Only you know what it will take to accomplish your goals. You can't do both. Come on; you know what's best. If you do the right thing, you won't regret it; trust me. Rome will be there today and tomorrow, but the local festival won't.

Always plan your time with no regrets. What you do today is where you'll be tomorrow. If you decide to do something, then just make sure your decision lines up with your goals. Sometimes you can accomplish multiple goals at the same time, and sometimes you have to make a choice. Don't forget about your *wait* time. Whether you're sitting in an airport or on a plane, train, or bus, you can spend this time wisely. Do your homework or get your readings done for class. Write in your journal or something else that helps you in your journey. This will allow you to have more downtime and to spend it more enjoyably. If you plan and utilize time well, then you'll have a lot more of it to enjoy than if you let time just happen to you. This is the great benefit of good time management.

Whereintheworld.co.uk – Adventure travel and events you never knew existed. A way for you to enjoy your down time.

51. Can my friends and relatives visit?

We are all visitors to this time, this place. We are just passing through. Our purpose here is to observe, to learn, to grow, to love... and then we return home.
~Australian Aboriginal Proverb

Sure, why not have your friends and relatives visit. Know the rules before inviting anyone to stay with you. It is common for residence halls to have restrictions and you shouldn't expect your host family to provide space. When my parents visited me in Ecuador, I recommended a family-run hostel that operated like a bed and breakfast. It was more pleasant for them than staying in my cramped quarters. It also gave them some necessary down time.

If your parents or friends are looking for more class and style than a hostel, consider asking your local arrangements person, at the host institution or provider, if they have any corporate rates for guests. Some universities have their own guest housing, available for free or much lesser than market prices. Go ahead and make reservations, but check the Internet at least two weeks before their departure, also. It may be that ratestogo.com or laterooms.com has a number of last-minute bargains that are better than your original reservation. Check traveladvisor.com and hotelchatter.com for reviews.

Some schools actually have programs for visiting parents. For example, the University of Queensland has a *Visiting Parents Program*, where the institution provides parents with a wealth of information, tips, discounts, a tour of the campus, and a complementary lunch for three. If there is nothing like this at your host institution, then check to see if the Visitor's Office can arrange for a tour of the campus. They might be willing to make other special arrangements for your parents beyond a mere campus tour.

It is ideal if parents and friends come to visit you during your vacation time or after the program has ended. That way you don't have to worry about your academic workload and you can have fun traveling. Also, you will have been there long enough to show them how to navigate the country/culture. It is no fun to try to entertain guests when you're in the middle of final exams or when you are juggling three to five classes. Entertaining and especially traveling with others can be quite exhausting. You'll know what I mean when the time comes.

One thing that you may not have thought about is insurance. As certain types of insurance were necessary for you, they are probably necessary for your guests. Visitors are not immune from health problems, various sorts of accidents, and other emergencies. The cost of their trip may be nonrefundable if they have to cancel or return early for a legitimate reason. Their current health insurance coverage and arrangements may not be adequate for medical assistance and medical emergency evacuation. There are lots of different policies for short-term travel out of the country. Advise your guests to do their research and buy something that suits their needs, before they travel abroad. See section #27 for more information.

Part VI.

Live in another Country

52. What exactly is culture?

As the soil, however rich it may be, cannot be productive without cultivation, so the mind without culture can never produce good fruit. ~Seneca

According to cultural anthropologist Edward T. Hall, culture is communication and communication is culture (1959). It is a culture that teaches us how to communicate, and it is how we communicate that binds us to a culture. People that don't stay in keeping with cultural communication practices, usually end up *excommunicated* from the culture in some shape or form. There are countless different cultures in the world and each of us uniquely fits into many that shape and mold our growth.

Culture (or conformity) is the opposite of individualism. Like the Chinese philosophy yin and yang, they oppose but unify each other through their duality. Without culture, there would be no community, and without individualism there would be no change and community would be changeless. While each individual is a one-of-a-kind life form, culture is what a group of individuals have in common. It is what make us different from animals and advances the human race.

Some cultures are stronger than others, for different reasons. Nations and religions tend to be strong because they share a common history. There's something about history that binds a people together in a way that is unparalleled to cultures that don't have it. History is the main ingredient to an unbreakable culture. Other cultures are strengthened by a common set of values and beliefs. When communities are committed with heart and soul, the culture is strengthened because of it.

Cultures are complicated because our understanding comes from what has been communicated about a particular culture within our own culture. For example, the media is a form of communication within our national culture, which shapes our understanding of the African continent. If we choose to add to our knowledge, then our understanding may be shaped by a book and whatever else we read. If we happen to visit Africa (or talk to someone who has visited), then we will be shaped by this new information. Depending on the length and quality of our experiences, we may never have a true understanding of Africa or how countries within the continent may differ.

On top of the complications we have in tying to understand other cultures from the vantage point of our own, there are many subcultures within a continent. Every region (originally divided by race) has its own culture, which houses national and religious cultures, which house countless subcultures. For example, Africa is known as the motherland of black people. Within Africa, we have the North, West, East, and South, all different from each other but similar within the larger context. When Europeans invaded Africa, the areas changed; the area in which we find South Africa changed in ways that other countries did not.

So what is the national culture of South Africa? It depends on who you talk to…a native African from a small, secluded village will see things differently than an immigrant African whose grandparents migrated to Cape Town over 100 years ago. To comprehend the culture is to perceive something different from the cultures within and around it. In the case of South Africa, the culture isn't a common set of beliefs or values, but rather experiences. For example, everyone from South Africa has experienced the Apartheid in one way or another, and while each of their experiences is different, there are some common bonds they share because of it.

Traveling keys us in to all the intricacies and layers of culture but it often pigeonholes us within the *concept* of our nation. There is no way to pre-determine all the cultural differences that you will encounter. Just because you're from a particular nation doesn't mean you're exactly the same as everyone else that lives there. You may be in South Africa when you meet an English chap who lives and works in the country. You may meet English people who have an appreciation and affinity towards the US. What you can attempt to learn in this cultural encounter is South African and English history, and how it has shaped the two cultures. What is South African culture? What is English culture? Is it really what you learned back home or is it different and more?

Just as mixing water with lemon juice and sugar gives you lemonade; mixing one culture with another can sweeten up your life (to say the least). When you leave your culture and enter into another, you will encounter many similarities, but you will notice many differences. People will think, live, and behave in ways that you are not accustomed to and don't understand. For example, people may not arrive on time; for you, it's disrespectful but for them it's just a normal part of their everyday living that stems from the way they understand time and use it. This is where we find what is commonly referred to as the *iceberg effect*. Although many differences are visible, there is more that is invisible, or under the water. This is where our communication can become hairy.

Let's look a simple example. Everyday, your professor is late to your two o'clock class. Through your cultural lenses, you interpret his perpetual lateness as disrespectful and you begin to construe him as lazy, disorganized, and inconsiderate. In reality, your professor has lunch with his friends everyday and finds it perfectly normal to take his time, finish his meal, and arrive a little late to class. After all, when class is right after lunch, it's understandable that both the professor and students will be running late. To rush to class and arrive on the hour would be disrespectful and unrealistic in a culture that values company and food with such passion. Even if he wanted to arrive on time, it would be unfair to all his students.

Culture is an interesting phenomenon. If you take the time to study and understand it, you will be amazed at how it flows throughout your life like water, taking on so many different forms and hiding in so many nooks and crannies. Culture is communication, but it is much more, it is the glue that binds us together as the human race. Culture is something you have but you don't know that you have until you stand face-to-face with another. Culture is the only thing (other than love itself) which allows us to have individual differences and still come together in community. It is what makes us different from the animal kingdom. Individuals bind culture, and culture binds individuals, and this is what makes the world go around.

One of my most interesting encounters with culture occurred in Africa, when my mother called a spirit doctor to treat her malaria. A man came to the house, threw out some stones, and examined where they fell. He then pointed to an area in the backyard and told her that the spirit causing the malaria was under the ground. As he started to dig, he located a small object in the hole, and threw it up in the air like a hot potato. Then he started chanting loudly and dancing around. My host mother ordered me to go into the house because she believed white skin was weak and the spirit could easily find its way inside of my body. Later, I was told that the spirit causing the malaria was connected to that object. The witch doctor had essentially cast it away, so that it could not return.

Further Exploration

Beyond Culture by Edward T. Hall

Studying Abroad/Learning Abroad: An Abridged Edition of Whole World Guide to Culture Learning by J. Daniel Hess

Survival Kit for Overseas Living by L. Robert Kohls

53. How will I adapt and adjust?

The most important trip you may take in life is meeting people halfway. ~Henry Boye

Cultural adjustment is the path to growth and development through study abroad and other international experiences. It is to international education as puberty is to growing up. There are various stages involved in cultural adjustment. They are high and low, and change over the course of time. Below are five stages you can look forward to experiencing, if you're immersed in the host culture for an extended period of time. If you're traveling on a short-term program and/or an island program (not immersed in the host culture), then know that you may never leave the first stage.

Stage 1, EUPHORIA
You started gearing up for this stage the moment you decided to study abroad. You've arrived and everything is grand! The orientation was exciting, the food is good, there are so many things to see and do. Wow, life doesn't get much better than this! Everything looks peachy, even better than you imagined.

Stage 2, DISTRESS
Life starts to normalize. You miss some comforts from home. You're finding it hard to communicate with your host family. You got sick from the food more than once. You don't like

the poor service at the university. You regret your decision to study abroad. Everything is getting old, and fast!

Stage 3, ADJUSTMENT

Different feelings start to surface in your life. One day you feel embarrassed, and another day you feel isolated, angry, and even hostile. Sometimes you feel depressed. It's normal; so don't worry. Your experience is not what you expected. These feelings come and go, and then they stabilize.

Stage 4, ADAPTATION

You become familiar with the culture and how to get around. You learn to communicate better and relationships with your family improve. While you don't like their teaching style so much, you've come to like your professors and have figured out how to get the information you need. You begin to adapt.

Stage 5, RECOVERY

You regain confidence and learn to appreciate the culture as a whole. You accept that which you cannot change, and find more good than evil. You may actually think the host culture is better than your own in many ways, and it may be hard to go home. You assimilate parts of the culture; you're renewed.

You may experience many emotions and changes...

Curiosity	Embarrassment	Communication
Excitement	Depression	Friendships
Elation	Isolation	Confidence
Surprise	Anger	Appreciation
Confusion	Hostility	Acceptance
Discomfort	Familiarity	Growth/Change

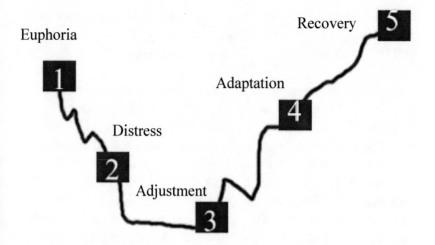

Euphoria

Recovery **5**

1

Adaptation

Distress

4

2

Adjustment

3

When I first arrived in Cameroon, it was thrilling! After the Peace Corps staff picked us up from the airport, they took us to a lovely little restaurant with delicious food. It was the first time that I had ever tasted real mango juice. After lunch, they escorted us to the training camp, where a traditional African dance group welcomed us with drums and other traditional instruments. It was absolutely thrilling to be a part of so much culture and change all at once, before we met our families.

My homestay family was African-Muslim (and Animist) and they spoke both Fulfulde and French. Although I had taken two years of French in high school and college, I didn't speak it well. Still I managed to communicate with them and enjoy the new environment. It wasn't until a week or two later when I started going into DISTRESS mode. I had gotten very sick and had to go outside many time in the middle of the night to relieve myself of diarrhea. It was dark, and I didn't feel very comfortable squatting over an open latrine.

On top of this, every time I turned on my flashlight to get up and go, there were two huge cockroaches (each three inches long) on the mosquito net above my head. There was also a very loud cricket somewhere in my bed that would suddenly start chirping every time I was beginning to fall back asleep.

I'd have to shake my sleeping bag to make it stop, and then 15 minutes later, it would start again. It was exhausting and night after night, I just couldn't seem to get enough rest.

One time, I got up to go to the latrine and found a huge spider on my wall, probably about two inches wide and long. Not very friendly with spiders, I searched my room frantically for something to kill it with, for fear that I would find it in bed with me if I didn't. Since it was enormous, I kind-of threw my shoe at it, but it moved. I ended up piercing its big round sack belly, and little did I know what was inside. Out of sack scurried hundreds of baby spiders, across the walls. At that moment, I just started sobbing. I felt like surrendering it all and going home. Even so, something inside convinced me to stay, and I did.

After this low point, I recovered from that terrible bout of diarrhea and learned how to manage the many bugs in my life. When I went to my site, I lived with all kinds of critters. I lived with strange flat spiders that suction-cupped the walls (to eat the algae), mice that would raid my kitchen at night, tarantulas that lived under my bed, and a snake that took a liking to my oven (actually, I had the snake killed since it was poisonous). The cockroaches raided my latrine at night, and I even found a scorpion in one of my shoes (luckily I knew to check before putting it on). I wasn't on Main Street anymore, but this time I managed.

Be sure to apply effective coping mechanisms abroad. While some ways are positive and effective, others are negative and ineffective. For example, avoiding the culture frequently and withdrawing on a consistent basis is negative and ineffective. Relying entirely on resources or other people all of the time is negative, but using resources to find your way is positive and beneficial. Coping is about finding balance and not allowing yourself to be distracted from what you came to accomplish.

When our coping strategies cause us to lose track of personal and academic goals, then they need to be reconsidered.

Everyone has bad days, but what makes bad days worse in the cultural adjustment process is that you don't have your usual support systems to help. Nonetheless, there are a few things that you can do to help yourself get through these days. One of the best things is to get away by yourself for a while so that you can think clearly. Temporary, *occasional* withdrawal is healthy and necessary to *recharge your energy* when you are culturally or linguistically challenged in some way. Living in another country and learning a new language is tough! Don't be too hard on yourself, and keep a healthy perspective.

After you've recharged, then it's time to assert yourself and learn more about the culture. Join clubs and groups, put yourself in structured situations to get to know people, go out with your friends, spend time with your host family (if you have one), and participate in extracurricular activities. Utilize the resources at the study abroad program or institution to help you get started, and then learn to manage yourself in the new culture. This is a marketable skill called *adaptability* that will help you to have a successful experience abroad, and in many other turning points of your life.

Be an active learner. Use information to guide you through your experience, rather than control you through it. Dare your friends to venture outside of their worldviews and don't be afraid to venture out, either. Study the culture and learn from it. Every culture has something valuable to offer, a new and improved perspective of yourself and the world. The whole experience can only develop maturity. Strive to maintain and expand your own identity, not to lose or dilute your inner self. Then, allow yourself to be a unique person. You don't have to become the culture and nobody expects you to, either. Simply allow the culture to make you a healthier and better person.

187

You can expect to miss some things from home, and this too is normal. It is hard to say what you'll miss the most. It really depends on your preferences. It may be McDonalds, it could be pizza, or it could be the mailbox. For me, it was *Berber carpet*; I could not lie down on my concrete floor. What you miss will depend on lots of things, namely the likeability and availability of certain items while you are abroad. When I lived in Cameroon, it was hard to find dairy products like ice cream and cheese. A few grocers carried it, but it was very expensive and didn't taste the same as it does in the States. Instead of being hard, it was soft, chewy, and gooey.

All you can do is make the best of whatever you miss. Try to find something you like in the culture to counterbalance what you miss from home. When I went to France, I had the most delicious crepes! Now I'm back in the US, and longing for a crepe stand again. It doesn't matter if you're here or there, you'll always miss something and you'll always be thankful for what you have at the moment, whether you realize it or not. Generally, the more experiences you have in this life, the more you'll have to appreciate (and subsequently long for) in your everyday world.

A few years ago, I received a post card advertisement from an Internet company called Home Sick Snacks, which seems to have gone under because its website is now a dead link. The advertisement read, "Your momma may be 5000 miles away, but homesicksnacks.com is just a click away." My colleagues and I got a kick out of that concept because we remembered those days of longing! It's amazing what you miss when you suddenly don't have it around you anymore. Some things that I missed a lot while abroad weren't American snacks, but my mother and my car.

Write down what you miss in your journal. Believe it or not, someday you won't even remember having gone without it. It is good for the soul to yearn. It reminds us of our humanness

188

and how delicate life really is, and it helps us distinguish our needs from our wants and put them into perspective.

Resources

The Art of Crossing Cultures
by Craig Storti

Campus Blues – An excellent mental health resource for college students. http://www.campusblues.com

---

54. How do I recognize differences?

Our greatest strength as a human race is our ability to acknowledge our differences, our greatest weakness is our failure to embrace them.
~ Judith Henderson

The problem we have with handling differences is we often don't see or recognize the differences. We don't recognize them because we think that our way is the way of the world. There are many ways in which people can be different from each other. *Maximizing Study Abroad: A Student's Guide to Strategies for Language and Culture Learning and Use* is a nice guide for understanding the differences that lie under the surface (www.carla.umn.edu/maxsa). Linear vs. circular time, direct vs. indirect communication, formality vs. informality, and individualism vs. community are just some of the major differences.

I once heard a story about a Peace Corps volunteer who was doing health work in Africa. She was teaching some village women about fertility and how to put on a condom. For demo purposes, she showed them how to slide a condom on the end of a broomstick and told them if they do this at home then they won't get pregnant. A few months later, a woman came

189

back and told the volunteer that the method didn't work. She put the condom on the broomstick in her home, but still got pregnant. Do you see where communication went astray? To the African woman, the volunteer's demonstration was literal, one of black magic and voodoo.

To recognize differences, you have to understand the cultures and worldviews that are involved in communication. Culture is to a group as worldview is to an individual. While culture is shared between one or more groups; worldview is unique to an individual and has to do with how he/she understands life, its inner-workings, death, the world, and the universe. For example, I culturally identify myself as an American, as do 300 million others. However, I must say my belief system and way of life is different from many Americans. This has to do with my unique biology and experiences, as well as what I'd refer to as my soul.

I believe that I was created by a loving god who helps and watches over my family and me. I think little dogs are mean and ornery (because I was bitten by one as a child). I don't like cats, but I love lions. I believe that my life has a purpose beyond my control. I now think spiders can be our friends. Finally, I believe that more women should be in positions of leadership. Many of our inner beliefs are unspeakable. These beliefs guide how we see and do things, our framework for everyday living. The more you can find out about people, the more you can attempt to understand them, only if they're truthful of course.

No matter how much you think you know about a culture or person, you will experience misunderstandings from time to time. These misunderstandings occur when communication goes astray or values clash between two or more cultures and worldviews. Good observation skills are critical because you just can't learn everything there is to know about people with books and television. When you notice that something has gone wrong, ask yourself what happened. Try to understand the other person's culture/worldview. Don't be afraid to make mistakes; just do your best and pick up any pieces that fall along the wayside.

Reading

American Ways: A Guide for Foreigners in the United States by Gary Althen

Distant Mirrors: America as a Foreign Culture by Philip R. DeVita and James D. Armstrong

Rethinking Worldview: Learning to Think, Live, and Speak in this World by J. Mark Bertrand

---

How American Are You?
(Self-Assessment Quiz)

Have you ever given much thought to what makes up your nationality? If you're an American, then you may consider yourself different from other Americans, but chances are you probably have more in common with your co-nationals than you think. Take the quiz on the next page and check the box next to every question that you answer yes.

Is the ideal person independent and self-reliant?	
Do you value your independence and career?	
Do you believe that church and state should be kept as separate institutions?	
Do you believe religion is an individual choice?	
Is the *first-come-first-serve* outlook fair?	
Do you believe that all people are created equal?	
Do you prefer informal over formal communication?	
Is being on time and punctuality important to you?	
Do money and possessions measure success?	

Are you accustomed to small talk?	
Do you have lots of different friends?	
Do you discuss your personal life openly?	
Is a preponderance of evidence necessary to prove something to someone?	
Are facts more important than hearsay?	
Do you avoid same-sex touch?	
When someone you don't know well touches you, does it make you feel uncomfortable?	
Do you welcome debate and arguments?	
Do you prefer that someone is at least an arm's length away from you when talking?	
Is it important that someone look you in the eye for you to know that he/she is listening?	
Are you uncomfortable with silence?	
Do you point with your index finger?	
Are you free to use both hands in the same way?	
Do you take a shower everyday?	
Do you notice stinky smells easily?	
Do you expect to be called by your first name?	
Is friendship always informal, regardless of age?	
Would you ask a child what he wants to be when he grows up or a senior what she wants to do after retiring?	
Do you believe in working and playing hard?	
Do you enjoy, welcome, and value competition?	
Do you have your own space and value your privacy?	
Do children have the right to disagree with their parents?	
Do you think that education is the key to success?	
Do you believe that everybody has the opportunity to succeed in life, regardless of background?	
TOTAL THE NUMBER OF CHECKMARKS (yes's)	

1-11	12-22	23-33
Not Really Sure	**American**	**Very American**

55. What about my classes?

Travel and change of place impart new vigor to the mind. ~ **Seneca**

First of all, university life is different in other countries. The institution may not have a campus, but rather buildings spread around the city. Students may be older and may live at home, thus obliterating the need for on-campus residence halls and university-sponsored clubs and activities. The Student Union may be totally independent. Young people may play different sports or engage in unfamiliar activities for fun. Students may spend more time with their families than they do with their friends. Their best friends may be family. Professors may not be *friendly* with students and the format of class may seem old fashioned.

In most foreign countries, the faculty give lectures and assign readings but students are responsible for how much work they do and what they accomplish. Most of the learning requires self-discipline and direction. Rather than being evaluated on class participation, pop quizzes, tests, and so on, students are graded on one or two final exams. This can be nerve-racking, but is a good indication of whether or not you've retained the information taught in a course. The relationship between a professor and his/her students is usually more formal than in the US, and there may be no explanation provided (or further negotiation acceptable) for assigned grades.

The system may be different as well. In the US, registration is usually a painless online process, a class meets in the same room for the entire quarter/semester, you receive a syllabus of some kind at the beginning, and good organization is usually apparent. In foreign countries, registration may be a painful paper-driven process, your classrooms may switch frequently, you may not be provided with a syllabus, and organization is not always apparent (from the American point of view). Also, students may follow a rigid plan of study with little to no say in their schedules. The same course may change substantially from one professor to another.

Libraries may not be the self-serve format that you're used to at home and access to materials may be limited. Usually, you have to request materials from a librarian or via a computer. The books are then retrieved for you and you can schedule a time to review them or pick them up. For security reasons, you may have to check your backpack at a desk upon entering the library and the library may not be open late at night. Once you get used to the schedule and procedures, you should be able to manage. Always allow extra time when learning new systems. If you're attending an American university overseas, then this information is probably irrelevant.

What is often considered normal practice in foreign countries may appear disorganized and strange to Americans. This is because higher education in the US is driven by capitalism, consumerism, and competition. In other countries, education is regarded as a privilege rather than a product. The more you know beforehand, the better prepared you'll be able to deal with the inconveniences and oddities of studying in another country. Higher education systems are very different around the world. In many countries, there is often no such thing as a *Grade Point Average*. In New Zealand, courses are called papers. Student Services is an American concept that may not even exist, especially at public institutions.

Understand that quality and service is usually dependent on funding. Public higher education is low cost or free in many countries, but it is also underfunded. Only prophets can make wine out of water; for the rest of us, it takes other ingredients. In higher education, the main ingredient is money. The best facilities and professors cost the most. This is why private education is so much better than the public education in many countries. Students who can afford to pay high tuition, get the best education and services. Sadly, families who don't have the money are forced to settle with whatever they can get. They have to put up with underpaid, unmotivated professors and administrators who don't feel valued and appreciated.

Consider the following resources to advance your learning:

- *Understanding the Education – and through it the Culture – in Education Abroad* by Linda A. Chrisholm and Howard A. Beny
- **Center for Global Education, WWCU** http://www.globaled.us/wwcu
- **Universities of the World** http://www.unesco.org/iau/world-universities

56. What about housing?

I long, as does every human being, to be at home wherever I find myself.
~Maya Angelou

Your housing options will vary dramatically, depending on the program, institution, and country. My advice would be to find out as much as you can about your housing options, so that you can make an informed decision. Of all complaints, one of the most frequent is housing. This is because students don't do enough research beforehand. Be careful to choose the best fit for you! Below are a few different options.

- **Homestay/Host Family** – Room and board with a family. A great way to acclimate to the culture.
- **Student Housing** – Residence halls or apartments that are owned or rented by the school/provider or are designated by another company for student use.
- **Independent Housing** – An apartment that you have sought and secured, usually with help or assistance from your home and/or host institution.

Look at student evaluations, specifically what they say about student housing in your program. Also, visit online sources of information where students from all over the world can post comments (www.iagora.com). Know that photographs seen in brochures and fliers are often taken with a wide-angle lens, so they look much bigger than they are up close and personal. Keep in mind that space is a luxury. While you may end up with a spacious apartment, I wouldn't count on it.

Housing is an individual choice. It all boils down to your priorities, preferences, and what's important to you. Your ideal housing situation may be 45 minutes from campus, but are you willing to get up early to make the commute? Living with a family can be beneficial to learning the language, but are you willing to sacrifice some privacy and space? Making decisions is all about making sacrifices, in keeping with your values, goals, and priorities.

You may decide that where you ended up living is not a good fit for you. Talk to your host institution or program provider to see if and how you can make a change. If you're miserable and you're not functioning well in the environment, then you should definitely make a change. Before you decide however, visit the rooms, flats, apartments, or families of your fellow international students. Make sure that there are other options that would suit your preferences and/or needs better.

57. How do I get around?

It is not down in any map; true places never are. ~ *Herman Melville*

Most students use public transportation while abroad. In fact, public transportation is generally the *preferred method* of getting around in foreign countries. Not many countries are afforded the kind of space and resources that we have in the United States, to depend on private transportation for all our needs. It is often easier just to hop on a metro, bus, or train, than it is to drive. In other countries, you'll find people from all walks of life using public transportation, not just people who can't afford otherwise.

For short trips, walking is great, or bicycling. Often times you can buy a used bicycle for $10 or so and ride it for your entire study abroad experience. Just be very careful in large cities where it's not recommended to bike. Before you return to the US, you can sell your bike or give it away. In general, you'll find that people walk and bike a lot more in other countries than they do in the States, not just for exercise and recreation, but for transportation.

If you're in Europe or the UK, the best way to travel to other cities and countries is via trains and planes. Believe it or not, it can sometimes be cheaper to take a flight than a train. Not too long ago, I paid €12 to fly from one European country to another. Citybird, Easyjet, Icelandair, Martinair, Ryanair, SkyEurope, Virgin Express, and Virgin Atlantic usually have low fares, except during the summer. Baggage limits may be low, while excess fees may be high.

Eurail (www.eurail.com) and Eurostar (www.eurostar.com) are some of the best rails to see and get around Europe and the UK. Eurail is for travel around Europe, and Eurostar is for travel within the UK. See *Rail Europe* (www.raileurope.com) for the major providers of rail passes. While not as swift as flying, you get to see the countryside and the journey is more enjoyable. Visit *Rick Steves* to download the latest rail guide: www.ricksteves.com/rail.

Planes

Citybird – http://www.citybird.com
Easyjet – http://www.easyjet.com
Icelandair – http://www.icelandair.is
LTU – http://www.ltu.com

Martinair – http://www.martinairusa.com
Ryanair – http://www.ryanair.com
SkyEurope – http://www2.skyeurope.com/en
Virgin Atlantic – http://www.virgin-atlantic.com
Virgin Atlantic – www.virgin-atlantic.com/en/us/index.jsp
Wizzair – http://wizzair.com
Student Flights – http://www.studentflights.co.uk
Itravel – www.iagora.com/itravel/tools/intl/aireurope.html
Skyscanner – www.skyscanner.net

Trains

European Train Query Page – http://bahn.hafas.de
Eurail/Eurostar – www.trenitaliaplus.com
Dutch Railway – www.ns.nl
Belgian Railway – http://www.b-rail.be
German Railway – http://reiseauskunft.bahn.de
French Railway – http://www.sncf.com
Spanish Rail – http://www.renfe.es/ingles

Of all transportation methods, taxis seem to confuse me more than any of them. This is because taxi drivers are skilled at identifying tourists and subsequently doubling the price. In Budapest, I took a taxi from my hotel to the train station (less than five minutes) and was forced to pay more than double or leave my precious bag in the trunk and run. I paid more than double but was not happy about it! When I returned to the US, I filed a complaint with the company. What I learned is that if you ask your hotel to call you a taxi, then you can expect to pay double what it would cost if you were to just wave down or call a taxi on your own, or if you were to have a friend call you a taxi. Taxi companies often have contracts with hotels, and hotels are making money off their higher rates, too! It's win-win for both of them, and lose-lose for us.

Taxi Tips

- Don't use unregistered (independent) taxis. You will need to find out how to identify an authentic cab in your host country before you get in one.
- Find taxi stands where usually only authorized taxis are allowed to stop and pick up passengers. Know how many passengers they are permitted to carry.
- Look for similarities among taxis, phone numbers, identification numbers, meters, radios, etc.
- Know what different rides cost in the city, and make sure you have enough cash to cover the cost.
- Make sure there is a meter running or negotiate a price before you get into the car, to avoid rip-offs.
- Know the general route to where you are going, so that you can confront a taxi that takes you for a ride.
- Be careful about sharing taxis with strangers, because scams are often attempted by pairs and groups.
- Avoid taxis in front of train stations and airports if you want to avoid high prices and rip-offs.
- Make sure there's an inside handle. Also, make sure it works and you can get out if it becomes necessary.
- Keep a watch on your bags. Leave your bag if you have to run in an emergency.
- Know who to call in an emergency (your local 911).

Some students choose to rent or buy a car when they travel overseas. I've commonly heard of a group of friends pitching in to buy something used and old, and then sharing it amongst themselves. While I have nothing to say about renting, I don't recommend that you buy a car for many reasons. You don't know the condition of the car, and it could be unsafe. Even if you're a mechanic, you may end up wasting a lot of precious time if it were to break. You have to worry about obtaining a special international driver's license, registration paperwork, license plates, insurance, operation, maintenance, repair costs, and much more. The laws are different in other countries and if you're in an accident, there may be a whole lot of trouble that you didn't see coming. The driving culture can be chaotic and difficult, especially for a foreigner.

Other Resources and Tips

Go to http://routesinternational.com for a cyber gateway to world transportation by road, rail, sea, and air. You can find links to local buses, subways, and ferries.

Go to http://www.youra.com/intlferries/index.html to link to ferry operations around the world.

Go to www.newspaperlinks.com, www.craigslist.org, and www.freecycle.org to search international classifieds for used bicycles or other items.

For a worldwide bicycling tour directory, and tons of bike information, visit http://www.bicycletour.com.

For over 2000 walks in the United Kingdom and Europe, visit http://www.walkingworld.com.

Finally, visit the world's largest walking and hiking trail database at http://www.traildatabase.org.

---

58. How about time and measurement?

Any measurement must take into account the position of the observer. There is no such thing as measurement absolute, there is only measurement relative.
~ Jeanette Winterson

Numbers are expressed differently around the world. In the US, the comma is used to separate thousands ($1,000) and the period is used for decimals ($10.95). In Continental Europe, it is just the opposite; the period is used to separate thousands ($1.000) and the comma is used for decimals ($10,95). Even more confusing is the *International Systems of Units* (SI), the new metric system of the world. It recommends that a space be used to separate hundreds, and doesn't distinguish between the comma and the period when it comes to decimals. For example, $15 500,50 is the same as $15 500.50.

The SI is not set in stone either. Definitions are modified and new units are created through international agreement, as the technology of measurement advances. Almost every country in the world has adopted it. However, the US still recognizes its previous system in addition to SI. Liberia and Myanmar have chosen not to adopt SI. For a detailed presentation, visit www.physics.nist.gov/cuu/Units. To see a printable brochure, visit http://www.bipm.org/en/si/si_brochure.

Worldwide Metric: www.worldwidemetric.com/metcal.htm

Length	Area
1 inch = 2.54 centimeters	1 square mile = 2.59 sq km
1 centimeter = .39 inches	1 square kilometer = .386 sq mi
1 foot = .30 meters	1 sq miles = 259 hectares
1 meter = 3.281 feet	1 hectare = 100 acres
1 yard = .9144 meters	1 sq kilometer = 247.1 acres
1 mile = 1.61 kilometers	100 acres = .01 sq kilometer
1 kilometer = .62 miles	*Kilometers (km), miles (mi), square (sq)*

Volume	Weight
1 gallon = 3.785 liters	1 pound = .45 kilograms
1 liter = .264 gallons	1 kilogram = 2.2 pounds
1 fl ounce = 29.6 milliliters	1 ounce = 28.3 grams
1 milliliters = .03 fl ounces	1 gram = .04 ounces
1 cup = 8 ounces	1 cup = 100 grams dry weight

Speed	Energy & Temperature
1 mph = 1.609 kmh	1 hp = 0.7457 kW
1 kmh = .62 mph	1 kW = 1.341hp
1 kn = 1.85 kmh	1 cal = 4.2 J
1 kmh = .54 kn	1 J = .24 cal
	C = (F − 32)/1.8
	F = (C x 1.8) + 32
Kilometers per hour (kmh), miles per hour (mph), international knots (kn)	*Horse power (hp), kilowatts (kW), calories (cal), joules (J), Fahrenheit (F), Celsius (C)*

Temperature

There are two main temperature scales: **Fahrenheit** (used in the US) and **Celsius** (part of the Metric System, used in most countries). Daniel Gabriel Fahrenheit (1686-1736) proposed his system first in 1724, whereas Anders Celsius (1701-1744) proposed his system in 1742, just two years before his death. Notice that Fahrenheit is 180 degrees between the freezing and boiling points of water and Celsius is only 100. You can easily make conversions between the two.

°C to °F Multiply by 9, Divide by 5, Add 32

°F to °C Subtract 32, Multiply by 5, Divide by 9

	Celsius	Fahrenheit
Freezing point of water	0 °C	32 °F
Ideal weather	21 °C	70 °F
Body Temperature	37 °C	98.6 °F
Hot bath water	40 °C	104 °F
Boiling point of water	100 °C	212 °F

Clothing (Pants)

Women

US	2	4	6	8	10	12	14	16
Australia	6	8	10	12	14	16	18	20
UK	4	6	8	10	12	14	16	18
Italy	36	38	40	42	44	46	48	50
France	32	34	36	38	40	42	44	46
Germany	30	32	34	36	38	40	42	44
Japan	5	7	9	11	13	15	17	19

Men

US	32	34	36	38	40	42	44	46
UK	32	34	36	38	40	42	44	46
Cont Eur	42	44	46	48	50	52	54	56
Japan		S		M	L		LL	

Clothing (Shoes)

Women

US	6	6.5	7	7.5	8	8.5	9	9.5
Australia	4.5	5	5.5	6	6.5	7	7.5	8
UK	3.5	4	4.5	5	5.5	6	6.5	7
Con Eur	36	37	37.5	38	38.5	39	40	41
Korea	235	238	241	245	248	251	254	257
Japan	22	22.5	23	23.5	24	24.5	25	25.5

Men

US	6	6.5	7	7.5	8	8.5	9	9.5
UK	5.5	6	6.5	7	7.5	8	8.5	9
Cont Eur	38	38.5	39	40	41	42	43	43.5
Japan	24	24.5	25	25.5	26	26.5	27	27.5

Calendars/Holidays/Time

Earth Calendar – www.earthcalendar.net
Time and Date – www.timeanddate.com
World Holiday Calendar – www.aglobalworld.com

Electricity

US current = 110 volts, 60 cycles of alternating current. Most other countries are between 220 to 240 volts.

Weather

In the Northern Hemisphere, seasons are opposite those in the Southern Hemisphere. When it's winter in New York, it's summer in Sydney.

59. What about food and drink?

The belly rules the mind. ~**Spanish Proverb**

Expect to eat some good food, and maybe some yucky food, too. Be careful about where you eat, to avoid getting sick, but try as many ethnic recipes as you can. A country's food is the hand of her hospitality. If you don't eat her food, you don't really accept her hospitality. Eating is the highlight of all my travels, both national and international.

Don't let your mind or customs fool you into thinking something might not taste good. I've eaten beetles, grasshoppers, snake, turtle, guinea pig, rat, and monkey. I've tried all sorts of fruits and vegetables, foreign to my US culture. Not only did I enjoy the food, but I got a real taste for the culture. Visit Chowhound.com for great tips on restaurants/cuisine.

When I lived in the Andes Mountains, I ate *chochos* at least once a week. Chochos are a high-protein legume. In English, the bean is *Andean Lupin* and the botanical name is *Lupinus Mutabilis Sweet*. Chochos come out of pre-Incan times. They were used to make beads and to control intestinal parasites in animals. They were eaten only after soaking and washing in water for several days to remove the bitter alkaloids.

While you will likely have the opportunity to eat special and exotic dishes, it probably won't be everyday. When I lived in Cameroon, I ate snake once and monkey twice. When I was in Ecuador, I ate guinea pig twice. Daily meals consist of many of the same foods we eat in the States (rice, potatoes, etc.); they are just preserved and prepared differently. It may be too bland or a lot spicier than you are used to at home.

Once in awhile, you'll get a real treat like *tripas*. Tripas are "animal guts" in Spanish. Surprisingly, they are tasty when smoked on the grill and served hot. You have to chew the organ tissue about twice as long as you would a regular piece of meat, but it's worth it. The people say that tripas make a tough stomach. I happen to think they build a strong jaw and a gutsy spirit.

60. What about bathrooms?

If I want to be alone, some place I can write, I can read, I can pray, I can cry, I can do whatever I want — I go to the bathroom. ~**Alicia Keys**

Bathrooms in other countries can be amusing, simply because they are different from what you may be accustomed to in the United States. Handles and buttons to flush the toilet may be extra-large or extra-small. Baths or showers may have strange mechanisms that you've never seen before. In Ecuador, for example, it is common to see a Frankenstein-like shower, one with a lever that you push up to turn on the electricity and make your water run hot. If you touch any of the metal in the shower while the lever is up, you get an electrical shock (it works much better than an alarm clock at 6am).

Bathrooms may also have different unspoken rules. In many underdeveloped countries, the sewer system isn't equipped to handle toilet paper, so people throw it in the trashcan rather than flush it down the toilet. In certain countries, people don't use toilet paper at all; instead, they use a teapot full of water and their left hand (which is actually cleaner than trying to wipe up a gooey mess with tissue). In other countries, there is no push button or lever to flush the toilet; instead, you have to throw a bucket of water in the bowl to get everything down. Finally, in some places, there are no toilets, just holes in the ground; there are no bathtubs and showers, only a bucket.

In the public arena, there may not be a separate bathroom for women and men, and you may have to pay money to use it. Typically, public facilities don't provide amenities like toilet paper and soap, so it is best to keep a stash of it in your purse or daypack. It is not uncommon for people to sell toilet paper at the entrance either. In Europe, the trains have bathrooms on them, but they are very small and cramped. It's always best to try to use the bathroom before traveling long distances. Also, don't eat any sketchy foods while on the road. It's no fun to get sick on a bus full of strangers (take it from experience).

Check out thebathroomdiaries.com, the world's largest database of bathroom locations, ratings, and reviews. This is a fun website with lots of information on toilets.

61. What about toiletries and laundry?

After enlightenment, the laundry. ~Zen Proverb

Try to figure out how laundry works before you arrive. Every program and country is different. If going to Western Europe, you'll probably be using machines, but in some parts of the world, be prepared to learn how to wash your clothes the old-fashioned way. Where there are washers, there are not always dryers, so beware. If dryers aren't common, then be sure to bring a clothesline or be prepared to buy one upon arrival.

Washing your clothes by hand isn't as hard as it looks. There are usually washboards or platforms that assist in the process and water flows directly into them. Only in underdeveloped countries may you have to wash your clothes, and take a bath using a bucket. Actually, your clothes come out cleaner after hand washing them than throwing them in a machine; so don't fret over it. Ask for assistance if you can't figure it out. People are usually more than willing and like to help.

If you dry your clothing on a line outside, be careful about when you do it and for how long. In parts of Africa, you can acquire certain diseases through flies laying eggs on your wet clothing. You can also get body lice and crabs if you dry your underwear on couches, chairs, or beds where people put their heads. I had a friend who got crabs from drying underwear on the arm of her couch. Also, if you are on or near the equator, beware of the sun, which can burn white clothing and turned it yellow or light brown.

Tip—if you're on the road, wash out your lighter clothing (underwear and socks) the night before and they should be dry in the morning. If it's cold, try putting them near the radiator or heat vent. If you are staying in the same place for more than two nights, then wash larger items, as long as they have two or three days to dry. There's no need for detergent because bar soap works fine. It is easy to wash clothes in the shower, too. In fact, I wash all of my clothes when I take a shower the night before.

62. What about cell phones and Internet?

If it keeps up, man will atrophy all his limbs but the push-button finger.
~ Frank Lloyd Wright

A cell phone is handy, but don't bring one with you unless it is *unlocked* and uses GSM standard, or it will not function.

Instead, do as the locals do; buy a phone there and pay as you go. Another option is to bring a global cell phone that you can unlock and swap out SIM cards. Buying pre-paid SIM cards overseas is much cheaper and easier than contracting with a wireless company at home.

Many cell phones that you buy overseas receive calls for free, unlike the US where you have to pay to place or receive calls. When we were in Ecuador, my brother-in-law lent us a phone and although we couldn't place calls, he was able to call us and keep in touch on a regular basis. I really liked the fact that we didn't have to pay to receive calls. Just like a landline, the call is paid for by the one who places it.

It really depends on your location, but most likely you will have access to the Internet either at school, in your apartment, or through a local cybercafé that offers access for a small fee. You can locate many of these cybercafés before you leave at www.world66.com/netcafeguide. It is sometimes possible to make international calls for very good rates. Because of high costs associated with Internet, cybercafés tend to be a more economical way for people to access the worldwide web.

Don't expect Internet access to be as prevalent or as fast as it is in the US. In the United States, many families have their own computers as well as Cable or DSL Internet access from their homes. However, for economic and cultural reasons, this isn't always the case in other parts of the world. Whether it is the high cost or the strong sense of community, Internet from home isn't priority, and people may not depend on email like they do in the US.

Once you arrive, you'll need to figure out how the phone system works and how to place in-country and international calls. You should do this right away, so you don't waste time trying to figure it out in the event of an emergency. Following are some examples, with facts and tips that may save you and your family some frustration and hassle.

Placing a call to Italy from North America
You need to call Rome, Italy.
Phone: +39 06 466229
Fax: +39 06 46622900

- Notice the fax number is longer than the phone number (not unusual for European countries).
- The + reminds you to add your international access code, which is 011 if dialing from North America.
- 39 is the Country Code for Italy
- 06 is the Area Code for Rome
- Dial   011   39   06   466229
  (Access Code)   (Country Code)   (Area /City Code)   (Local Number)

Placing a call to North America from Italy
You want to call home from Italy.
Phone: (217) 556-5678

To call North America, just dial 001 (the 00 is the direct dial prefix, and the 1 is the country code) and then 217-556-5678.

Placing a call to Germany from Italy
You want to make reservations at a hotel in Germany.
You see the phone number written two different ways:
+49 69 7578-1130 and 069 7578-1130

- The first way assumes you're calling from another country. The + reminds you to add your international access code, which is 00 if dialing from anywhere in Europe (except for Finland).
- The second way assumes you're calling from within Germany. Since Germany uses an area code, drop the first "0" when calling from another country.
- Dial   00   49   69   7578-1130
  (Access Code)   (Country Code)   (Area Code)   (Local Number)

Placing a Call within your Host Country

Some countries use area codes and others use direct-dial. For those that use area codes, you have to dial the area code first. For those that use direct-dial, you just dial the same number no matter where it is in the country. There may still be long-distance charges, so check before you dial.

Other Options to Consider

Phone cards can be the most economical way for your parents and friends to call you from home. There are many different companies on the Internet. When you pay online, you get a calling card number and a pin. My husband uses callcasa.com because they allow him to buy just one card at a time for $5 each. A card usually allows him to talk to family in Ecuador for 30 to 45 minutes, which calculates between 11 and 16 cents a minute. Another option is uniontelecard.com. If you'd rather have a calling plan, vonage.com is just one example.

Another option is to buy calling cards in the local kiosks and use them as desired to place phone calls internationally. When I visited France, I bought an international calling card for seven euro. It allowed me to talk to my husband in the States for three hours, with time leftover. Depending on the country, these can be the best rates to call home. Do not use your cell phone unless you're a millionaire and you don't mind paying outrageously expensive rates! Reserve your cell for emergencies or for receiving calls (if free).

A new way of phoning is through the computer (skype.com, messenger.yahoo.com, pc-telephone.com, talktohome.com). You can call PC-to-PC for free or PC-to-Landline for a small fee. PC to cell phone is more expensive. Communications are encrypted so nobody can intercept or listen in on your calls. If you want to take advantage of these services, then you need a microphone. If don't want to listen through your computer's speakers, then you will also need a headset. You can buy a microphone headset in most office stores and online. There are lots of different kinds from small to bulky, so shop around before you buy. Bring an extra pair, in case one breaks while you're away.

To determine when to phone home (and not upset your mom at 3:00am) visit www.timeticker.com. Think of west as future time travel and east as past. In other words, the time increases as you go west and decreases as you east.

Country/City Dialing Codes
http://www.usa.att.com/traveler/services/codes/index.jsp

Steve Kropla's Help for World Travelers – Worldwide Electrical and Telephone Information. www.kropla.com.

---

63. How does snail mail work?

What a lot we lost when we stopped writing letters.
You can't reread a phone call. ~ Liz Carpenter

The postal service can be very different in other countries. In the United States, you are probably accustomed to a postal worker dropping off mail, in a box outside of your home, on a daily basis. You are likely inundated with junk mail and bills, along with a few personal letters here and there. Well, that's the USA! Fortunately, many countries don't use the postal service as much as we do or in the same way. For example, in Ecuador, I had to physically go to a building to pay my water and electric bill, and so did everyone else.

Thanks to email, you probably won't have to send as many letters via post. However, you may wish to receive packages. In many countries, *duty* is imposed when you pick up your packages. The amount depends on weight, content, and value. The best thing to do is learn more about the postal service in your host country, before asking your family and friends to send care packages. Certain things are prohibited for political or health-related reasons. Food is usually not allowed. Also, it is not recommended to send anything of great value, unless you purchase theft, loss, and damage insurance.

The US Postal Service has an online International Resource Center where you can find a wealth of information. Visit this Center at www.usps.com/international/intlresourcecenter.htm. The *International Mail Manual* has lots of country-specific information about prohibitions, restrictions, observations, size limits, customs forms, and more. This manual can be found at http://pe.usps.gov/text/imm/welcome.htm.

Keep in mind that foreign postal systems may take longer. I sent a large package to a South American country via airmail (always send via air and not boat---yes, it can still go by boat if you don't specify "airmail" on the package), and my party didn't receive it until three months later. It is not uncommon for letters and packages to take several weeks or months for delivery. Just have faith and be patient, and hopefully the package will arrive.

Avoid sending perishable or irreplaceable valuables or money in the mail. If sending more than $50 worth of stuff, it is best to ascertain that the contents are insured for theft, loss, and damage. You will probably have to pick up your package at the post office and pay some sort of duty. As a rule of thumb, if you can get it where you are, even if it costs a little more, then don't have mom, dad, or someone else send it. The cost of shipping makes it ludicrous.

When I was living in Ecuador, a friend of mine sent me a care package full of used clothing and snacks. On the customs form, she had to write a value of the contents in the package. Consequently, she wrote what she thought—$100. It cost her about $50 to send and it cost me about $20 in duty fees (20% of the value) to get it out of customs. Lesson learned: if the value of the package is relative, then estimate low (ex. used clothing could have a $0 value). If your sender writes "0", then most of your packages should be free to pick up.

On another note, when I was in Africa, my mom sent me a pair of *tevas*. Tevas were a very popular and stylish sandal in my day, which averaged from $50 to $100 a pair. Anyway, my mom did a smart thing; she sent each shoe in a different package. After all, who would try to steal just one sandal? I ended up receiving the second one a month later, but I can't complain because it arrived! Had she not done that, I'm sure my shoes would have been conveniently lost or stolen in the mail. The black markets love to get their hands on any kind of valuables from abroad.

If you don't have an address right away, no worries. Most of the time, you can have mail sent *in care of* the International Programs Office until you find a place to live and set up a mailing address. In some countries, there are no mail carriers or addresses, so you'd have to get a P.O. Box to receive mail.

64. What about markets and bargaining?

Don't bargain for fish which are still in the water. ~ Indian Proverb

Bargaining is a social and business practice in most countries around the world. By virtue of the fact that you're a tourist, you have to learn to bargain if you want to pay a fair price. It seems to scare tourists to bargain because they don't want to appear cheap, but if you don't bargain, then you're spreading the old belief that tourists (or Americans) are rich and you're raising the price for all of us! (GRRR) Please learn to bargain. It's actually pleasant and fun once you get the hang of it.

1. Know where to shop. Some markets in or close to tourist locations are higher in price. Unless you want to buy gifts and souvenirs for your trip home (which shouldn't be until the

end of your program anyway), then you'll probably want to shop where the locals shop. Any local can tell you about the shopping, just ask. All the locals know where to get clothes, produce, etc. for a good price.

2. Know the fair market value for whatever it is that you want to buy. You can ask the locals (friends), or you can check in a few stores to see what kind of price they give you. People are more than willing to help. Don't stand in your stiff, proud, cultural shoes and pretend to know everything. Let people assist (but not the same people who you are negotiating with).

3. Decide what it is that you want to buy and the most that you're willing to pay according to the information you know about fair market value. Then, look at several different items without letting on to the one you really like. Ask for prices. Pick an item that you want, and then start negotiating below the price or below what you're willing to pay, whichever is less. Don't let the salesperson see your enthusiasm for the item. Make it look as if you're *kind-of* interested but not sold because there are other options you can consider elsewhere.

4. There's no rule about where you should start negotiating. If you know the fair market value, then you should start below it, so that you can arrive/agree on something fair. If you don't know the fair market value, then you should know how much sales people typically mark up their prices (which may vary per city, market, and store). I usually subtract 60% in hopes of arriving at 50% off the price, or start below what I am willing to pay and go no higher. If they don't agree with my highest price, then I thank them kindly, and walk away. If the salesperson is willing to take my price, but was bluffing to see if he could get more, then he'll call me back or send his son or daughter to call me back and sell it to me right there. If not, then I can decide to return later, if and when I really want to buy the item (knowing the final price).

5. Be careful not to go too low when you start negotiating or the sales person will either be insulted or will assume that you don't have a clue about the market or how much to pay for things. He'll probably start trying to teach you about market prices, and he'll do it in a way that puts him in control of the situation, again marking the price up, above the fair market value, but making it look as if he's giving you a deal. If you know your limit, then you can agree to pay it or walk away, but you still may end up paying more than the fair market value, which is okay but not ideal. It's always best to know about the markets and prices before you attempt to buy.

6. If you're having a hard time getting a price down, look for a reason it should be reduced like a flaw or defect. Tell the sales person that he is going to have a hard time finding a buyer for an imperfect product that needs fixing or work.

7. If you're buying several items, ask for a discount, and if they won't give you a discount, then ask for a free gift. If they won't give you a free gift, then just forget it. At least you got what you wanted at a price you were willing to pay.

8. Don't buy antiques! Antiques are often considered national treasures and are illegal to take out of the country. People are arrested at airports every year for innocently trying to export antique coins, paintings, sculptures, etc.

9. Always take your purchase with you… don't let them ship it home. If you have to ship it, make sure that you're covered by insurance or secure, money-back guarantees if it were to conveniently be damaged, lost, or stolen in the mail.

Part VII.

Get along with the Locals

65. What are the unspoken rules?

Before you go abroad, it is important to know the unspoken rules within the customs and culture. Most of the time, we don't think twice about what we're doing, let alone how it might be offensive. If you knew that direct eye contact was aggressive and rude, then by all means, you would avoid it. If you had known that putting your feet on a chair would have resulted in someone spitting on your shoes, then you would have kept them on the floor.

Unspoken rules usually revolve around etiquette and protocol, which can carry severe unspoken consequences when violated. We all live by unspoken rules and we're all learning new rules everyday. When we enter a new job, school, church, etc. there are rules to learn that nobody can articulate; they just know. You have to observe carefully and sometimes make mistakes before you learn the rules and can socially manage yourself in the environment.

While I can give you some general ideas about what not to do abroad that you would normally do at home, you'll need to learn the specifics from the materials you read about your host country and culture. Normally, people from other cultures will excuse our errors, because they know we are ignorant of their ways. It is when errors are not recognized within the context of culture that they can send unintended messages to our hosts.

Let's say you are in a culture where formality is high. You feel like you have known your professor for a while and call him by his first name. For you, calling him by his first name means you are comfortable with him and like him as a person. You notice your professor's character changes. He seems irritated with you and has more rigid expectations. What do you think might be going on? Well, you called him by his first name, and your doing so has inadvertently communicated that you do not respect and honor him as one should his professor.

Presentation – Be careful about what you wear. For example, wearing shorts in a church could be considered disrespectful. Wearing flip-flops, sweat pants, a t-shirt, and baseball cap is like wearing an orange sign that says "I'm an American... look at me...whoopee, yippee!"

Manners – Be careful about your table manners and how you conduct yourself at meals. For example, in East Asia you should NOT finish everything on your plate. In Belgium, you should never put your hands under the table. Be respectful of people. Ask locals before taking pictures of them.

Gestures – Before you go, learn the different gestures. It's especially important to know the lewd gestures, so that you don't inadvertently swallow your shoe. The PEACE sign or the A-OKAY sign may be quite vulgar in some countries! Shaking your head "No" can mean, "Yes, I hear you" in Asia.

Body Language – Be careful about your body language. If you're visiting an African authority figure, don't cross your legs in front of him (a sure sign of disrespect). The way we bow or shake hands may speak volumes about our character.

Touching – In some countries such as China, any kind of public affection (including hugs and kisses) is considered rude and inappropriate. Be careful about how you greet people and say goodbye when you depart. Think twice about hugging.

Personal Space – In some countries, personal space is much less than in the US, and people stand and sit very close to each other. While you may feel invaded, know it is a part of the culture. Italians and Spaniards often use less personal space.

Facial Expression – Smiling at a stranger could be considered weird or inappropriate in the UK. Making eye contact could be considered aggressive or rude in many Asian countries. Lack of facial expression doesn't always mean lack of interest.

Culture Matters Workbook – Developed by the Peace Corps to help new Volunteers acquire the knowledge and skills to work successfully and respectfully in other cultures. peacecorps.gov/wws/educators/enrichment/culturematters

World Citizen's Guide – Interesting facts and practical advice about the world. www.worldcitizensguide.org

---

66. How should I handle stereotypes?

To travel is to discover that everyone is wrong about other countries. ~**Aldous Huxley**

As for any large group of people, there are plenty of stereotypes about Americans: outgoing, noisy, friendly, informal, egotistical, immature, hard-working, extravagant, wasteful, overly confident, wealthy, disrespectful, prejudiced, ignorant of other countries, uninterested in foreign languages, generous, always in a hurry, and oblivious of class and/or status. While I can identify with only some of the things on this list, some of the time, applying it to a whole nation is ridiculous.

When I was living in Ecuador a number of years ago, my host family was lavishing me (and not themselves) with imported canned foods from the US. I didn't particularly enjoy or want to eat canned foods everyday, so I asked them curiously, why I was eating canned green beans while they were eating fresh ones from the market. As it turned out, my host mother was trying to do me a favor. She thought that canned food would be easier on my stomach, since she presumed it was all that Americans are accustomed to eating. ☺

Stereotyping is never a good thing, but it happens because we are uninformed about people that are dissimilar from us, and our brains don't know how to differentiate universal, cultural, and personal characteristics and behaviors with the limited information we receive. What is personal characterizes an individual; *Larry is obsessed with winning*. What is cultural characterizes a group of people; *Americans value freedom* or *Christians believe in God*. What is universal applies to all human beings; *human beings can love and hate*.

With only the mass media and society to look to for answers, stereotypes can and do proliferate. In the home of my host family, only a handful of television shows aired from the US, and most of the US foods in the grocery stores came in cans. Honestly, if I had grown up in Ecuador, never knew someone from the US, and looked to my environment for clues about what US people are all about, I'd probably conclude that they look like the folks from *Baywatch*, they act like the folks on *Jerry Springer*, they have a lot of money, and they value what is quick and easy. It would then take real Americans to show me otherwise, to teach me what Americanism is really about.

Still then, I might grasp American culture mixed up with the personal attributes of the people I meet. To an Ecuadorian who has not had much personal contact with Americans, Joe Kerns might seem to be very giving, but does that mean that all Americans are generous? I wouldn't know until I came in contact with more Americans and could start comparing and contrasting their attitudes, characteristics, and behaviors. In the process, I might learn that not all the Americans I meet are generous, but they all own expensive hiking shoes and backpacks, so all Americans must have money! Or is it just those Americans that travel abroad who have money or have been given money for the purpose of traveling abroad? I would never really know unless I traveled to the US and saw the different socioeconomic classes. Still then, it would be hard to understand Americanism as a national culture.

When you travel internationally, don't be frustrated by all the stereotypes you encounter. You may have to explain time and again that you are not your country's foreign affairs advisor, and you do not have a lot of money. On the other hand, do you know what characterizes you as American? What are the characteristics of American culture? Aha! If you don't know, then how should they? Or should they just recognize that you are an individual? Maybe your thinking that they should view you as an individual, is your American culture speaking loud and clear. Maybe this is what you'll learn when you travel abroad; *Americans do not like to be stereotyped because they value individualism.* Remember that America was founded by the individualists (rebels) of the world! Also, remember that not all America is individualist (some brought in against their will via slavery). So again, what is America?

Did you ever wonder why people from the United States call themselves American? There are two Americas (North and South) with lots of countries throughout the two continents. Yet, when we say the word "American," what we really mean is someone from the US. Other countries call themselves by their national title: *French* for France, *Spanish* for Spain, *Ecuadorian* for Ecuador, *Brazilian* for Brazil, *Mexican* for Mexico and *Canadian* for Canada, etc. United States is the only country in the world that has an adjective for its people that does not stem from either the national language or the primary name of the country. This speaks to the identity of United States citizens from inside to out. It says something about the way we see nations and ourselves among them. We are American, not United-*Statians.* America is the land of the free and brave, and its people are not bound.

Traveling can help you identify and shape your own identity because it brings to consciousness and separates what is universal from what is cultural-personal. One of the reasons why culture is so hard to separate from what is personal is that there are so many different cultures, in so many different layers and degrees working in each one of us. You aren't only shaped by your national culture; you are shaped by your race, your gender, your sexual orientation, your religion, your jobs, your experiences, your family, your friends, your education, etc. Multiple cultures, in different, ever-changing degrees, mixed with the mysteries of the soul, attempt to define your character similar to the way your fingerprint identifies your body. Our culture becomes the juncture where we seek our identity as individuals and grow as a collective whole.

When we travel, others pigeonhole us by our race, gender, nationality, and religion (if they know it). This is how they make sense of who we are in the context of their world. Race and gender is usually obvious, as we cannot hide physical characteristics. Nationality is somewhat of a guessing game, based on stereotypes, although I've noticed that one of the first questions people ask is where I'm from, even before they ask my name! Religion is sometimes visible and sometimes not, but people generally assume my religion once they know my nationality. Unless it comes up in conversation, and it usually doesn't, I'm compartmentalized into their concept of Christianity and all the preconceived notions that they have about it. The dance comes as we try to step into each other's reality and understanding.

All said, you can't change the stereotypes of the world, but you can challenge them and alter them ever so gently. For example, US women have a reputation of being promiscuous. If you are a US woman, then you have the power to alter that stereotype, or reinforce it in everyone you meet. Rosa Parks changed American history by sitting down on a bus. Will men who come into contact with you say, "Now, she didn't really meet my expectations of an American woman," or will they say "Now, that's exactly what I expected—an easy lay"? We only have two options; we can either weaken a stereotype or we can reinforce it. The power lies within each one of us. If enough people weaken a stereotype over time, then it may cease to exist in the future. Maybe someday, all men will say, "Those American women are really hard to get and smart, too!" I'm looking forward to that day! Do you think it will ever come? Don't underestimate your power for change.

The layers and complexities of culture are endless. It is only by exposing ourselves to a group of people that we can better understand their many attitudes, beliefs, characteristics, and behaviors. If we do this correctly, then we must be *forgiving* enough to understand their reliance on stereotypes, *hopeful* enough that they can abandon their stereotypes for something more genuine, and *caring* enough to make a real difference by being honest with ourselves and the people we meet in this world. The first travelers set out to discover new lands; we set out to discover ourselves and help others discover us along the way.

67. What about anti-American sentiment?

I like to see a man proud of the place in which he lives. I like to see a man live so that his place will be proud of him. ~Abraham Lincoln

Anti-American sentiment is the feeling of opposition and/or unfriendliness toward the US government, people, or culture. It is nothing new to American travelers, but it does seem to be intensifying rather than diminishing. In a March 2007 survey conducted by GlobeScan and the University of Maryland's Program on International Policy Attitudes, it was found that only three other countries (Israel, Iran and North Korea) were perceived more negatively than the United States. Most think the US is unilateral, and responsive only to its own interests.

What is hard for some people to understand is that Americans are not their government. Most Americans are just trying to make the best of life and want the best for their families and humankind. Many give to charity and provide time as well as

225

money to those in need. Many like to travel and learn about other cultures and people. All the while, the media spews out lies, loud and clear, leaving out critical pieces of information, providing inaccurate facts, twisting the biases, and forming stereotypes in the minds of people who watch and listen.

Most Americans travel abroad without incident, and most of the sentiment is just that, sentiment (feelings) without action. Usually, civilized people do not like violence, and they don't like to hurt others, even when there is disagreement. Since we hope for change, but don't know what's going to happen with the US in the world, it's important that you learn how to be safe in your travels abroad. Below are a few tips to help you guide your safety when it comes to anti-American sentiment. Being safe is being smart about your actions and behaviors.

- Be alert and know what's going on around you at all times. Never drink more than you can stay alert.
- Be well informed about US foreign policy and how your host country has been affected by it.
- Don't be defensive; listen to people and put things in perspective.
- Be open to other viewpoints to develop a more global perspective and understanding.
- Don't flaunt your Americanism in public. Keep a low profile when it comes to your nationality.
- Avoid clothing and accessories that make you stand out as an American (ex. USA ball caps, sweatshirts, bags, and flags).
- Avoid conversations about politics and religion in crowded public places where you can be overheard, and do not voice your opinions to the media.
- Avoid demonstrations and other sticky situations where anti-American sentiments can be expressed and acknowledged.

- Stay away from American hangouts and other establishments, as they are prime targets for terrorism and for identifying and trapping Americans.
- If you sense anti-Americanism and someone asks you where you're from, you can always say that you're from Canada. Pick a city you're familiar with, like Toronto or Quebec (if you know some French).

68. What about prejudice among locals?

Be the change you want to see in the world. ~ **Mahatma Gandhi**

Prejudice and discrimination is a widespread sickness that has infected every country in some way, shape, or form. This is because ignorant people have great power in large groups. If you don't experience prejudice directly, you will experience it indirectly. For example, in many of the large, modern cities of Latin America, the *mestizos* (the mixed Spanish bloodline) frown upon the *indigenous* (the pure Indian bloodline). The mestizos are not outwardly cruel, in the sense that they spit on or attack the indigenous. Rather, they stereotype and treat the indigenous people as uneducated, dishonest, dirty, and pitiful, and they distance themselves physically and psychologically.

Discrimination is usually aimed at nationality, gender, race, sexual preference, or religion, and is a byproduct of fear. My mother-in-law is a dark-skinned indigenous lady who married a very white mestizo man. I believe she internalized so much prejudice that it turned her against herself. She did not cherish her roots. In fact, she worked very hard to despise them in herself and others. She scolded her sons for going out in the sun, and hated all the dark-skinned women they dated. I think she liked me, not for my personality, but rather for the color of my skin (also very white). In her mind, white skin was the remedy for the curse of indigenous roots.

As a student, you have a unique opportunity to *stand up to* persecutors and *stand up for* the victims of discrimination. You can do this in small ways by befriending, respecting, honoring, and cherishing those who are persecuted, in plain view of those who do the persecuting. Like my mother-in-law, people who experience prejudice often develop a form of self-hatred. This poisons their inner beings and families, and sets them up for failure. Either they get distracted with trying to fit another mold or they completely give up and submit to the negative stereotypes that bombard them on a daily basis. It is the rare victim of prejudice who finds strength to fight.

---

101 Ways to Combat Prejudice – An excellent online book, compliments of Barnes & Noble and the Anti-Defamation League. http://www.adl.org/Prejudice/closethebook.pdf

---

69. What about unwanted attention?

The road to truth is long, and lined the entire way with annoying bastards.
~ Alexander Jablokov

Unwanted attention is bound to result when the gender roles of two different cultures collide. In certain areas of the world, behaviors associated with gender equality may be interpreted as promiscuous by the local men. For example, making eye contact and smiling in a way that you consider friendly and polite, may mean "Come on, Baby" to a local man who is not accustomed to communicating with American women. Just wearing shorts in some areas of the world could label you as a prostitute in their minds, even though it means no such thing in yours. Watch how local women deal with local men, and dress on the conservative to avoid catcalls and come-on's from men you're <u>not</u> interested in getting to know better.

If unwanted attention is in the form of words, ignore it. If it escalates to touch, then pull away right at that moment and project an attitude of confidence along with authority. When I worked with the Peace Corps, I was harassed daily by men. I learned that if I responded to the verbal harassment in any way, they'd harass me all the more. However, if I ignored it, they'd either leave me alone, or on rare occasions grab my arm to make sure I was paying attention. Whenever a man would grab me, I'd *quick release* (pull away, escape), squint my eyes, straighten my back, raise up my shoulders, bring my fists/arms up in front of me, and reveal my teeth with a snarl. Then, I'd look at him as if I was going to tear his head off. At that point, he'd usually cower away quietly.

If unwanted attention ever results in a struggle, then it is good to know some self-defense strategies. First, scream. Second, strike, grab, twist, and pull anything you can get a hold of on his body. Third, as soon as you can get away, run! Forth, go to the authorities and get help. Pulling back fingers, poking eyes, kicking a shin, grabbing some hair, scratching a face, and twisting ears all cause an attacker to feel pain. This pain distracts his attention, and makes him more likely to let go of you to deal with his own injury and distress. Never go to a secondary location with an assailant. Most likely, the attacker has a sick, perverted, or angry intention to rape or kill you; otherwise, he wouldn't be trying to take you somewhere else.

For a great travel resource just for women, check out *Journey Woman* at http://www.journeywoman.com.

70. What about gender issues?

Sometimes I wonder if men and women really suit each other. Perhaps they should live next door and just visit now and then. ~ **Katharine Hepburn**

The rights, roles, and responsibilities of gender are unique in every country. When I was living and working in Cameroon, I observed the character and strength of the African woman. I was amazed by all she did. She farmed in the hot son, cooked, cleaned, and cared for many children. Her arms and legs were strong, and were much bigger than those of her husband. She was generous, friendly, capable, and joyous. Her attitudes and behaviors commanded nothing but my utmost respect.

As you can imagine, there many abuses...husbands drinking in the bars, cheating on their wives openly with prostitutes, the spread of HIV/AIDS via unfaithfulness, and more. It was truly heartbreaking to see women and children degraded and destroyed this way. In one case, my friend's husband passed away, and she was forced by tradition to sleep with her dead husband's body for seven days. She wasn't allowed to bathe, wash, or even change her bloody menstrual cloth.

This brings me to the fact that most of the world is patriarch, with men on top, running everything. You certainly wouldn't find a man sleeping with his dead wife's body for several days. Although more countries have permitted certain women to rise into positions of power, the masses haven't changed their attitudes or behavior. Chile, Bolivia, Argentina, Liberia, the Philippines, Panama, Ireland, Iceland, and more have all seen women presidents, but they are not egalitarian or even close. Women are still produced, packaged, and played.

How your gender factors into your experience will depend on many circumstances. If you are a woman (and this section is mainly for women), you may be expected to follow the same rules, but you may also have a free pass because you are not a part of the culture. I was not treated as African women were treated; I was treated differently and in some cases with much more respect because of where I came from and the color of my skin. Not only did women treat me differently, but men did also (both positive and negative).

I didn't like being treated differently, so I did everything that I could to appear the same. I wore African clothing, I learned how to cook African foods, I did all my household chores African-style, and I found an African boyfriend or two. Still, I couldn't seem to escape the particular treatment for outsiders. Sometimes it worked in my favor, but other times it just made me mad. I once got a ride, a meager place to stay, and meals, at no cost, while there were many Africans who walked, slept on the ground, and ate scraps for several days. At some point, I realized that I did not have the strength to be African.

It wasn't all positive treatment either. While the African men seemed to grant me more freedom and respect on the outside, they were always trying to wiggle their way inside for more. African men were everywhere and hard to ward off. I'd open the door in the morning, and there'd be a man sitting on my porch. I'd close the door at night and some man would start knocking. Looking back, I see that many of the men thought that American women were easy. Even so, there were many unthreatening and good-natured men, too. I turned down too many marriage proposals and broke a lot of hearts.

While I can't go into too much depth when it comes to gender roles (because it is such a relative topic), I can give you some guidance when it comes to being female in another country. First, you must have simple but firm boundaries in your life. You can choose to enforce these boundaries with a graceful, neutral, or serious tone, depending on the circumstances. If you're a person that doesn't like to say no, then this may be uncomfortable for you at first. However, the more that you practice taking care of yourself, the easier it will get.

Exercise: Kendu is in your class, and he's been helping you with your French. The two of you went biking together a few days ago, and he is coming over to your house every night now. You don't want to upset him or risk your friendship, but you're not comfortable, and the last thing you want to do is send the wrong message. How would you confront Kendu, and tell him that you don't want him coming over at night?

---

71. How will we communicate?

Language forces us to perceive the world as man presents it to us.
~ Julia Penelope

You'll be amazed at how well you can communicate, even if you don't speak the language. However, you should still try to speak the language and learn as much as possible. Even if you say, "May I have some agua, por favor?" in Spanish, it's better than saying "May I have some water, please?" in a Spanish-speaking country. It's the effort that is appreciated, and the practice that helps you learn. If you want to take a course that might help, consider enrolling in a local language school. Classes are inexpensive and may really help!

Imagine sitting in a coffee shop in Springfield, Illinois, when someone approaches and asks you a question in Chinese. You don't speak Chinese, and a variety of thoughts race across your mind. *He must not speak any English at all. How can that be since he's obviously in the USA for one reason or another? What in the world is he trying to say to me?* You may want to help him, or you may just tell him "No Chinese" and walk away. Either way, you probably think he should at least know a few words and phrases in English if he's in your country. He didn't even try to speak it!

Don't make a bad first impression of yourself or your country by not speaking enough of the host language to get around the city that you're visiting. People are willing to help, especially when you can show some appreciation of their language and culture. Even if the language is limited to the host country or region, and everyone speaks English, you should still make an attempt to learn some. You may notice that the locals speak their own language with each other and insiders, and English to outsiders. Learning the language will enhance your relationships and experience. It will get you on the inside of the fence, where you can truly learn and grow.

Sure, you'll make mistakes, but it's okay; that's why humans were created with a sense of humor. Your mistakes actually help form good relationships because others feel like they can help you, and most people like to assist. I once told my host family that I was *pregnant*, rather than *embarrassed*; "Estoy embarazada" means, "I'm pregnant" in Spanish. I was dating their son, so we had a good laugh. Lighten up; have a sense of humor about yourself and you'll be fine. Here are just a few big-money bloopers that have happened around the world:

- The Dairy Association's success with the *Got Milk?* campaign ended up in Mexico, but it didn't do so well because in Spanish it read "Are You Lactating?"
- A sign in an Italian Laundromat translated as "Ladies, leave your clothes here and have a good time."
- In China, Pepsi's slogan *Come Alive* translated into "Pepsi Brings Your Ancestors Back from the Grave."
- A detour sign in Japan reads "Stop: Drive Sideways."
- Gerber baby food wasn't doing well in Africa, with a smiling baby on the label. Later the company learned that in Africa, pictures on the label often indicate what's inside, since many people can't read.
- An advertisement for donkey rides in Thailand reads, "Would you like to ride on your own ass?"

Beyond language, you need to be aware of non-verbal forms of communication. Greetings, gestures, eye contact, personal space, facial expressions, posture, touching, and behaviors are forms of communication. These many communication forms can take on different meanings in different cultures. Learning them requires good observation ability and a lot of practice. Since non-verbal communication often occurs unconsciously, it can be difficult to change. Develop awareness of the major differences to avoid embarrassing and offensive mistakes.

72. Can I really learn the language?

Language is the dress of thought. ~Samuel Johnson

Before you leave, get some language tapes from your library and buy a good, small dictionary/guide with entry words and phrases. Try to learn some *basics* at the very least. Although pricey, RosettaStone (www.rosettastone.com) is supposed to be one of the best language learning tools available. Another interesting site is http://how-to-learn-any-language.com/e, all about teaching yourself foreign languages. It introduces you to Mezzofanti, an Italian who spoke 38 languages fluently.

When you arrive, be sure to take a language course and study everyday. Participate in the classroom and take advantage of personal help like tutoring, buddy systems, etc. One thing you can do to help with your vocabulary is to put sticky notes on everything in your home, with the written word in the host language. When you practice the vocabulary, from sentences with different verb tenses. Carry flashcards and practice when you have *down time* or *wait time* (section #50).

Read the local newspaper, listen to the radio, watch television (with subtitles), listen to popular songs and write down the lyrics, and read children's books/stories in the host language. Practice speaking out loud, even when you study by yourself, and don't be afraid to make mistakes. Interact with your host family and other locals. Again, don't worry about mistakes; most are understood and forgiven, and in some cases, create a little laughter for everyone who hears them, including you!

Resources

Language Learning Resources – This site claims to be the best language learning resources, tips, and advice on the web. http://www.language-learning-advisor.com

---

LinguaGuide – More resources. http://www.linguaguide.com

RealAudio Language Station – Look up and listen to radio and television stations around the world, in the language you're trying to study. http://www.word2word.com/real.html

Thousands of world newspapers – Read newspapers around the world. http://www.onlinenewspapers.com

Maximizing Study Abroad: A Student's Guide to Strategies for Language and Culture Learning and Use. Minneapolis, MI: Center for Advanced Research on Language Acquisition

73. What about my host family?

The family is one of nature's masterpieces. ~George Santayana

If you have the good fortune of staying with a host family, then you will inevitably learn about the culture and hopefully have an opportunity to practice the language. You will get to eat what the locals eat, sleep like the locals sleep, and interact with the locals on a daily basis, from the time you wake up to the time you pass out in utter exhaustion. You can't have a more authentic experience than with a host family. There is absolutely no better way to learn a culture and language than to live with a family and experience their day-to-day life.

Because you are living in such close proximity with locals, your different cultures are likely to collide from time to time. These cultural collisions bring out the various ways in which we interpret actions, events, and behaviors, based on cultural attitudes and beliefs. For example, a young, American student invites her host father and mother out to dinner. The whole family, and even the extended family show up, and the bill is handed to her to pay for everyone. The American is clearly upset. She is just a poor student, and doesn't understand why her Mexican family would take advantage of her in this way. She pays the bill begrudgingly, and resents them for it.

What she didn't know about Mexican culture is a restaurant invitation to some family members is an open invitation to all and anyone who invites is expected to pay the bill. It is very rare that a couple would go out to dinner without the rest of the family. They weren't taking advantage of her; they were following their own understanding of the invitation. When something doesn't go as planned, figure out what happened, do your best to repair any damage that it caused, and learn from the experience. Don't get too emotional about it because it won't do any good to the damage that's already done.

Good things can come from cultural collisions, too. When I was training for the Peace Corps, I spent a lot of time with my host family, despite my inability to speak the language well. One day I got sick with a mild typhoid fever and the Peace Corps staff decided to keep me in the health center overnight. The staff informed my host mother that I would not be home, and she came to visit me before I went to sleep. While it was nice to see her, I later learned that it was highly unusual for an African Muslim woman to go out at night, even to visit her own children. All I could fathom is that she must have really cared about me to risk her reputation this way.

When you're living with a family that is not your own, you should make a concerted effort to be humble, considerate, and respectful of their ways. Get excited (rather than discouraged) about the differences you encounter. Help out with household chores. Ask permission to take items from the refrigerator or to use the phone (especially since there may be charges for every click, even with local calls). Don't use too much water (since it is very expensive in other countries). Fit in with their customs, lifestyle, and routine. If they don't wear shoes in the house, then you shouldn't either. Listen and observe; don't just see and hear. Always remember, you're a guest.

74. How do I meet people, make friends?

The most beautiful discovery true friends make is that they can grow separately without growing apart. ~ **Elisabeth Foley**

Being social is an important part of life. It is said that students with satisfying social lives are usually successful in academic work and beyond. For this reason and more, it is important that you meet people and make friends when you're abroad. Some of those friendships may come and go, but others will be with you for a much longer part of your life. While it may be difficult to leave your social network at home, you'd be wise to take advantage of this opportunity to start fresh and develop new and different relationships.

Our friendships shape our personalities. While we all want to be accepted and integrated into almost any social circle, real friendships among people are the most important part of life. Fact is you won't be accepted in every social circle, but you will have true friends that you can count on when you need them. When you don't have real, true friendships in your life, it's easy to become anxious and depressed. We need people to accept us for who we are and we need to accept others, too. We also need advice, help, and favors from time to time.

Everyone has flaws; nobody is perfect. If you want friends in your life, then you must realize that none of them can or will measure up to your expectations, and you'll probably be let down once in awhile. This is normal; just be you, be honest, allow for imperfection, and give a little respect. While not as easy as it sounds, there's no reason why you can't develop good friendships with internationals and locals, as well as co-nationals studying abroad in your host country. All you have to do is be real with yourself and others.

Before you start befriending everyone that you meet, realize that time spent in one relationship is sacrifice in another. If fostering friendships with locals is important to you, then you should be careful about how much time you spend with your American friends. When you're in close contact/proximity with Americans, all the time, you run the risk of becoming a *ghetto* that dissociates you from the locals. Be mindful that all individuals lead to circles and groups. One relationship with a local can lead to many doors for potential friendships.

How do you start conversations and make friends with locals? Well, it's similar to how you start conversations and friends with all people. See the following tips.

- **Initiate greetings and conversations**. A good way to start is to ask a question. "Excuse me, can you tell me what time it is?"; "That's a nice umbrella, where did you get it?"; "Aren't you in Dr. Amaya's class?" There are hundreds of different questions you can use to start a conversation with someone.
- **Know what topics are open for conversation** at each stage of the relationship. Politics and religion, as well as socioeconomic status, are never good conversation starters. You should get to know people better before jumping into these discussions.
- **Try to find commonalities right way**. Look at socio-economic backgrounds, education, interests, attitudes, and values. Good friendships presume similarities in how we live and do things. If you don't have anything in common, then you probably don't have much basis for a friendship.
- **Attempt to meet people in everyday places** (your classroom, school, cafeteria, neighborhood, market, job, etc.). It's not a good idea to meet people in the bars, because of many predators hungry to devour unwary prey. If you want to go to pubs and bars, then go together with people you know and trust.

75. What about friendship and dating?

Friendship is born at that moment when one person says to another: "What! You, too? Thought I was the only one." ~ *C.S. Lewis*

In many parts of the world, the friendship and dating scene is similar to that of the United States. However, expectations and expressions may be different. You may be expected to behave and not behave in certain ways towards good friends and dates. For example, in parts of Africa, same-sex friends hold hands in public, as a symbol of their friendship. It's not uncommon to see two males (or two females) walking hand-in-hand, and seeming to be touchy-feely with each other. This affection has nothing to do with their sexual orientation, but is rather an expression of friendship.

Before you go grabbing your friend's hand, you had better know the customs. The best way to find out is by conducting research before you go. Another thing to be careful about is showing affection in public with the opposite sex. In several parts of the world, namely Japan and Cameroon, expressing any kind of public affection between the sexes is forbidden. However, in other parts of the world, you'll see quite the opposite. In Latin America, for example, certain parks are full of couples *making out* and sometimes doing a lot more. You get used to seeing it after awhile and just turn the other way.

While you will probably find lots of opportunities to make friends and maybe even find a significant other in your host country, there are a few networks that can help. Friendship Force is an international organization whose mission is to facilitate friendships across international boarders. It is made up of close to 400 clubs all over the world. Information can be found at http://www.friendshipforce.org. Establishing an international penpal before you take off for a host country can be another great way to get started. Check out *International*

Pen Friends (http://www.ipfeurope.com) or *Penpal International* (http://ppi.searchy.net).

Know how people flirt in your host culture. In some parts of the world, eye contact is a sign of interest. If you're a woman and a man is buying you drinks at a bar, the expectation could be that you agree to sleep with him later in the night. If you're a man and you're visiting a local woman's home after dark, it may mean that you want to get sexual. A man once shook my hand, and wiggled his finger inside. It felt like he was tickling my palm. I thought it was strange, and later learned that he was asking me to sleep with him. If I had wiggled my finger back, then I would have agreed.

If you are interested in pursuing a romantic relationship with a local, then you should probably know what to do. If you're a man, is it customary to walk your date to the door and give her a kiss goodnight? In many parts of the world, such an act could be pushy and overbearing, wanting sex en lieu of love. You may be surprised to know that in some countries, like Australia and New Zealand, women will often pick up the tab on dates. In Arab countries, there isn't much dating, and a marriage proposal requires a very large down payment to the family of the bride.

With the exception of the US, dating is often a family affair; the two families take time to get to know and approve of each other long before a marriage takes place. Individuals don't get married, families do. Maybe that is why there seems to be less bickering between family members and in-laws; they are part of the decision. Big cities are usually modern in their thinking and behaviors. Smaller cities and villages in the rural communities are more inclined to following old traditions, like arranging marriages, or murdering an unmarried daughter who has lost her virginity.

While hard to believe, there was no such thing as dating in the early ages. Men would raid villages and capture women they wanted for wives. Dating, and male counterparts paying for dates, was born from the concept of chivalry in medieval times. However, marriage was still more about men finding women who could bear children and help with the workload than it was about romance. Before 1228, it was against the law for women to propose marriage. It wasn't until later that dating became more about women and romance.

Quick Facts on Dating and Friendship Customs

- In Iran, it's illegal to date.
- In Afghanistan, dating is rare because parents arrange most marriages.
- In Russia, it is customary to ask the parents for a woman's hand in marriage.
- In Australia, women often ask out men and pay for the date, too.
- In the Philippines, when a man decides to wed a woman, his parents usually visit her house and present an extravagant gift.
- In some parts of Europe, dating is usually a group event (i.e. Finland).
- In parts of Europe, Greenland, Asia, the Middle East, and Africa, same-sex affection is presumed to be friendship, not homosexuality.
- In Northern Africa and the Middle East, opposite-sex friendships and homosexuality are shunned.
- In Spain, dating is a one-on-one event and both parties ask each other out and share costs.
- In parts of East Asia, only men ask and pay.
- In Native American cultures, blood-brotherhood rituals are common.
- In East Asia, young people don't date until they go to college, or are in their mid-20s.

- In India, dating is serious business for permanent relationships, not just for fun.
- In France, it is common for women to share the tab with their date (50-50).
- In Ukraine, men offer women their arms, not their hands. Men and women in general do not hold hands.
- In most of the world, friendship isn't taken lightly. It is a serious commitment.
- In African cultures, there are formal friendship rituals.

76. What if I fall in love with a local?

Love: a temporary insanity, curable by marriage. ~**Ambrose Bierce**

Getting married overseas is romantic and exciting, but not without headaches. You and your fiancé will need to present specific documentation, and then after you marry, you'll have to figure out how to get residency. If your spouse is returning to the US, he/she will need to apply for permanent residency, which takes a lot of time, labor, and money; information is available from The Bureau of Citizenship and Immigration Services in the Department of Homeland Security. If you are planning to stay in country, you will need to get a residency card from the appropriate government office.

According to *Title 22, The Code of Federal Regulations 52.1*, American diplomatic and consular officers are not permitted to perform marriages abroad. This regulation exists primarily because the laws of a country govern the legal agreement of marriage. Hence, it makes sense that Bolivia's civil and/or religious officials perform a marriage ceremony that takes place in Bolivia, between a Bolivian and an American citizen. As far as documentation is concerned, you will typically need to present an affidavit from the US embassy stating that you are not presently married in your country, and you are legally capable of entering into a marriage contract.

Marriages of US citizen(s) abroad are always registered in the country where they occur. The US government doesn't play part in the registration of marriages overseas. Be sure to bring a few copies of your certificate home with you if returning to the United States permanently. It will usually be accepted as official evidence; nonetheless, if it is written in a foreign language, the requester of evidence may require an official translation. If you have problems proving the validity of your marriage certificate, the US government can authenticate your foreign marriage documents for a fee.

The best source of information about marriage in a particular country is the tourist information bureau of that country and the American embassy and/or consulate. In some countries, there are two separate ceremonies. I was married in Ecuador where the *legal* ceremony is viewed as a semi-commitment, and the *religious* ceremony is the serious, lifelong endeavor. Many people will marry *in the law* to see how things go for a few years before involving religion.

Name-change customs are also very interesting. In Ecuador, for example, women keep their maiden name and add on their husband's name. Both husband and wife have their spouse's name written on the back of their government identification card. Also, children take the last names of both their mother and father. We chose to continue this Ecuadorian tradition and my children now have two last names that recognize both their father and their mother's lineage.

- **Dual Citizenship (Department of State)**
  travel.state.gov/travel/cis_pa_tw/cis/cis_1753.html
- **Immigrant Visa for Spouse** – http://travel.state.gov/
  visa/immigrants_types_marriage2.html
- **Vital Records Services, Birth, Death, & Marriage**
  http://www.cdc.gov/nchs/howto/w2w/w2welcom.htm
- *Intercultural Marriage, Promises and Pitfalls*
  by Dugan Romano

77. What about alcohol and drugs?

Alcohol removes inhibitions — like that scared little mouse who got drunk and shook his whiskers and shouted: "Now bring on that damn cat!" ~ **Eleanor Early**

Never, ever use illegal drugs in a foreign country, or in any country for that matter! If you choose to consume alcoholic beverages, always do so legally and in an appropriate manner. Also, know that you don't have to drink alcohol in order to be culturally appropriate. If you don't drink for whatever reason (religion, addiction, nutrition, medication, etc.), it is okay. Many people don't drink alcohol or beverages with caffeine because they are taking anti-depressants or other medications. You don't have to specify why you choose not to drink, just say it's for personal reasons if you want to maintain privacy.

If you choose to drink alcohol legally, in accordance with the laws of the host country, there are some social and cultural implications to think about when doing so. In many areas of the world, alcoholic beverages are a part of everyday life. In West Africa, it's palm wine or corn beer; in Europe, it's grape wine; and in Latin America, *sangria* tends to be made from a variety of fruit. Especially in Europe, fine wine is viewed as sacred, and may accompany group meals, social gathering, or celebrations; drunkenness is not tolerated, and people don't have the desire or need to drink excessively.

When consuming alcohol, drink slowly and drink with food, so you don't get wasted. One drink per hour (with food) is a good formula to use. Never drink more than four glasses per hour. Also, know the potency (proof) of whatever you drink. Obviously, a glass of tequila will go farther than a glass of wine. Beer in other countries may be a lot stronger than it is in the US, not to mention the big bottles. Don't drink alone, either. If you or someone else is drinking alone, it may be a sign of depression, an emotional problem, or an addiction. If you think you have a problem with alcohol, then get help. See http://www.alcoholics-anonymous.org.

Warning: Alcohol is one of the most widely used social drugs in the world and affects the mind and body. In short, it raises blood pressure and triglycerides; impairs judgment, reflexes, and coordination; and displaces nutrients from the body after consumption. Research also links the use of alcohol to brain damage, heart damage, nerve damage, stomach inflammation and bleeding, tremors, dementia, stroke, cancer, malnutrition, hepatitis, liver disease, cirrhosis, obesity, and more. Do not use alcohol during pregnancy and in case of other medical conditions, as recommended by your Doctor.

Drinking Age	Countries
No age limit	China, Poland, Thailand, Vietnam
21	United States
20	Japan, Iceland
19	South Korea
18	Argentina, Australia, Barbados, Brazil, Chile, Canada (age 19 in some provinces), Czech Republic, Ecuador, Hong Kong, Israel, Malaysia, Mexico, New Zealand, Peru, Philippines, Puerto Rico, Ukraine, UK (16 in restaurants), Russia, South Africa, Venezuela
16	Austria, Belgium, Italy, France, Germany, Greece, Netherlands, Norway, Poland, Spain, Switzerland, Turkey

78. What's happening to me?

Nothing in life is to be feared. It is only to be understood. ~ *Marie Curie*

What is happening to you is probably *cultural awareness*. You are uncovering your own culture and learning a culture new. Some ways seem better and refreshing and others don't mesh with your worldview. You are frustrated with your own culture for just *not getting it*, and you are frustrated with the host culture for not being efficient. These frustrations may go back and forth for a while until you find yourself within them. Learning to be *you*, apart from many social pressures takes soul searching, practice, and courage. It's when you find the confidence to be who you are, that you can become more.

One of my biggest moments abroad had to do with letting go of arrogance, but not pride, about my home country/culture. I applied for and got into the Peace Corps because I wanted to make a difference in this world, to help people. I'm ashamed to admit this, but I thought we were better and even superior to the rest of the world. Anyway, after a few days of living with my African host family, I thought I was going to return home… HUGE cockroaches on my walls, no electricity, no running water, no toilets, little foreign language skills, illness, no silverware, and much more, etc.

Because part of me wanted to make conversation, and part of me wanted to know how to live without all the luxuries that Americans treat as necessities, I attempted (with a dictionary in hand) to ask my host mother how to take a bath with no running water. After going back and forth, pointing to words in the dictionary, and acting out my question with gestures, she finally said "AHHHHHHH" and wrote four words on my notepad in French, "I show you tomorrow." I didn't know what to expect, but figured she would indicate where/how to take a bath the next morning.

246

When I got up in morning and went to the latrine, my mother came in with a bucket of cold water, to which she poured a pot of hot boiling water, stirred with a stick, and asked me to check, presumably to see if it was warm enough or not too hot. Then she told me to remove my clothing. I was hesitant, obviously! Because I was staring at her with a dumbfounded look on my face, she must have thought I didn't understand, and so she took off her shirt to show me. As if the look on my face didn't say "Please STOP!" she started removing her skirt to further illustrate. I quickly nodded "oui, oui" indicating that I had understood. No further words were necessary.

So, here happened one of the most embarrassing moments of my adult life…I took off my clothes and she began to wash me. She gave me the soap and told me to rub it on my body, and then she scooped out some water from the bucket with a teapot and poured it on me to rinse. She put some shampoo on her hands and washed my hair, and then told me to bend forward (with my head upside down) and poured water over my head. Naked, I stood before this African woman, as she washed me like her own child. It was clear to me that she was just trying to be is helpful, and when we were done, she asked if I needed anything else. Then she smiled tenderly, gave me a small towel to dry, and left me to dress, while she prepared my breakfast for training (school).

From that day forward, I was very careful about when I asked for help. As the days passed, my host family taught me how to wash my clothes, iron, cook, fetch water from the well, collect rain water in a big barrel (to avoid trips to the well), and a whole horde of other skills that I took to my site. Not only did that day in the bathroom teach me how to bathe in a bucket, but also it showed me how foolish I was to think that I was more capable and knowing. I didn't know how to do anything without the luxuries of modern-day technology. I had to ask how they manage without toilet paper; although a no brainer (soap and water), it was just weird for me to use a teapot on the toilet. My African host family and all of my African friends taught me more about life than I could have ever taught them (unless baking banana bread and chocolate-chip cookies counts for something). Lesson learned: there isn't *better* when it comes to culture, there is just *different*.

I suppose that I did impart some knowledge and skill to the people I knew in Africa. However, I feel like they gave me so much more. Even today, I *think* the way that I learned in Africa. Not long ago, I was talking to my husband about the yard work at our home. He was convinced that we needed a weed eater to trim some grass around the edge of our porch and garden. We had already gone through two weed eaters at our previous home that both stopped working after a couple of years. I told him that I didn't see the point of buying yet another when it wasn't a large area and we could just trim it by hand. After all, in Africa I cut my lawn with a machete! At first he didn't agree, but I ended up getting my way, and he has come to find that it is possible to live without everything.

Religion	Politics	Beauty	Rituals	Ceremonies
Education	Economics	Gender Roles		Family
Stories	Ideals	Heroes	Values	Law	Space
Individuals	Community	Non-Verbals		Work
Holidays	Play	Arts	Children	Time

Part VIII.

MAXIMIZE
your Trip:
Top Secrets

79. What should I overcome?

You are wise to ask this question because obstacles are what keep us from our destinations in study abroad and in life. If you want to succeed in anything that you set out to do, then you must meet challenges and overcome obstacles in the way. The more you overcome, the better you feel about yourself, and the more you will conquer in the future.

Insecurity is an obstacle to purpose and fulfillment. If you are not secure in yourself, and/or if you do not like yourself, then you need to do some soul searching and find out why! First, you are unique and have something special and precious to offer people in the world. If you don't know what it is, then I encourage you to start a quest. Low self-esteem occurs when people measure their self-worth by manmade markers instead of by their inner beauty and life source. Study abroad can help you identify these often *invisible* manmade markers (or distracters) and boost your self-esteem.

Peer and social pressures can also be big obstacles. When you follow the herd, you fail to go off the beaten path (where one finds gold). To be a gold digger, you have to follow your gut instinct, your spirit, your drive… not the crowd. You have to go where the gold is, even if you don't know your way. Just get a treasure map and learn to do what you (not your friends) believe is right, good, appropriate, etc. Don't befriend people because you want to be in the *cool* crowd, make friends with people who can get past the façade and to the heart of what it is you're all about.

No matter your age, you probably fear something that is good for you. When I was a child, my mom used to give me cod-liver oil on a great big spoon, and I feared the taste. As an adult, I used to be afraid to say the first "Hello," and to start a conversation with an acquaintance or stranger. I also feared face-to-face confrontation. Really, I was afraid of rejection, so I didn't expose myself to it at all! In fact, I still struggle in this area and when I overcome that fear, I realize that new doors and friendships are opened, as well as opportunities. So I recommend that you fear little and live large.

Luxuries and comforts are nice, but are not necessary. Going without them can actually strengthen your body and mind, and make you a healthier, more adaptable person. The less you depend on, the more you can do. For example, when I was in Africa, I needed a special kind of shoe for hiking, but the Africans just needed their feet. I needed a fork, spoon, and knife to eat food, but the Africans just needed their hands and fingers. I thought that if someone couldn't walk they needed a wheel chair, but an African proved me wrong again, when he pulled himself along the ground with his arms and something with wheels that resembled a skateboard.

Overcome the need to be conventional and let your individual fruits to rise. Allow your branches to move and stretch in the ways that they wish to grow. People who are always worried about what their neighbors think, don't go very far in life, and don't live life to its fullest. They get so occupied with their image, and always doing the proper thing, that they forget how to connect with what's real. They don't see, smell, taste, hear, read, write, touch, and soak up life. They're too busy trying to fit into a mold. Have you ever tried to put a square in a circle? It doesn't fit right, and it never will.

Don't be ethnocentric. Ethnocentrism is the belief that your cultures are superior to others. You will not learn and grow if you don't open your mind and allow yourself to see the good in all people and things. Find in other cultures what suits you better than your own; this is true freedom.

80. What should I seek?

The traveler was active; he went strenuously in search of people, of adventure, of experience. The tourist is passive; he expects interesting things to happen to him. He goes "sight-seeing." ~ Daniel J. Boorstin

Seek the journey, not the destination. You certainly want to see all you can muster, and learn all that you can stand, but not at the sacrifice of your local experience. If you hop on a tourist bus where you can stop at 20 different sites in only a few hours, then you miss the authentic and *real* experience of walking the streets, looking in shops, dining in a local café, seeing the families commune in the park, etc. because you're too busy racing to conquer as many destinations as you can. I like to take at least one day per week to meander (safely) with a map and some money. I let destiny carry me that day.

Live in the moment; take what you can and enjoy it. One of the things I admire about some countries that I've visited is that people know how to live life to the fullest. The systems may not be as smooth and efficient, but the quality of life is higher and better quality than what we experience in the US. It is evident that relationships with family/friends mean more to people than their accomplishments. Time is used to nourish social atmosphere instead of personal successes. People make time to stroll, smell the roses, visit with loved ones, and really taste the good things in life like food, arts, etc.

No matter what the circumstances, find joy within your inner being. This is not only *my* recommendation, but also that of spiritual leaders; it is taught in various religions (even those that don't believe in God). It is joyfulness that has driven you to want to study abroad and its patience and hope that will get you through the difficulties. Know that challenges are normal in study abroad, and big obstacles only make you a better and stronger jumper! I think I can… I think I can… get the point?

YOU CAN! Don't say the word *can't*; just eliminate it from your vocabulary.

As much as you can muster, live as the locals do. When I was abroad, I met many missionaries from American and Europe that lived way above the standard of the locals, with modern homes, SUVs, etc. If you can't live at least somewhat like the locals, then you'll have a tough time relating to them, and subsequently, you'll miss much of their culture. I once knew a European couple who built and ran a new health center in my small African village. When I asked a local friend why most people still go to the old center, she replied, "Come on, Wendy...their dogs eat better than our children."

It's easy to get caught up in the pressures of tourism, at the expense of experiencing everyday life. Don't let it happen to you. Life is not fast-paced because there's no sense in racing against time. Focus on BEING rather than DOING, and you will still manage to see new places, do your homework, and get all your chores done. When you *experience* the values in another culture, above and beyond just knowing they exist, you authenticate your understanding. You won't remember all the places you see, but you will hold on to the values you found through people who crossed your path along the way.

81. How can I learn the most?

When we allow ourselves to become vulnerable, to take chances, and to risk our pride, that is when we find our own glory. ~ **Richard Corman**

Take small, healthy risks that improve the quality of your life. A risk that is good for me may be very different from a risk that is good for you. What is it that you would like to do, that you know you can do, but haven't mustered up the discipline, courage, or strength? Your risk may be as simple as saying "Hello" to someone or going to the market by yourself.

Be patient with yourself. Don't expect to learn everything, all at once. Language and culture learning take a lot of time. If you want to learn more, then you have to give yourself more time! Students always tell me that their experiences weren't long enough. Planning for a year and deciding to come back early is much easier than planning for a semester and later deciding to stay for a year.

Be vulnerable, and don't be afraid to try new things and make mistakes. Have a sense of humor about yourself and laugh! When I was in Ecuador, my now mother-in-law asked me if I liked *jugo de carne*, which literally means *meat juice*. Having no clue what I was about to receive (at worse, a glass of blood with my rice and beans); I received a plate of delicious beef stew with homegrown tomatoes. Then, I laughed at my initial thought and told my family, who laughed, too.

Be spontaneous; seize opportunity! If you can only operate on a rigid plan that you made several days or weeks before, you will miss some great experiences. My host family decided at the last minute to go to the beach for the weekend. At first, I was hesitant because I had some books to read and reports to write, but I didn't want to miss anything. So, I threw some stuff in a bag, hopped in the car, and went to the beach. It was a great time that I remember very clearly to this day.

Be assertive with your learning. Don't be afraid to ask when you don't understand something. For most people, helping others makes them feel wanted and needed. As a foreigner, you're at an advantage because some types of ignorance are understandable and excusable. Believe it or not, when you ask a question, you give someone an opportunity to converse, to show her understanding, to share her experiences, etc. You open opportunities for more conversation. Others jump in and your question is suddenly a group discussion.

Read historic or contemporary novels, identify great figures that traveled the same road, choose a new-founded hero, and follow him/her on a journey to discovery. If you're in Paris, read *Hemingway: The Paris Years* by Michael S. Reynolds, and experience what it's like to live in Hemingway's Paris. If you're in Great Britain, read works by Elizabeth Hamilton or Jane Porter. Going to South Africa? Read *Cry, the Beloved Country* by Alan Paton. There are many fine options.

82. Should I keep a journal or blog?

Journal writing is a voyage to the interior. ~ **Christina Baldwin**

Yes, you should do both if you can, but keep a journal if you have to choose between one or the other. Electronic blogging is harder to preserve for keepsake. You may not be able to access the Internet to blog as frequently as you can jot things down. I have lots of photos, personal letters, and journals from my Peace Corps days, but since email has taken over, I can't get organized enough to save my e-thoughts and e-ideas for memories anymore. I cannot even get organized enough to print digital photographs on a regular basis. If you've found an easy way to preserve your experiences electronically, then email me. I could use some advice.

When I refer to journaling, I do not mean a time-consuming process of summarizing your experiences day after day; I'm talking about recording memories in a systematic way that enables you to find information ten years from now, without having to read your journals front to back. Sadly, I was never taught this concept when I was young, and I missed a lot of important information in my journals that I can't recall or find anymore. Most of what I missed had to do with identities and contact info, and interesting foods and recipes that I wanted to remember how to make. I also lost track of the places that I visited. Take it from me and keep a *smart* journal.

Buy a notebook, something small that you can carry with you wherever you go. Divide it into four sections. Use these four sections to safeguard your memories. As we get older, we tend to forget more, and the *information age* certainly doesn't help. You will be very happy that you have such a resource and record of your experiences later in life. Had I only done things differently back in the day, I'd be a lot happier with what sits on my shelf at home. Believe it or not, I don't even remember some of the people I wrote about and some of the things I did, let alone details. I dated a guy for six months and don't even have his last name!

Smart Journal

People – Use this section to record information about friends, professors, host family, significant others, strangers you meet on the train that you don't expect to see again, people you are keeping in contact with back home, etc. Leave the first page blank for a table of contents later. Then, start adding people. Reserve at least two pages per person and use them over time to gather personal information like full name, how you met each other, birthday, address, phone, your relationship, etc. Paste in photos, email messages, etc. Be creative.

Facts – This section is reserved for facts you want to recall in the future like recipes, names of dishes you likes, places you visited, where you attended school, your address/phone in the host country, bizarre foods, stores you like, restaurants you enjoy, trains, hostels, airlines, holidays, routes, unique words you learn, museums, historic sites (and significance), etc. You can draw pictures, maps, or you can paste information into your journal. Anything factual can go in this section.

Ahha's – Questions, thoughts, feelings, discoveries, ideas, and cultural differences, which come to you as result of your study abroad experience. This is your GROWTH section and how you are changing mentally, emotionally, intellectually, spiritually, physically, etc. It's your record of transformation. Use it for joyfulness, frustration, humility, pride, anger, etc. Whenever your writing is motivated by deep thoughts and feelings, it should probably go in this section.

Activity – Reserve this section for activities and stories. Do you want to remember a day in the life? Or, did something exciting, hilarious, or bizarre happen to you? An activity may be your everyday walk to school. A story could be an annual festival, a trip to Auschwitz, a child you befriended, a good time with friends, an embarrassing moment, your personal experience with a historical event, a journey to the rain forest, etc. Activities and stories are what make our experiences real. So, record your mundane to extraordinary activities.

Tips: Consider bringing a few glue sticks to paste memoirs into your journal like photographs, tickets, etc. Don't throw away your maps; mark where you live, the paths you walk, where you go to school, the places you visited in other cities, the routes you followed, etc. You can use a color-code system with markers to distinguish routes and locations. Over time, you may forget this information and be thankful you have a record. If you don't have a city map, then draw one with a pen. In addition to your journal, get a small binder to keep your maps, categorized by city or trip.

Other resources (blogs):

- http://blogger.com
- http://blogsearch.google.com
- http://blogstream.com
- http://facebook.com
- http://myspace.com
- http://mytripjournal.com
- http://palsabroad.com
- http://www.toadfire.com

83. How can I connect with people?

...there is nothing in the world as interesting as people, and one can never study them enough. ~ Vincent Van Gogh

The real beauty of international travel is not in the places we see, but in the people we meet. It's through our relationships that we give and take, and subsequently change, which can be for better or worse. Consequently it's important to connect with the right people who can help you grow and change in a positive direction. There are several things that you can do to meet the right people and connect.

Look for similarities before you pursue a connection. Does the person look like someone that you'd want to know? Are you often in the same places? Based on your observations and interactions, what are your most obvious similarities? Friends have characteristics that pull them together (values, hobbies, work, goals, etc.). Try to find at least three or four things that you have in common with someone before getting serious.

Be transparent (real) with people. Don't put on a façade and pretend you're someone that you are not. Too many people mask who they really are because they want to look cool and fit in with peers. Fakes tend to flock together; when nobody is real, you end up with a bunch of incompatible, fake friends that like you for who you aren't! There is nothing worse than being stuck in fake-mode and unable to get out. If this sounds like you, start over and this time do it right.

Share yourself with others. People are usually as interested in you and your culture as you are in theirs. When I was living with my African family, my host mother often saw me doing push-ups (I was a workout fanatic). One thing led to another and before I knew it, I was teaching my African mama how to do pushups. She did a few and we all laughed. I also taught

259

her some card tricks, how to make spaghetti, and much more. She ended up loving my perfume and so I gave her a bottle.

In the course of all this, she opened up to me. I found out that the man I thought was my host father was actually her secret lover. Her husband lived in another city with several other wives. I never figured out why she was separated from them. She told me not to tell anyone because it was very shameful for her and could have fatal consequences. My mother also shared with me why she didn't have too many female friends; "They talk too much and are too clingy," she said.

Listen and pay attention. Do you forget people's names? Do you usually formulate your response before someone is done talking? If you answered *yes* to either of these questions, then you could probably use some tips on listening. Try to hear what is said rather than what you want to hear. Try to read between and around the words by observing non-verbal forms of communication. To listen, you have to think; you can hear and not listen (through one ear and out the other).

Since listening in a foreign language means more thinking, it's easy to get tired and start daydreaming. Try to avoid this by letting your host family and friends know when you are mentally worn and need a break (or need them to slow down). Always give 100% of your attention, don't be afraid to seek clarification when you don't understand, and never pretend to understand when you don't or it may come back to haunt you. Show comprehension by offering respect and affirmation.

Expect and accept differences. Everyone is different and it's okay not to agree on everything. Agree to disagree and focus on the things you have in common. Most married couples are completely opposite in many ways; one likes it hot, the other likes it cold or one is outgoing and the other a homebody. The truth, however, is that they have more similarities than they have differences; the differences are just more obvious. It's important to realize that differences in our relationships can help us grow and develop into better people.

Finally, step into other people's shoes. When you step out of your own experience, and into another, you learn and grow, but you also nourish that relationship. You can better relate with others by asking them lots of questions and doing things their way. Show interest in just getting to know people and what makes them tick. Visit their homes, eat what they like to eat, ask them the *getting-to-know-you* questions, etc. There's nothing more honorable than when people show interest and curiosity in your person.

84. What is there to gain?

I soon realized that no journey carries one far unless, as it extends into the world around us, it goes an equal distance into the world within. ~ **Lillian Smith**

You can gain awareness, knowledge, and skills. Awareness about yourself and others is important, and the more you seek to know of other people, the more you learn about yourself. Knowledge about the world, and a more authentic worldview, is also important because "Knowledge is not information, it's transformation" (Osho). Skills that help you communicate (both written and verbal), think outside of the box, and take more initiative, are good to carry in life. Many employers and parents love this stuff!

You can gain a sense of freedom and become what you are meant to be in life. Whenever you start a new school, a new job, or move to a different community, you have a chance to start fresh. Nobody knows you or what you are like; you haven't been labeled in a particular way or slotted into some grouping. The opportunity to start anew is greater when you study abroad because you're no longer confined by your own culture. In essence, you can gain a *new you*, which means your whole life can change for the better.

Regardless of what there is to gain, we usually only gain what we desire to obtain. If you have no interest or desire to learn the language, then you probably won't do what it takes to make that happen. The best thing you can do is to have clear goals, and a solid understanding of what you hope to bring home from your experience. Do not *let* life happen to you; instead, *make* your life happen. You're probably paying a lot of money to study abroad, so take it seriously. You will reap what you sew.

While you can't change the wind, you can adjust your sails to get anywhere that's accessible by sea (assuming a tidal wave doesn't whip you away). I think this is one of those principles that you learn through international education. You may feel lost in culture, but right about your choice to go abroad. You may feel smaller in the world, but bigger in life. After four years in the Peace Corps, I felt weaker in the greater scheme of things (like changing the world), but stronger in my ability to move forward and make small changes for the better.

85. What is there to lose?

I've grown certain that the root of all fear is that we've been forced to deny who we are. ~ **Frances Moore Lappe**

Whenever we are cut off from what is familiar, we are offered an opportunity to rise up and meet challenge. Wherever there is challenge, there is potential for growth. Wherever there is growth, there is something gained and lost. We have to let go before we can move on. This is what makes change difficult to process and accept. This is what makes study abroad an opportunity for growth and development.

You may be motivated to let go of certain things when you study abroad. Some of these things may include stereotypes, ethnocentrism, your formerly constructed worldview, inner fears, self-consciousness, certain relationships (that no longer seem healthy), innocence, etc. You have as much to lose as you have to gain and this is precisely why study abroad can be so transforming. A butterfly must leave its cocoon.

When I realized that life was going to go on with or without me, I stopped resisting change. My fear of abandonment and death just washed away, and I was set free. Suddenly, I was able to be the person that I think I was meant to be, and do the things that made my spirit soar. It didn't matter so much what other people thought of me, because I knew in my heart that *who I was* and *what I choose to do* was all right.

Don't be afraid to let go; it's a natural part of life that we all must experience. Healthy growth takes time and sets you free. Being different is not the end of the world, but a beginning. Lose what prohibits you from coming into your *bona fide* self. Lose whatever keeps you from traveling in a positive direction. Lose the façade and graciously accept what is real, for the time that it's real, in the place that it has become.

86. What about global issues?

There's enough on this planet for everyone's needs but not for everyone's greed.
~Mahatma Gandhi

One of the greatest transformations that this world has seen can be summed up in a word: *globalization*. Globalization is the integration of economic, cultural, and political systems around the world. It is caused by international investment, trade, and technology and has created interdependency among the nations. For the first time in history, a ripple in one major economy can shake the entire world. For more information, visit www.globalization101.org (a student's guide).

Since the world is evolving into one system, it is important that we learn how to manage it for the good of people and earth. Although we are globally dependent, we do not possess enough global awareness, knowledge, and skill to effectively manage our planet. It is our mismanagement of everything that has created an array of global issues. If we don't deal with and effectively resolve these issues in the future, then it will eventually be our demise.

The American Forum for Global Education has done a super job of identifying the major global issues that students need to learn about today and compiling an array of resources and publications. While mainly geared towards K-12, much of the material is also good for college students who didn't get the information in high school, and for Education majors who hope to teach. Explore their website at globaled.org. Another excellent resource is *The World is Flat* by Thomas Friedman.

Given the array of information on global issues, and how they're interconnected, it will be necessary for all nations to work together on resolutions. Since you will be the next and most globally competent workforce on the planet, you may be involved in this process. Take some time during your study abroad experience or after to focus on the issues that interest you the most. Learn about these issues, and see if you can fathom any solutions. Here are a few thoughts and ideas...

How to stop Conflict and Abuse – Violence, terrorism, guerrilla activities, war, arms trafficking, weapons of mass destruction (biological, chemical, nuclear), ethnic cleansing, and genocide both within nations and between nations of the world, gender power, abuse of women and children, sex trafficking and trade, prostitution, ethnic-racial-political-religious abuse, and government corruption.

Ideologies, philosophies, and religions are deeply imbedded in culture and politics. It is important to study the major world religions, political philosophies, and cultural ideologies in order to better understand and/or empathize with different people, to influence change. It's equally important to study human commonality and diversity to reduce stereotypes, prejudice, and discrimination, as well as solve problems that stem from ethnic and racial tensions.

How to manage the Global Economy/Planet – Trade politics, currency exchange rates, foreign assistance barriers, foreign debt, exportation of jobs, rising economic disparity (between rich and poor), environmental pollution, natural resource depletion, ozone depletion, toxic/nuclear waste, deforestation, acid rain, global warming, environmental disasters, climate change, drought, and species eradication.

Learn about alternative energy sources and conservation. Learn about international bodies and structures like the UN, NATO, SEATO, OAS, and OAU. Learn about alliances (such as NAFTA), treaties, and negotiations, devolution of the nations, political disintegration, secessionism, separatism, irredentism, and the opposing trends of regional integration and increased democratization. Find ways of redistributing wealth, to decrease the gap between the rich and poor, and promoting fair trade practices. Guard biodiversity/resources.

How to Sustain Life and improve Quality – Lack of health care, food shortages, nutrition deficits, massive famines, infectious diseases, inadequate sanitation, drug use and abuse (trade, prevention, prosecution), inadequate shelter/housing, illiteracy, shrinking economic resources, lack of social safety nets, illegal aliens, high populations in the cities, political asylum, dependency ratios (percentage of population under 15 or over 65 years old), mounting numbers of refugees worldwide, growing crime, and identity theft.

Research and gather data on growth, patterns, movements, and trends in populations around the world. Discover the causes of poverty. Examine the role of science and technology in the lives of all human beings. Learn about the information revolution. Learn sustainable development methods/practices.

A hot topic in study abroad is sustainable travel. If you want to learn more about how you can leave the world a better place, then look into Sustainable Travel International, a 501(c)(3) non-profit organization whose mission is to promote sustainable development and responsible travel. www.sustainabletravelinternational.org

How to solve International Development Issues – Broader dependency that includes increasing foreign debt as well as economic imperialism, explosive urban growth in the cities (megacities) which overpower the countries, cartels among developing nations that possess raw materials needed by industrialized nations, and international security/immigration.

Look into why such problems are happening and how they interconnect with other global issues. Research how solving one global issue (like the redistribution of wealth) could impact international developments and relationships. Find solutions to US dependence on foreign oil and rising cartels.

Multinational Organizations

United Nations (UN) – This international organization strives to solve problems that challenge humanity. It was founded in 1945 to stop wars between nations and to provide a platform for dialogue. www.un.org and www.unsystem.org

United Nations Education, Scientific, and Cultural Organization (UNESCO) – A specialized UN agency that promotes international cooperation among its Member States and Associate Members in the fields of education, science, culture and communication. www.unesco.org

The World Bank Group - The World Bank is a vital source of financial and technical assistance to developing countries around the world. Its primary focus is to help the poorest of the poor. It is one of the largest sources of funding for the developing world. www.worldbank.org

Other multinational organizations include:

- **The African Development Bank (AFDB):** www.afdb.org
- **Asian Development Bank (ADB):** www.adb.org
- **Bank for International Settlements (BIS):** bis.org
- **European Bank for Reconstruction & Development (EBRD):** www.ebrd.com
- **Inter-American Development Bank (IADB):** www.iadb.org
- **International Court of Justice (ICJ):** www.icj-cij.org
- **International Labor Organization (ILO):** www.ilo.org
- **International Monetary Fund (IMF):** www.imf.org
- **Organization for Economic Cooperation & Development (OECD):** www.oecd.org
- **Organization of American States (OAS):** www.oas.org
- **The Organization of the Petroleum Exporting Countries (OPEC):** www.opec.org
- **United Nations Conference on Trade & Development (UNCTAD):** www.unctad.org
- **United Nations Industrial Development Organization (UNIDO):** www.unido.org
- **World Health Organization (WHO):** www.who.ch
- **World Trade Organization (WTO):** www.wto.org

The UN Millennium Project
(www.unmillenniumproject.org)

At the 2000 Millennium Summit, UN world leaders adopted the *Millennium Declaration*, committing their nations to a global partnership to reduce poverty and set out a series of time-bound targets by 2015. These Millennium Development Goals (MDGs) will address extreme poverty (income, hunger, disease, lack of adequate shelter, and exclusion) and promote gender equality, education, environmental sustainability, and basic human rights for all.

1. Eradicate extreme poverty and hunger.
2. Achieve universal primary education.
3. Promote gender equality & the empowerment of women.
4. Reduce child mortality.
5. Improve maternal health.
6. Combat HIV/AIDS, malaria and other diseases.
7. Ensure environmental sustainability.
8. Develop a global partnership for development.

87. How can I make a difference?

Too often travel, instead of broadening the mind, merely lengthens the conversation. ~ Elizabeth Drew

When you decided to take a leap of faith and study abroad, you were probably focused on what it could do for you, and rightfully so! It is my sincere hope that you have a wonderful, life-changing experience. If you haven't already realized it, this experience is about much more than you, as it spills over into the lives of other people. Your choices and decisions can change lives for better or worse, richer or poorer.

When I was in the Peace Corps, a friend from home came and visited me. I was working in a village with a local doctor in a small health center. To make a long story short, Dr. Miguel and my friend Krista fell in love, and were married shortly thereafter. Miguel just finished his second round of medical school (in the US) and is now a practicing MD. If it weren't for *my* choices, the two of them would have never even met.

While you may not find a husband or wife, your experience will have an impact on the present and future for many people with whom you know and encounter. Find good mentors and be good mentors to people around you, and you can make a real difference in this world. People are always watching and listening for those who are different, who stand out from the crowd and shine.

One of the things we like to talk about in higher education is global citizenship. It's our hope that international education will cultivate this attitude-behavior in participants. A global citizen has a sense of responsibility in the global community. He/she cares for human beings and the entire world, supports the well-being of others, works to alleviate global inequality, and avoids actions that damage the planet.

Look at your experience as intensive training to save some aspect of humanity or planet earth, and earn a living on the side. Get knowledge and share your self, life, and experience wherever you go. As much as your study abroad opportunity has helped you, it has the potential for a far greater impact! Just let it flow and be who you're meant to be. Realize that life is greater than me, myself, and I.

Commit yourself to lifelong learning. The more you learn, the more you can become, and the more you can do. There's so much to learn, and you can't get it all from school. Lifelong learning keeps our minds vigorous and our bodies young. We cannot learn enough, and it's never too early or too late to learn more. The drive to discover and grow keeps us alive and kicking in the many stages of life.

Part X.

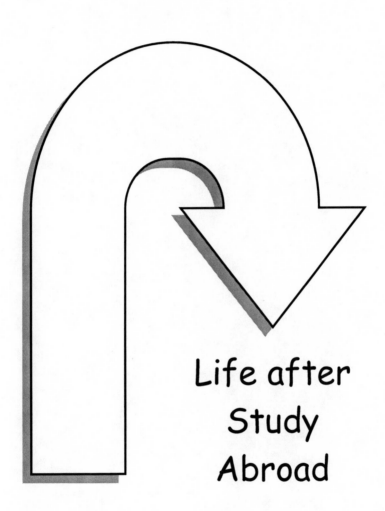

Life after
Study
Abroad

88. How will I say goodbye?

Don't cry because it's over. Smile because it happened. ~**Dr. Seuss**

When I left Cameroon, I didn't know that I wasn't returning. I was sent to Peace Corps Washington to treat a bout of what was thought to be malaria, and while I was away, the Peace Corps decided to close my site for safety reasons. When I was better, they gave me the choice of returning to a different site in Cameroon or going to another country. I decided to take a new assignment in Ecuador, and consequently I never had the opportunity to say goodbye to friends in Cameroon.

Afterwards, I wrote many personal letters to my Cameroonian and Peace Corps friends. I tried to explain what had happened and did what I could to keep the relationships alive, but there was always confusion, and I never experienced true closure in the relationships. Had I known that I would not be returning, I would have said my goodbyes, acquired permanent contact information to keep in touch, taken more pictures, organized my personal possessions, and given away many gifts.

I always thought that one day I would return to Cameroon, but it hasn't happened yet, and I don't know if it ever will. Even if I do have an opportunity to return someday, I don't know how to find my Cameroonian friends who have since divorced, moved, etc. I don't even know if the same people would be living in my village, as the children would be all grown up. There were some expats in my area, too, and I lost touch with them about a year after my departure.

The lesson I took from this experience is to always say good-bye, even when you think you will return. Life has a way of taking turns, and with all good intentions, you may not have the opportunity to go back to your host country/city for a long time, if ever. It's important to bring a certain closure to your relationships (even if you will be in touch via email), and do so in a culturally appropriate manner. It may be expected that you give gifts, or that you have a goodbye party. Your goodbyes are final impressions in people's hearts and minds. Be sure to say goodbye to everyone, even the store clerk, and the bus driver you see on a regular basis. Goodbyes are just as important, if not more important than your greetings/hellos.

89. What about gifts to bring home?

Every gift from a friend is a wish for your happiness. ~*Richard Bach*

Good international gifts are usually exclusive to a particular country or area of the world. If the country is known to have beautiful wall art, then a small painting might be nice. If the country is known for its woodworking, then a small mask or cultural artifact would suffice. It also depends on how many family members and friends you have, how much space you have in your luggage, and how careful you can be with fragile items. (*Tip: If transporting fragile items, wrap them up in your clothing and put them in the middle of your bags*).

In *Aix en Provence* (Southern France), people make a great spice mix called *Herb de Provence,* packaged in small burlap bags. I bought several bags, and my family and friends loved them. Think carefully about what you carry (size and weight); you can't bring everything with you. If you're not running an import/export business, you probably have $800 of duty-free personal exemption, depending on the country. You can bring more; you just have to pay duty on it. Make certain you know before you go, so that you aren't stuck with a large bill.

Keep in mind that although you can bring items back to the US, several things are prohibited or restricted. Products that could be a detriment to community health or public safety are prohibited. Certain kinds of toys, illegal substances, firearms, animals, vegetables, textiles, and cultural artifacts may have embargos. Alcohol is restricted (to only a certain number of bottles). Fruit and meat is prohibited. The US Customs puts out a *Know Before You Go* brochure that answers everything in detail. Go to www.customs.ustreas.gov/xp/cgov/travel.

90. What about US Customs?

Immigration is the sincerest form of flattery. ~**Jack Paar**

You will have to fill out a *declaration form* on the airplane. Fill it out honestly and thoroughly. Never, ever lie. Customs officials have the right to search you and your luggage. Even if they don't check your bags, they often have dogs that sniff out illegalities. Penalties for lying to government officials are stiff, so just don't do it. The rules and regulations are there for your own safety and that of the American people. They aren't there to make your life miserable. Things that seem harmless may in fact be dangerous.

You have to declare everything you are taking home that you didn't take with you before you went. Whether you bought the items or they were given to you as gifts, you still have to declare them. For everything you bought, keep receipts and sales slips. On the declaration form, you will have to state what you paid for each item, including taxes. If you received an item as a gift, then you need to estimate *fair market value*. Be sure to pack declared items in a way that you can easily access them if necessary.

Do customs officials know if you bought something outside of the US? Well, they don't know for sure but they have the right to presume. The burden of proof is on you. For example, if you bought a camera in the US that was made in Japan, then you may have to pay duty on it unless you can prove you owned it before you went on your journey. Legitimate proof would be an official document such as a receipt, insurance policy, appraisal, etc. You should also register your valuables before you leave, just to be on the safe side.

On the plane, you will be given a declaration form to fill out, and at your first port of entry in the US, you will have to go through two processes before you can either leave or catch your next flight. You will have to pass immigration with your passport. They will check to make sure that you, as a person, are okay to enter the country. You will then have to go to the baggage claim, grab a cart, pick up your checked luggage on a conveyer belt, and carry it through US Customs with your declaration form. It is their job to make sure that you're not bringing anything illegal into the country and that you pay duty that may be owed. Once you get past Customs, you'll drop off your luggage again and go to your next connection.

- **US Customs and Border Protection**
  http://www.customs.ustreas.gov
- **Immigration Requirements and Forms** – cbp.gov/ xp/cgov/travel/id_visa/immigration_linklist.xml
- **How the US Customs Services Work** – http://www. howstuffworks.com/us-customs-service.htm

91. What should I do when I get back?

We become what we do. ~*May-lin Soong Chiang*

Here are a few things that I suggest you think about doing when you get back to the States:

- Fill out a program evaluation for your study abroad office so that they can monitor program quality. It is more important than you may think. In many offices, evaluations are made available to students who are thinking about going to an institution where you studied. Your insight can be invaluable, so share it.

- Be sure to have an official transcript of your study abroad coursework sent to the right office at your home institution. Sometimes a transcript ends up in the wrong office and isn't processed efficiently as a result. Allow a few weeks for it to arrive and then check to see if the appropriate person received it.
- It is a good idea to schedule a checkup for a full physical with your doctor. You may have picked up a bug you don't even know about, such as a parasite. Amoebas and giardia sometimes don't present any symptoms. Finish your malaria pills (if required) and request a TB test just to be on the safe side.
- If you are finding it difficult to adjust and reconnect, then don't overburden yourself with six classes and a part-time job. Take it easy and allow yourself some time to relax. If you're still having a hard time, after a month or two, visit the counseling center on campus.
- You may have some new ideas or different academic and career goals. If you're unsure about your next step, your major, or your career, talk to your advisor or a career counselor. They can help you map your new-founded direction.
- Get involved! You can participate in your campus's study abroad fair, pre-departure orientations, clubs and organizations (with an international flavor), etc. Just sharing stories and talking to people can help you feel better. It can also help you better articulate your experience for job interviews.

92. What is reverse culture shock?

The whole object of travel is not to set foot on foreign land; it is at last to set foot on one's own country as a foreign land. ~*G.K. Chesterton*

After you've been through the stages of cultural adjustment and return from your study abroad experience, you may be concerned about *reverse culture shock.* You've just had this amazing journey in life, and now you're back to the old grindstone again. If you feel gloomy, find it difficult to communicate your experience to family and friends, miss the country, the culture, and friends you made abroad, and replay the memories over and over again in your mind, then you're probably going through a case of reverse culture shock.

You had a life-changing experience, but nobody really seems to care. Your attitude and values are different, but you don't really know *how* or *why.* As you readjust to your own culture and nation, the sadness will subside and the *old* and *new you* will eventually come together. It just takes time. While your body may have come home, remember that your heart, mind, and soul are still lagging behind in the country you visited. Eventually the rest of you will catch up and you will *bring yourself together* again; so don't worry about it.

In the meantime, there are a few things you can do to speed up the process: talk with other students who have studied abroad, get involved in international clubs and organizations, volunteer at study abroad fairs, talk with your study abroad advisor, write stories for a campus publication, take a course with an international focus, create a website about your study abroad experience, send your photos into contests, participate in international events and functions on campus, and think about traveling again.

Try to understand your friends and family, too. They didn't have the experiences that you had, and it's hard for them to relate. However, they did have their *own* experiences. They may have gone through stages and changed in ways that are different from you. New partners, marriages, divorces, births, deaths, illnesses, living arrangements, graduations, jobs, etc. all have a major impact on people's lives. Your family and friends may be frustrated with *you* for focusing too much on your own experiences, and not paying attention to theirs.

I'm sure you learned this while studying abroad, but try also to remember when you get home; the world doesn't revolve around you. It is important that people notice you and how you've grown and changed through your studies abroad, but it is also important that you pay attention to them. As hard as it may be to understand, life didn't stop when you were gone. After serving in the Peace Corps, I was wrapped up in my own journey—what I gained from it and what I missed about it. I thought that my experiences were more significant than the experiences of my family and friends. It took me awhile, but I eventually learned otherwise.

Incorporating study abroad growth and development into our lives is about giving, taking, and balancing ourselves with the world. It is about changing and staying the same. It is about seeing how big and how small we really are, all at the same time. The amazing thing about study abroad and international travel in general, is that it affects every area of our lives and challenges us in everything we are and do. You are blessed and fortunate to have had such an experience, such an opportunity to grow and develop into a better person. Look on the bright side of things, try to see the glass as half-full rather than half-empty, and enjoy the rest of your life.

Reading

The Art of Coming Home by Craig Storti

---

93. How hard is the readjustment?

I met a lot of people in Europe. I even encountered myself. ~ *James Baldwin*

Any adjustment to change is difficult. However, the degree of difficulty really depends on you as an individual. Once your eyes are opened, it is hard if not impossible to close them. We experience this with lots of things in life—our first love, our first intimate encounter, our first vehicle, the first time we are living on our own, our first spouse (hopefully the last), our first child, etc. If this is your first time living and studying in another country, then your eyes were probably opened to the realities of another world. You had a chance to experience something wonderful. Look at it as a privilege because not all students study abroad. Typically, only 1% of all US college students take advantage of this awesome opportunity.

The best thing you can do is *think* on the bright side. You have a lifetime ahead of you to do whatever you want with what you have been given, so if you're going to think, then think about all the things you will do and all the experiences you will have. It doesn't do any good to focus and dwell on the past; however, it is exciting to live in the present, and from time to time, think about how the present might unfold into the future. Siddhartha Gautama once said, "The secret of health for both mind and body is not to mourn for the past, not to worry about the future, not to anticipate troubles, but to live the present moment wisely and earnestly." We cannot change the past, and we really don't have any control over the future, so let's make the best of the here and now.

The process of readjusting to the US is difficult, to say the least. When I returned, after four years overseas, I had to get used to free enterprise again. I remember feeling so frustrated because nobody would rent me an apartment. I didn't have a job, but I had enough money in the bank to pay for a full year. It was a huge shock that people would be so brainless and heartless. I mean gee-whiz, I had just served my country for four years in the Peace Corps. All I wanted was to pay for my apartment and go to graduate school. Having just come from countries that treated me with great honor and respect, I could not understand why my own fellow citizens wouldn't give me a break. I had never missed a bill in my life and had always been responsible with money. Until I found my equilibrium, it was challenging to make it through the days.

94. How can I share my experience?

The greatest gift is to give people your enlightenment, to share it. It has to be the greatest. ~**Buddha**

There are so many ways you can share your experiences with others. Look at me; I wrote this book! The reason I wrote this book is because I like sharing my attitudes, knowledge, and skills with all kinds of people. Being a quiet person, I'm more comfortable writing than I am speaking in front of groups or staring in documentaries. My point is that everybody has their own ways of sharing; all you have to do is find what works for you, and then do it.

Living and working abroad molded my life and shaped me into the person I am today. Nonetheless, I had a hard time articulating how it changed me, especially to people that did not have international experience. In these situations, I would try to find something we had in common. This would build a bridge of communication whereby I could slip in my thoughts here and there, using one of my infamous experiences, sure to awe and dazzle.

What I've found is that people relate to stories better than they can often relate to experience. In fact, people love stories especially when you weave in some humor here and there! I once had a conversation with someone who asked me, "So what was Africa like?" Needless to say, I didn't know how to answer such a vague question, and so I said, "It's not what you'd expect." Then, I went on with a story that exemplified my point, with just a taste of my experience in Africa.

Shortly after I started my training in Africa, I traveled north to visit a village that farmed cotton for a living. There was a gathering in the evening among the villagers, to celebrate the end of the season. The group of families had a big room, full of cotton, and I was invited to lie down in it. I laid around in the fluffy cotton for a while, until summoned to a campfire where the respected *Elders* were ready to speak. There were all kinds of villagers at the meeting, from babies to seniors. There was a lot of noise, and then suddenly, it stopped. It was so quiet that all we could hear were the bugs and crackling fire. A traditional Elder stood up slowly, and started to speak. Her voice was coarse and deep, filled with experience.

While I didn't know who the woman was, I could sense that she was someone of great importance. All eyes were on her and everyone was silent as she spoke with authority. One of the younger men agreed to translate for me, since she spoke the native language of her tribe. She started with a few short remarks about the season and thanked everyone for their hard work in gathering the cotton. She warmly welcomed me to her village and thanked me for taking time to come. Then, she proceeded with a story about different cultures and how they can benefit from each other.

She claimed it was a true story about a young African boy from their village. Many years ago, there was an American family living in the village. They were missionaries and had young children. One of the American boys gave the African boy a stick of chewing gum. Since Africans view everything in life as being practical, the boy couldn't understand how the gum was useful, when you chew but don't swallow it. So, he put it away and forgot about it until one day he got sick with a bad case of diarrhea. It was so bad that he couldn't sit in class without running to the latrine every few minutes. Suddenly he remembered the chewing gum! He chewed it up and stuck it in his asshole. This helped him stay in school.

All the villagers laughed, and of course, I was baffled. I guess I was expecting some wise story about the spirit world, or something more fitting to my image of an elderly African. A joke about chewing gum as a plug for diarrhea was not on my radar screen. I did learn that Africans can have an interesting sense of humor. I also learned that they are not afraid to talk about such things that we find distasteful. The rest of the trip was pretty normal, and I can't remember too much about it, but I never forgot this experience.

95. Will others think I've changed?

Time is a dressmaker specializing in alterations. ~ **Faith Baldwin**

Most parents and professors will note the difference in your everyday attitude and in your commitment to life, academics, and career goals. The Peace Corps induced great change in my life. Obviously, people notice the change in everything I am and do. It isn't something that I can conceal.

- **Personal** – married to a native Ecuadorian, raising a bilingual/bicultural family, in-laws in another country
- **Academics/Career** – work as a study abroad director, study international education and communication
- **Social** – have many intercultural, international friends and interests, travel the world, eat weird foods, etc.

Personal Transformation

	Life Development	
Career	Self Perception	Academics
Transformation	Understanding of your cultural values & biases	Transformation

Social Transformation

96. How will credits/grades transfer?

But there are advantages to being elected President. The day after I was elected, I had my high school grades classified Top Secret. ~**Ronald Regan**

The concept of measuring credit by contact hours developed in the US as a way to determine faculty-teaching loads. It's a costing system that isn't entirely relevant to students. In many other countries, credit is perceived as something the student achieves and cannot be measured by the number of contact hours spent in a classroom. The burden is on the student to learn the material, rather than on the faculty to lecture.

Nonetheless, many US colleges and universities still employ contact hours for determining the number of credits that will be received from study abroad. Since this formula doesn't always work, because hours spent in class are not listed on most foreign transcripts, it is commonplace to rely on official conversion scales. For example, *European Credit Transfer System* (ECTS), has determined that six ECTS credits convert to three or four US credits. The best thing that you can do is to ask your advisor. Every institution is different.

In addition to the credit conversion scales, US colleges and universities account for schedule differences in their terms. This would apply when an institution that functions on three terms transfers to a system that functions on two, or vice versa. There is typically a 3:2 ratio when transferring quarter credits to semester credits and a 2:3 ratio when transferring semester credits to quarter credits. When calculating quarter credits to semester credits, divide the quarter ones by 1.5 and round to the nearest whole number for semester equivalents.

When it comes to evaluating your credit, some study abroad offices will give you credit/no-credit and some will give you letter grades that may or may not affect your GPA. Others recognize your courses as transfer credit. Grade conversion practices are not standard across colleges and universities. A good resource that many higher institutions use to convert letter grades is the *WES Grade Conversion Guide* published by World Education Services (http://www.wes.org). If you go to their website and locate this resource, you can sign up for free access online, subject to user guidelines. You can then choose from more than 120 countries to see grade conversion scales. Not all institutions use WES. See the examples below.

Australia

High Distinction	A+
Distinction	A
Credit	B
Pass	C
Conceded, Conditional or Compensatory Pass	D
Failure	F

United Kingdom

70-100	A
65-69	A-
60-64	B+
50-59	B
45-49	C+
40-44	C
0-39	F

Spain

Matrícula de Honor (with Honors)	A
Sobresaliente (Outstanding)	A
Notable (Notable)	B+
Aprobado (Pass)	B-
Suspenso (Failure)	F

Chile

6.0-7.0	Muy Bueno (Very Good)	A
5.0-5.9	Bueno (Good)	B
4.0-4.9	Suficiente (Sufficient)	C
0.0-3.9	Insuficiente (Insufficient)	F

Germany

1-1.5	Sehr Gut (Very Good)	A
1.6-2.5	Gut (Good)	A
2.6-3.5	Befriedigend (Quite Good)	B
3.6-4.0	Ausreichend (Satisfactory)	C
4.1-4.3	-	*
4.4-6	Nicht Ausreichend (Insufficient)	F

France

16-20	Très Bien (Very Good)	A+
14-15.9	Bien (Good)	A
12-13.9	Assez Bien (Quite Good)	B
10-11.9	Passable (Satisfactory)	C
8-9.9	-	*

97. How do I build my credentials?

If opportunity doesn't knock, build a door. ~ *Milton Berle*

The key to building your credentials is to match employer's wants/needs with what you've acquired through international education and beyond. Think about what you have learned and how it can be valuable to prospective employers. Then, weave it into a resume and cover letter. Your resume is a fact sheet, a brief presentation of *you* as an asset. If your resume is well written, a prospective employer should be able to glance over it, and determine whether you have what they need for the position that they are trying to fill.

I'm amazed at how many people don't know how to create a quality resume. First, don't put your birth date, your weight, your height, your age, or your social security number on your resume. Your resume should include your name, address, and contact information (phone, email). It should also include an objective, your education, your work experience, any relevant activities, professional associations, professional research or presentations, publications, technical abilities, and languages. List your study abroad program in the education section. List volunteer/field work and related internships under your work experience. Don't forget start and end dates for each job.

While your resume is generally fixed, your cover letter should change for every position in which you apply. For each job description, highlight key action words, desirable skills, and experiences. Then think about how you can best demonstrate these in your letter. Your letter should never be longer than one page. Part of high-quality writing is being able to pack the most information into the fewest sentences, similar to packing light when you travel abroad. Your goal should be a face-to-face interview, and if your cover letter is long-winded and your resume does not provide needed information, then you'll be quickly discarded from the pile.

Your cover letter should not simply repeat what is in your resume. Instead, use it to strategically summarize, highlight, extract, and detail attitudes-knowledge-skills that match the job description. Mention your study abroad experience, and how it relates to the job. For example, let's say I'm applying for a job that requires strong communication skills. Although my resume lists my work experience in Latin America, I don't assume that the employer understands everything I did there. I might talk about how learning Spanish on the job improved my English and communication skills in general. I might talk about my book, and highlight its popularity and selling rank among other related books.

If you are called for an interview, be prepared to talk about your experiences. While employers may believe that study abroad is a fine undertaking, its relationship to the workforce is not always apparent. It is your responsibility to articulate that relationship. Employers want to know what you learned, how your attitudes changed, the skills you acquired, and most importantly, how all of this makes you their best choice for the job. Build stories into your conversations. For example, when interviewers ask me if I've had any experience working with groups, I tell them that I formed and organized a united women's group, to unite African women from different tribes, with business projects. We produced soap, banana bread, and much more to sell in the market.

You should have three to four references, professional and academic in nature. It might not be a bad idea to include an international reference if it would be easy for the employer to contact him or her. Generally speaking, you shouldn't include more than one personal reference or relative. Don't forget to write down your relationship to each of your references, and include at least one direct supervisor. It's very annoying when people don't put the relationship on their list of references. Maybe the employer is only interested in calling one or two of your previous superiors.

Questions to help you Build your Resume

Do you have foreign language skills?	How are your communication skills?
Do you know firsthand another culture and its customs?	Are you a good listener?
Are you flexible and adaptable?	Do you have strong organization abilities and skills?
Do you respond well to change?	Are you fair and open-minded?
Are you good at solving problems?	Are you a good student and worker?
Do you appreciate people?	Are you well rounded and balanced?
Can you work independently?	
Do you value cultural diversity?	Are you responsible and mature?
Are you focused and directed?	Do you deal well with difference?
Do you actuate self-discipline?	
Are you a self-starter?	Are you self-confident and motivated?
Can you set and achieve goals?	Do you have leadership skills?
Are you patient?	Can you commit and follow through?
Do you understand global issues?	Do you work well independently?
Are you a good traveler?	
Are you a quick learner?	Are you a problem-solver?
Can you manage change?	Do you manage conflict well?

98. What do I need to know about jobs?

There is a way to do it better...find it. ~ *Thomas Edison*

Now that you've finished your credentials, it's time to talk about jobs in general. First, it's best to be honest... if you find a job that suits you well, then by all means, sell yourself as the best for the position. However, if you're reaching pretty far to meet the requirements, and you stretch the truth or lie on your resume, then you'll be sorry later on. Even if you get the job, chances are you don't have what they wanted and needed and you won't do well, or even worse, you'll be fired. If an employer ever discovers a lie on your resume, then you can expect an immediate dismissal. This can ruin you for life.

The interview is a chance for you to evaluate them as much as it is a chance for them to evaluate you. Again, be yourself and don't put on a big show or façade. Ask them questions and pay attention to the environment and office dynamics. Does if feel like a place you would enjoy working? I know so many people who hate their jobs due to unhealthy and dysfunctional environments. It's important that people get along, that your supervisor is someone you can work with, and that there is an atmosphere of respect. When people don't feel valued, all hell breaks loose. Remember, you're with these people every day!

When I was applying to become a director of study abroad, I was offered two positions at the same time. I liked both the positions and environments, and there was no right or wrong choice. Instead, I had to decide which one was better suited for me and my family, which was the better fit. It wasn't just a matter of salary or benefits, either. In fact, the job that I turned down was offering me 15K more than the job that I accepted. What it came down to was the office structure, the reporting lines, the people I'd be working with, the autonomy that I desired, the location relative to my parents, etc. It was a tough decision, but I'm confident that I made the right choice.

99. Can I have an international career?

Choose a job you love, and you will never have to work a day in your life.
~ Confucius

Yes, you can. There are many options available in just about every field. When you're looking for long-term employment, pay careful attention to salary and benefits, as well as the cost of living in the job location. Make sure that your health needs can be met, and that your housing/transportation is adequate. Also, make sure you understand the lifestyle you will have in view of the cost of living and salary you will earn. Below you will find resources to help you get started in a search.

Department of State – Various positions, including the Foreign Service. http://www.careers.state.gov

Europass – A great resource that can help you highlight your assets in an effective way. It can help to remove barriers to working, studying or training in Europe, and it's all free. http://www.europass.com

International Careers – Career information for volunteers. peacecorps.gov/rpcv/career/education/pdf/international.pdf

International Jobs Center – International jobs for professionals, including international development jobs http://www.internationaljobs.org

iWork at iAgora.com – An excellent starting point for entry-level jobs. http://www.iagora.com/iwork

Overseas Jobs – Lots of international jobs in different sectors. http://www.overseasjobs.com

The Paper Boy – Search world newspapers for jobs.
http://www.thepaperboy.com

Peace Corps – Federal employment in grass-roots
development. http://www.peacecorps.gov

United Nations Children's Fund – Grass-roots health and
education work. http://www.unicef.org

Work Abroad – An excellent online resource by William
Nolting at the University of Michigan.
http://www.internationalcenter.umich.edu/swt/work

Work Abroad (Monster) – International job postings.
http://workabroad.monster.com

More Reading

- *Best Resumes and CVs for International Jobs*
  by Ronald L. Krannich and Wendy S. Enelow
- *Careers in International Affairs* by Maria Pinto
  Carland and Candace Faber
- *International Job Finder: Where the Jobs Are
  Worldwide* by Daniel Lauber and Kraig Rice
- *Teaching English Abroad* by Susan Griffith
- *The Big Guide to Living and Working Overseas*
  by Clay Hubbs
- *Work Abroad: the Complete Guide to Finding a Job
  Overseas* by Clay Hubbs
- *Work Your Way Around the World* by Susan Griffith
- *Work Worldwide: International Career Strategies for
  the Adventurous Job Seeker* by Nancy Mueller

100. What about graduate school?

Curiosity may have killed the cat, but it sure has earned a lot of people graduate degrees. ~ **Robyn Irving**

If you studied abroad as an undergraduate, and now you are considering graduate school, there a few opportunities that I'd like to bring to your attention. In addition to all the grants and scholarships to which you can apply, there are some programs and opportunities that are worth a second look.

The Erasmus Mundus program strives to attract top students to Europe. Its mission is to promote mutual understanding between Europe and other areas of the world, and to enhance Europe's international reputation in higher education. The program supports high-quality European Masters Courses and provides scholarship monies to student participants. These scholarships are significant (€ 24,000), and are comparable to US Fulbright and other prestigious programs. To learn more, visit http://ec.europa.eu/education/index_en.html.

SIT Graduate Institute (www.worldlearning.org) is known for preparing graduates as critical thinkers, good communicators, and intercultural *managers* of cross-cultural awareness and skills. SIT offers master's programs in Social Justice and Intercultural Relations; Teaching, Intercultural Service, Leadership, and Management; Conflict Resolution; NGO Leadership and Management; International Education; Sustainable Development; Language Teaching; Community Development; and Organizational Management.

Another program is the GlobalMBA offered by a consortium of four good universities (Fachhochschule Köln, Uniwersytet Warszawski, Dongbei University of Finance & Economics, and the University of North Florida). This unique program offers graduate students an opportunity to combine intensive classroom study with residential experiences in four different countries: Germany, Poland, China, and the US. For more information, visit www.unf.edu/coggin/intlbus/GlobalMBA.

A reasonably new graduate opportunity is Future Generations (http://www.future.org). Their motto is to research, teach, and demonstrate how communities change. They have a process for equitable community-based change and a Master's degree program in *Applied Community Change and Conservation*. They also have fieldwork demonstrations in Tibet, China, two states in India, Peru, and Afghanistan.

There are many dual/joint international degrees available. For example, the MBA students at the University of San Diego (USD) may enroll in a program to earn two masters degrees, one from USD and one from the Instituto Techológico y de Estudios Superiores de Monterrey (ITESM). The Columbia Law School has a joint-degree program with the University of London (JD-LL.B. and JD-LL.M) and the Université de Paris I (JD-Maîtrise en Droit). Don't worry, there are many more.

The Master's International Program (MIP) through the US Peace Corps (http://www.peacecorps.gov) offers students an opportunity to combine Peace Corps service with a master's degree program. Depending on the college or university, your assignment may consist of a thesis, project, service, or paper. MIP may also cover tuition and/or fees for graduate credit. Many colleges and universities participate in this program. Check the Peace Corps website for more information.

If you're looking exclusively outside of the US, the following resources may be helpful:

- **Australian Education Office**
  http://studyinaustralia.gov.au
- **The British Council**
  www.britishcouncil.org/usa

- **The Canadian Bureau for International Education**
  www.cbie.ca
- **SIU (International University Cooperation, Norwegian Council for Higher Education)**
  www.siu.no/en
- **DAAD German Academic Exchange Service**
  (Deutscher Akademischer Austauschdienst)
  www.daad.org

101. How do I get a job in study abroad?

Be careful what you wish for, lest it come true. ~ *Unknown*

While working in study abroad may look glamorous from the outside (because you get to travel once in awhile), it's really not as fun as it looks. There are a lot of policies, procedures, legalities, and processing that need attention on a daily basis. For example, a coordinator may spend time advising students, but he/she spends more time processing paperwork and taking care of problems that come up. Such and such a university lost someone's paperwork. Johnny is having problems getting his visa. Sally can't find a program that meets her needs. Joe needs a note taker at his host institution. Jill needs to find a counselor overseas. Professor Jim is having problems with a student who is misbehaving on a program. I can't begin to tell you how much we deal with on a daily basis, but if you can imagine the difficulties that you had, multiplied by 300, then you probably have a good idea of the daily grind. If you're still up to it, then consider the following tips:

- Get as much international experience as possible.
- Learn to speak one or more foreign languages well.
- Get experience working with college students in an international capacity. For example, become a *Peer Advisor* in your study abroad office or try to get a job

in International Student Services. Surround yourself with people and programs in International Education.
- Go back to school and get a Master's degree in an international field or in Student Affairs (since you'll be working primarily with college students).
- Study mentoring resources such as Allabroad.us.
- Become a member of NAFSA, The Association of International Educators (www.nafsa.org)
- Go to conferences put on by NAFSA and its regional and state branches. These conferences often provide grants for students who otherwise cannot afford to go (so, no excuse for lack of money getting in the way).
- Subscribe to the best study abroad administrator's listserv, SECUSS-L. See www.geocities.com/secussl to sign up or to view archived postings.
- Read journals, books, and research in the field:
  o ForumEA (Research): www.forumea.org
  o Frontiers: www.frontiersjournal.com
  o IIE Open Doors: opendoors.iienetwork.org
  o International Educator: www.nafsa.org
- Keep abreast on what is going on in higher education around the world. A good source of information is the higher education section of the United Nations Educational, Scientific, and Cultural Organization (UNESCO) at unesco.org. UNESCO is the only body in the UN with a mandate in higher education.
- Check for jobs at least once a week on the Internet. Good places to look are:
  o Academic360.com: www.academic360.com
  o Association of International Educators (NAFSA, The Job Registry) www.nafsa.org
  o Chronicle of Higher Education http://chronicle.com/jobs
  o HigherEdJobs.com: www.higheredjobs.com

Books

The Alchemist
by Paulo Coelho

All God's Children Need Traveling Shoes
by Maya Angelou

Around the World in 80 Days
by Jules Verne

Borges: Collected Fictions
by Jorge Luis Borges

The Complete Short Stories of Ernest Hemingway:
The Finca Vigia Edition
by Ernest Hemingway

Death in the Afternoon
by Ernest Hemingway

Following the Equator: A Journey Around the World
by Mark Twain

The Great Railway Bazaar
by Paul Theroux

Hemmingway: the Paris Years
by Michael Reynolds

The Innocents Abroad
by Mark Twain

The Journals of Lewis and Clark
edited by Bernard DeVoto

Leaves of Grass
by Walt Whitman

Lost in Translation
by Eva Hoffman

Monique and the Mango Rains:
Two Years with a Midwife in Mali
by Kris Holloway

Mountains Beyond Mountains: The Quest of Dr.
Paul Farmer, a Man Who Would Cure the World
by Tracy Kidder

My Journey to Llasa
by Alexandra David-Neel

On the Road
by Jack Kerouac

One Hundred Years of Solitude
by Gabriel Garcia Marquez

Out of Africa
by Karen Blixen

The Romance of the Rose
by Guillaume de Lorris and Jean de Meun

The Sun Also Rises
by Ernest Hemingway

A Tramp Abroad
by Mark Twain

Glossary

Consortium – A group of colleges and universities that have joined forces in offering one or more study abroad programs.

Credit Evaluation – The process of evaluating a foreign transcript for credit and/or grades at your home institution.

Direct Enroll – A student enrolls directly in a host institution without going through a third party.

Dual Degree – The articulation of a college degree from two or more institutions, each awarding its own.

Faculty-led Program – A travel course led by faculty members from the home institution. There may be a mix of lectures, exercises, excursions, and group time.

Globalization – The integration of economic, cultural, and political systems around the world.

Host or Host Institution – A foreign institution from which you may take classes to count toward your degree at home.

Home or Home Institution – The institution from which you are seeking a degree, whose requirements you must fulfill.

Integrated Program – A structured program that integrates students with the local language, community, and culture.

Island Program – A highly structured program that clusters American and/or International students together within a tight framework that encourages integration with each other, rather than with the local language, community, and culture.

Joint Degree – More than one college or university's name is on the diploma, which is offered jointly and awarded by two or more different institutions.

Passport – An international identification issued by a country to a citizen that allows the person to exit and enter the home country.

Power of Attorney – A legal instrument used for the primary purpose of delegating lawful and signature authority to another.

Primary Insurance – The first policy or coverage to apply.

Resident Credit – Credit earned at the home institution or at a host institution through which you are enrolled for home institution credit. It is not *transfer credit* because the home institution accepts it as its own.

Secondary Insurance – The policy or coverage to apply after the primary insurance determination of benefits.

Third Party or Provider – A company that contracts with overseas academic institutions and housing, to *package* study abroad programs. They provide additional, logistical services to students whose other option is to direct enroll.

Transfer Credit – Credit earned at a host institution, which is accepted by the home institution toward a degree. It is not *resident credit* in the sense that it is not treated by the home institution as its own.

Visa – An official document, stamp, or seal affixed within a passport, which allows the person to enter a foreign country for a particular purpose.

Index

Printed in the United States
121624LV00001B/238-243/P

9 780972 132848